COUNSELLING
AND THERAPY
WITH REFUGEES

WILEY SERIES IN
PSYCHOTHERAPY AND
COUNSELLING

SERIES EDITORS
Franz Epting *Dept of Psychology, University of Florida, USA*
Bonnie Strickland *Dept of Psychology, University of Massachusetts, USA*
John Allen *Dept of Community Studies, Brighton Polytechnic, UK*

COUNSELLING AND THERAPY WITH REFUGEES

Psychological Problems of Victims of War, Torture and Repression

Guus van der Veer

with contributions by
Victor Vladár Rivero *and* **Mia Groenenberg**

John Wiley & Sons
Chichester · New York · Brisbane · Toronto · Singapore

Other Wiley Editorial Offices

John Wiley & Sons, Inc., 605 Third Avenue,
New York, NY 10158-0012, USA

Jacaranda Wiley Ltd, G.P.O. Box 859, Brisbane,
Queensland 4001, Australia

John Wiley & Sons (Canada) Ltd, 22 Worcester Road,
Rexdale, Ontario M9W 1L1, Canada

John Wiley & Sons (SEA) Pte Ltd, 37 Jalan Pemimpin #05-04.
Block B, Union Industrial Building, Singapore 2057

Library of Congress Cataloging-in-Publication Data

Veer, Guus van der.
   Counselling and therapy with refugees : psychological problems of
victims of war, torture, and repression / Guus van der Veer, with
contributions by Victor Vladár Rivero and Mia Groenenberg.
      p.   cm. — (Wiley series in psychotherapy and counselling)
   Includes bibliographical references and index.
   ISBN 0-471-93414-3 (ppc)
   1. Refugees, Political—Mental health.   2. Refugees, Political-
-Counseling of.   3. Post-traumatic stress disorder—Treatment.
I. Title.
   [DNLM: 1. Counseling—methods.   2. Psychotherapy—methods.
3. Refugees—psychology.   4. Repression.   5. Torture—psychology.
WA 305 V419c]
RC451.4.P57V44   1992
616.89'14'08694—dc20
DNLM/DLC
for Library of Congress   91-47561
                                                                      CIP

British Library Cataloguing in Publication Data

A catalogue record for this book is
available from the British Library.

ISBN 0-471-93414-3

Typeset in 10/12pt Times by APS, Salisbury Wilts.
Printed and bound in Great Britain by Biddles Ltd, Guildford and King's Lynn

Contents

Series preface

There is no scarcity of books which deal with theoretical and philosophical issues in counselling and psychotherapy. Indeed, even to established professional and advanced students, it often seems that the proliferation of theories and models results in bewilderment and confusion. The Wiley series in Psychotherapy and Counselling aims to establish a clear balance between theory, research and practice. What unifies the books in this series is the importance attached to presenting clear authoritative accounts of theory, research and experience in ways which will inform practice and understanding. Each author is not only a subject specialist but an established counsellor or psychotherapist well able to draw upon a wealth of clinical experience and share this with the reader. In order to deal adequately with their chosen topics authors have drawn upon different conceptual frameworks and these are presented in ways which are clear, rigorous and accessible to a wide readership.

The scope of the series includes books offering reviews of different approaches to counselling and therapy; textbooks on theory, research and modes of practice; books which examine work with specific client groups; titles concerned with professional issues and books which examine emerging strategies or situations for innovative and effective psychotherapy and counselling.

This volume is a unique and timely one. Contemporary political upheavals are preceding in ways, and at a speed, that few, if any, could have foreseen. The long-term implications of these profound changes are even more difficult to anticipate. However, one thing is certain. As throughout history, an increasing number of people are becoming the victims of repressive political regimes and institutions. Throughout the world those who seek to escape from these regimes form the growing army of political refugees. Dr Van der Veer's book provides a comprehensive examination of the psychological experience of refugees and the ways in which counselling and therapy may be used to ameliorate the traumatization consequent upon such experiences.

What impressed me most about this book was the skilful and insightful way in which the author shows how we may gain understanding of this client group by drawing upon a range of theoretical perspectives including; psychodynamic, family therapy, learning theory, and cognitive approaches. Throughout, the book is admirably illustrated with well chosen case material drawn from the author's extensive practice and experience.

However, this is far from just a well written theoretical review. Issues such as cultural differences, the risk of suicide, the special problems of children and adolescents and sexual violence are all treated in a detailed and eminently practical way. The book ends with a careful examination of the particular difficulties associated with working with refugees which should be read by all helping professionals working in this field.

John Allen
Series Editor

Preface

The influx of refugees into the Western world has increased drastically in the last few years. As a result the number of people who are confronted with refugees' mental problems has grown. These mental problems may, for example, be manifested during contacts with social workers, therapists, lawyers or government officials.

Many of those who are professionally involved with refugees are not (fully) aware of the nature and background of their mental problems, and they usually do not have the time or the opportunity to acquire a deeper understanding.

These problems may lead to exasperation and suspicion on the part of officials who are involved in both providing assistance and exercising control, and in the case of professional therapists and social workers and volunteers, not only to irritation but also to feelings of helplessness and disappointment, because their tried and tested methods often do not have the expected result. The intensity of these negative sentiments is related to the inability to empathize with the refugee, and empathy requires expertise and knowledge.

Scientific knowledge relevant for understanding the mental problems of refugees has increased greatly during the last few years. For instance, a lot has been written about the effects of violence exercised by government officials in dictatorships. It is well known that torture is not only torment at the moment that it is inflicted but that it leaves painful physical and mental traces for years to come; that the relatives of those who are arrested and subsequently disappear find it hard to cope; that the experience of violence on the battlefield can lead to serious mental problems for the soldiers concerned; and that life in exile produces many practical and personal problems.

But the literature is not easily accessible to many of those who are interested. Many of the publications are not available in English or are only distributed internally by organizations which provide assistance to refugees, or appear in the form of photocopies of congress papers.

In this study as much as possible of the available scientific literature on the effects of torture, terror, battlefield experience, disappearance of relatives and exile have been reviewed. The emphasis will be on the mental effects. This scientific information will be related to the experiences acquired by psychologists and psychiatrists in the provision of assistance to victims and their relatives. An attempt will be made to connect the various contributions to each other by placing them in a more general theoretical framework.

The discussion of facts and theory will, wherever possible, be related to practical experience. Practical examples are not, however, presented to prove the theory, but rather to illustrate the theoretical concepts and related mode of thought. In these examples personal details have been excluded or altered to prevent identification.

The book is meant to help professionals, particularly those in the mental health sector. But it also provides information which can be of use to government officials, lawyers, interpreters and volunteers who are involved with refugees.

In order to make this book accessible to people with little knowledge of psychology, some basic concepts from various psychological theories relevant to the understanding of mental problems in general will be discussed. While these concepts are familiar to most psychologists, they will be explained and related to the specific experiences of refugees on a level that can also be understood by an educated lay audience.

A practical chapter on the use of psychoactive drugs in the treatment of refugees has been writen by Victor Vladár Rivero, a psychiatrist, for the benefit of general practitioners, psychiatrists and medical specialists. Mia Groenenberg, a psychologist, contributed to the chapter about the specific problems of female refugees. The responsibility for the other chapters rests entirely with the main author.

Such frequently occurring terms as refugee, social worker, therapist, client, generally refer to both men and women.

Guus van der Veer
Amsterdam, August 1991

Acknowledgements

I would like to thank my colleagues Mia Groenenberg and Victor Vladár Rivero at the Social-Psychiatrist Service for Refugees in Amsterdam, whose cooperation has contributed greatly to the realization of this study. I would also like to thank the Chilean psychologists Elizabeth Lira and Juan Manuel Perez, the Argentinean psychiatrist Dario Lagos and my Sri Lankan colleague S. Selvaratnam, who took the time and trouble to share their experiences with me.

Finally, I would like to express my appreciation to the refugees who were prepared to tell me about their lives and their psychological problems, and who showed me how they overcame their troubles.

Part I

REFUGEES AND THEIR PROBLEMS

Introduction

This study is about refugees who, as individuals or in small groups, came to live in the West, far from their native country. The term refugee refers to people who have had to leave the country in which they lived because of violence and repression by the state. They are usually people who have felt threatened for some time by the authorities, or violent groups cooperating with, or operating under the protection of the authorities.

The meaning of the term refugee could be extended in various directions. Some prefer to apply it only to those who were politically active and who, as a result of activities ranging from armed struggle against dictatorship to shouting slogans at a demonstration, were persecuted to such an extent that they were in mortal danger for an extended period of time, and would again face similar danger if they were to return.

In this study a broader definition of refugee will be used. Those who were not politically active, or only active to a limited degree, but were nonetheless persecuted or banished are also included. For example, draft dodgers and deserters who refused to participate in (what they saw as) a cruel and meaningless war, or those who were persecuted because they belonged to a certain ethnic group (like the Tamils in Sri Lanka or the Kurds in Turkey), or because they were known to have certain political, religious or cultural tastes (for example as socialists, Baha'is, supporters of liberation theology or fans of Western pop music), or because they were considered deviant in some way (because of homosexual preference, for instance). These people have in common that the state in their native country considers them to be dangerous or without rights.

In this study, the term refugee also refers to those who had to flee their country because they accidentally became the victim of state repression.

Finally, there are also the relatives who accompanied the refugees as defined above. They have often suffered under the tensions caused by the political activities of their relative or his experience of repression, and have sometimes themselves become victims of reprisals. If the refugee has developed mental problems as a result of his experiences then this will also be a burden on his relatives (cf. Daly, 1985a; Figley, 1985). In this study these relatives also are considered to be refugees.

The term refugee can refer to people of different ages, with different personal histories and from different ethnic and cultural backgrounds. They have in common that they were forced to leave their own country for political reasons, but they differ with respect to their knowledge about political issues and their political orientation. Not all of them have the same legal status: some have become citizens of the country of exile, others remain illegal and live in constant fear of being repatriated. There are those who experienced much popular sympathy when they arrived and asked for asylum (such as some of the Polish dissidents who settled in Western Europe in the early 1980s), though some of them were aware that this positive attitude quickly faded when more of their compatriots arrived. Others had to face mistrust, rejection, or even hostility, insinuations and racism from the beginning (for example African refugees and Sri Lankan Tamils who came to Western Europe).

Moreover, refugees differ with respect to the amount and quality of political education they have had before leaving their country, the presence of conditions that support or obstruct their ability to cope with traumatic experiences and the capacities they have for dealing with new stressful experiences and adapting to new circumstances in the country of exile.

The aforementioned differences are reflected in the behaviour of refugees in everyday situations, in their attitudes to the professionals and volunteers who try to help them, in the content of the problems for which they seek assistance, in the way they think about the nature of their problems and have tried to cope with them themselves. These differences force us to be very careful when generalizing about refugees and their problems, whether from scientific research, or from clinical experience. Such generalizations can never do justice to the complexity of individual cases, and by making them in this study only a rough sketch is drawn, in order to reduce a very complex reality to less complex abstract statements. This can be done in different ways, depending on the psychological theory one has in mind while attempting to sum up what many refugees have in common.

In part I of this study some generalizations will be presented about refugees and their psychological problems on different levels of analysis and from various theoretical perspectives. It starts on the level of common sense: in chapter 1 the particular experiences of refugees are discussed, and examples are given of the various subjective meanings these experiences can have for the individual refugee who seeks assistance.

The following chapter (2) is about what psychological theories can contribute to understanding the problems of refugees. It contains descriptions based on the conceptual frameworks provided by various theoretical approaches of psychological problems and disturbances that are currently accepted by professionals who provide assistance to refugees and which present useful points of departure for counselling and therapy.

It is of course impossible to do justice to all the theoretical approaches that might be relevant for understanding the problems of refugees; that would require the writing of a massive encyclopaedic overview of the whole field of psychology and psychiatry. Not many social workers, psychologists and psychiatrists working with refugees would find the time to read it.

This study is not meant to be complete, but to provide a didactic approach which introduces a scientific way of thinking about the problems of refugees and shows the practitioner some examples of the many ways in which theoretical knowledge can inspire clinical work by offering different sets of spectacles through which he can look at the problems of refugees.

As a result, in this study the vast domain of psychology and psychiatry is crudely and frivolously reduced to five approaches. These are: the approach of psychiatric classification, the psychodynamic approach, the family-therapy approach, the learning-theory approach and the cognitive approach. A summary will be presented of the basic assumptions and central concepts of each approach which have proved helpful to us in reflecting on and describing clinical experience with refugees, followed by a discussion of what that approach can contribute to the understanding of the problems of refugees. Part I concludes with a chapter (3) on the diagnostic appraisal of the problems of refugees, in relation to the aforementioned theoretical approaches.

1 The experiences of refugees

A first glance

Refugees have in common that they have suffered from the abuse of power by the authorities of totalitarian regimes which systematically violate human rights. They have often undergone various hardships before and during their flight. Many have been imprisoned, maltreated during arrest or tortured during detention. Some have experienced situations in which death and violence were the order of the day. At a first glance, the following kinds of experiences can be distinguished.

Political repression   The person who decides to flee to the West does not usually do so on a momentary impulse. His decision is nearly always preceded by an extended period in which he is increasingly exposed to repression by the regime. This repression may include limits to the freedom of speech or education and intimidation by the police, the army or para-military groups of anyone who is criticizing the government or belongs to a particular minority. Such experiences may have caused a great deal of fear and tension which it proved difficult to cope with.

Detention   Many refugees have been arrested or abducted by police, military or members of para-military groups in their native country. The experience of detention often included the refugee being subjected to violence; being threatened; being isolated for some time from his family and friends; missing important events or ceremonies (like the wedding of a brother, the birth of a child, the death of a parent); and being temporarily unable to take care of his normal responsibilities (like earning money to support his family, or to look after the children). In many cases, being arrested came as an unexpected shock, and the experiences during detention often made the refugee lose his last illusions about the possibilities for political progress in his country, and about his own capacities to cope with the present political situation.

Torture Detention sometimes includes torture. The term torture refers to violence directed against the physical and mental integrity of the individual. This involves extended and repeated physical and psychological torment which is aimed at persuading the detainee to provide the authorities with information which will incriminate himself or others, or intimidating him and his social environment to such an extent that he will renounce further political activity. The aim is also to humiliate the victim and to deprive him of his self-confidence, his sense of identity, his willpower and his affect, thus reducing him to a numbed and helpless being (Santini, 1987).

According to Smeulers (1985) it is estimated that 30% of the refugees resident in the Netherlands have undergone torture. More than 50% of the clients to whom the author attended reported having been tortured.

Torture takes place in a situation in which the victim is helpless and totally at the mercy of his torturers. Generally speaking, torture forms a part of a systematic government policy which is directed at intimidating or destabilizing certain communities or ethnic groups (see for example Garcia & Rodriguez, 1987 for a description of the policies of the military governments in Argentina in the period between 1976 and 1982).

The physical torture undergone by the refugees to whom the author attended involved the conscious and premeditated application of various forms of torment which cause pain and/or physical damage. This was often accompanied by the threat that the physical damage would be permanent. Physical torment included hitting, kicking, burning with cigarettes, cigars, cigarette lighters or other hot objects; stabbing with knives and other sharp objects; the administration of electric shocks; holding the victims head under water (which was often polluted with urine and faeces); hanging the victim up by the wrists or feet or both at the same time; making him stand, do tiring exercises or adopt uncomfortable positions for long periods; exposing him to cold, heat, strong sun or very intense artificial light; administering chilli pepper to open wounds, failure to treat wounds caused by previous torture; the forced administration of psychotropic drugs by doctors who participated in the torture (see Cathcart, Berger & Knazan, 1979; Domovitch et al., 1984; Kosteljanetz & Aalund, 1983; Reid & Strong, 1987; Van der Veer, 1987a for enumerations of the various techniques).

Psychological torture can be defined as the creation of situations or conditions which are meant to evoke emotions which are difficult to cope with. For example, the refugees to whom the author attended mentioned the following forms: imprisonment for an extended period of time without the possibility of contacting family or friends; long-term solitary confinement; sensory deprivation (Daly, 1985b); having to listen to the screams of fellow prisoners who were being physically tortured; deprivation of sleep; having to witness friends, relatives or fellow prisoners being threatened, executed or tortured; being forced to eat excrement, to abuse or execute a fellow prisoner, or to do things which the victim considered 'strange' or immoral; sham executions; sexual violence. sexual violence.

Sexual violence is, of course, also a form of physical torture, but the psychological consequences are at least as drastic as the physical effects. The refugees to whom the author attended mentioned the following varieties: being insulted and humiliated by sexist remarks; being touched in indecent ways; being forced to undress in front of guards; being forced to watch or take part in sexual activities, with guards or with fellow prisoners, either heterosexual or homosexual; rape; mutilation of the sexual organs. Sexual torture is often accompanied by the threat that the victim's sexual functioning will be permanently impaired.

Torture is directed primarily at individuals. But it obviously also affects those in the victim's social environment. This matter will be discussed in the following chapter.

Other kinds of violence The other kinds of violence refugees report can, from a psychological perspective, be divided into two kinds. The first involves being subjected to *terror*, which is the systematic use of violence against specific local communities (a village, a neighbourhood), or ethnic groups (Tamils, Kurds). For the victims it is quite clear that they are victims and not perpetrators. They have not personally used violence, or have only used it if they considered it necessary for self-defence. Terror includes the killing of unarmed civilians, public display of the dead and mutilated bodies to serve as a 'warning', abduction of relatives or members of the immediate family of politically active persons (for further examples see University Teachers for Human Rights, 1989).

The second kind of violence will be referred to as *combat experiences* or *battlefield experiences*. Some refugees were confronted with bloody violence when they were guerrillas or soldiers. These people feel that they have been afflicted by the violence because, for example, they have seen their friends die. Sometimes they feel that they are partly responsible for unjustified violence, or guilty of atrocities. Some refugees with combat experience have become addicted to drugs which were forced on them by army doctors or commanding officers.

The disappearance of relatives Some refugees, particularly those from Latin America, but recently also those from Sri Lanka and Eritrea, have relatives who disappeared several years ago.

In the Spanish literature about the consequences of political violence, these missing persons are referred to as *desaparecidos*. The term *desaparecido* (disappeared person) was introduced in Guatemala in the early 1960s by the relatives of people who had been abducted by the special services of the army and police and detained in unknown locations. The army and police continued to deny, in spite of many statements by witnesses, that they were involved in the disappearances or that they even knew those who had disappeared. In Argentina, according to estimates by human rights organizations, 30 000 people have disappeared since 1976. They were almost certainly murdered.

The refugees who have a *desaparecido* in their family do not know whether he is still alive or how he might have died. This situation causes many uncertainties.

Research has shown that refugees who have a 'missing' relative have more mental problems than other refugees (Allodi & Rojas, 1985). Years of uncertainty as to the fate of the missing person cause inner problems which cannot easily be solved.

Separation and loss　All refugees have been forced, by their flight, to break important affective relationships: they have been separated from friends and loved ones, have had to leave familiar surroundings and pets behind and lost many of their material belongings. They therefore have enough reason to feel homesick.

Hardships　Refugees have often undergone various hardships before or during their flight. This also applies to those for whom the last leg of the journey was relatively comfortable, for example, an aeroplane flight. Many refugees have suffered hunger for an extended period, or have been exposed to extreme temperatures. Others have not had a normal social life for a long time, because they were imprisoned or in hiding. They were separated from family and friends, unable to receive education and in a constant state of fear. By the same token, children and adolescent refugees sometimes have experienced pedagogical neglect.

Exile　Life in exile entails all kinds of adjustment problems. Those seeking political asylum experience a long period of uncertainty in which they are not sure whether or not they will be accepted as refugees. During exile refugees generally continue feeling involved in what is happening in their native country, and if they receive bad news it may affect their psychological well-being. Various feelings, sometimes contradictory, related to the possibility of returning 'home' also play an important role in everyday life (Santini, 1986a) and may generate personal problems.

Traumatization and uprooting

The terms traumatization and uprooting will be used to summarize refugees' experiences with repression, torture and other kinds of violence, separation and loss, hardships and exile. Traumatization refers to extreme, painful experiences which are so difficult to cope with that they are likely to result in psychological dysfunction both in the short and in the long term. Uprooting refers to the experience of being forced to leave one's familiar surroundings and to settle in a new and unfamiliar environment for an indefinite period, which brings stress and can cause various long-lasting adjustment problems. Many refugees experience both traumatization and uprooting.

They share this experience of traumatization with other groups, such as war victims, veterans and some victims of natural disasters and violent crime, etc. They share the experience of uprooting with some emigrants who left their country for economic reasons. Therefore information gathered in studies of such groups may help in understanding the problems of refugees. But in making use of this kind of knowledge it is necessary to keep in mind the fundamental differences between refugees and the other groups.

Refugees and emigrants have in common that they have to adapt to a culture they experience as strange and sometimes hostile, and they may have ambivalent feelings both towards their original cultural background and their present environment. But the mere fact that emigrants had at least some freedom of choice when they left their country, while refugees generally felt forced to leave without much time for preparation, can make a lot of difference. The feeling of having been forced to leave familiar surroundings does not enhance adaptation to a new environment and new customs, whereas the ambition of an emigrant who wants to make it in the West, certainly can be adaptive.

Refugees also differ from people who where traumatized by natural disasters. The process of overcoming a man-made disaster is different because the victim has to come to terms with the fact that human beings caused and organized his suffering. Refugees certainly have something in common with the victims of violent crime, but the fact that the crimes of which they were the victim were justified by the authorities and not effectively opposed by large groups of their compatriots makes a psychological difference.

Refugees have sometimes had combat-experiences. But the exact content of these experiences may be very different to that which is found in the literature on Vietnam veterans or Israeli soldiers, due to the specific circumstances on the battlefield.

Scientific evidence on, and practical experience with, groups of people who have something in common with refugees can draw our attention to interesting details, but it may also blur our vision, and we must be careful in the way we utilize it.

Not all refugees seek help

According to an estimate by a government commission, about 30% of the refugees in the Netherlands ask for help because of psychological problems (Boekhoorn, 1987). What accounts for the resilience of the majority of refugees? What is the difference between those who request assistance because they are haunted by the memory of traumatic experiences and those who do not? And what is the difference between those who adapt to the situation in exile and those who do not? These are intriguing questions, to which several—speculative —answers can be given.

Differences in sensitivity   When large groups of people experience comparable traumatic events, there appear to be striking differences in the immediate psychological reactions of individuals. Tyhurst (1951) described three reaction patterns

1. Disturbed behaviour, such as confused or disoriented reactions, or being paralysed by fear (10–25% of the victims).
2. Stunning and bewilderment (about 75%). The victims' awareness of what is happening is restricted, they are not fully conscious of their emotions, but manifest a physiological fear reaction.
3. Controlled behaviour, aimed at restricting the consequences of the trauma (10–25% of the victims). These victims are able to retain their awareness and react adequately.

These differences are ascribed to differences in vulnerability, related to personality factors such as the capacity to endure fear and control one's behaviour under difficult circumstances. Vulnerability to traumatic experiences seems to be dependent on a large variety of variables (cf. Van der Kolk, 1988). It may be asssumed that its distribution follows a normal probability curve (Op den Velde, 1989).

Of course, the use of terms such as sensitivity or vulnerability does not explain which psychological or other mechanisms are responsible for individual differences in reaction to traumatic experiences.

Protective factors   The fact that people generally show enormous differences in their reaction to stressful events and deprivation has become a popular topic for discussion in developmental psychology. The adaptive reactions of children to stress are thought to be related to *coping skills*, which in their turn are seen as the result of a balance between more or less permanent *stress factors* and *protective factors* (Garmezy, 1985; De Wit, 1987).

The term stress factor (or risk factor) is commonly used to refer to factors such as traumatization in early childhood, marital conflicts between parents, delinquency or psychiatric disturbance in one of the parents and the like. These factors are thought to interfere with normal personality development, and may also make the individual more vulnerable to traumatic experiences. Davidson et al. (1985) have, in a retrospective investigation, shown that 66% of the people in their sample who were suffering from a psychiatric disorder after a traumatic experience, came from a family in which one of the members had a psychiatric disorder.

The term protective factors can refer to individual characteristics that are observable from early childhood, such as activity, social responsiveness, intelligence and quick recovery from illness, and which can be considered congenital. Another group of so called protective factors is related to favourable family conditions, such as the availability of at least one competent adult, opportunity for autonomous behaviour and the absence of disrupting conflicts. A third group of protective factors consists of conditions outside the family: a supportive school environment, for instance. Some authors subsume both family conditions and protective factors outside the family under the single heading *social support* (Oei, 1987; Parry & Shapiro, 1986). However, some *material* conditions, whether inside or outside the family, may also be more protective than others.

Finally, the term protective factor may be used for individual characteristics which are the result of a process of personality development in which experience and interaction with the environment played an important part: a positive self-image and self-respect, the experience of 'required helpfulness' (that is the experience of competence as a result of the necessity to help others: Rachman, 1979), or an attitude that invites favourable reactions from the social environment. An illustration of the importance of the latter can be found in a study of the adaptation of young Vietnamese refugees who arrived in the Netherlands as unaccompanied minors (Tuk, 1988). In this study three groups are distinguished: a small group of individuals who had many conflicts with the adults in their environment, a second small group that tended to social isolation; and a majority which adapted well. This majority manifested ambition and a wish to adapt to Dutch culture. Their behaviour could be characterized as polite, modest, industrious and achievement oriented. Their behaviour seemed to evoke more social support and appreciation from Dutch people than that of the other two groups.

In summary: the presence of protective factors in their personal history and present life-environment makes some refugees more stress and trauma resistant than others, and therefore enables them to integrate their traumatic experiences and adapt to life in exile without having to ask for help. But 'protective factor' is a post factum construct: the ways in which these factors protect, and the psychological mechanisms that make them effective, have hardly been investigated.

Delayed reaction   Some refugees have been adapting adequately for many years, but then suddenly seem to collapse. They manifest a form of delayed reaction to their painful experiences. This may happen when a particular occurrence unexpectedly confronts them with their traumatic past, or echoes the original trauma (cf. Amen, 1985). It may also occur when an accumulation of stressful events like being turned down in a job application, losing a job, retirement, contracting a physical illness, undermines their power of endurance. For example, the arrival of a relative from, or the discussion of plans to return to, the refugee's native country (cf. Weinstein & Ortic, 1985), pictures of that country on television or in films, news of asylum seekers being expelled, rejection of a request for asylum, may contribute to a refugee getting into a condition of psychological crisis.

A.A. had lived in exile for 10 years without having any manifest problems. When he came to the therapist, he had been suffering from nightmares and concentration disturbances for six months. Three occurrences seemed to have triggered these symptoms. The nightmares started after he had paid a visit to his native country. He remembered that he had become upset when he passed the prison where he had been detained for several months and tortured.

The visit to his native country, especially the meeting with old friends, had increased his desire to return. But he was afraid to do so, because of the unstable political situation. He had discussed the matter with his wife and children, but they did not want to go back.

He had made the trip immediately after his retirement, and when he returned he had little to do and felt useless.

One could speculate here that A.A. was a rather resilient man, but that retirement had placed him in a new stage of life with new problems, and that, probably partly as a result of his re-experiencing of traumatic experiences and the pressure to continue his life in exile, he was unable to cope with these problems.

Obstacles to counselling and therapy   The fact that some refugees do not seek help does not necessarily mean that they do not need help. It is possible that they need help but cannot find it, or that they do not feel attracted to the kind of help mental health institutions usually offer. The mental health care sector is, generally speaking, not adjusted to providing assistance to different kinds of foreigners and to all those who have experienced extreme violence. Language problems and cultural differences sometimes form a barrier between refugees and health care institutions. Some refugees do seek assistance for somatic complaints, but doctors may not be aware of the possible psychological roots of their complaints. Refugees from certain non-Western cultures sometimes deny their mental problems because these are not readily accepted in their culture, or because they are less well known (Boekhoorn, 1987). And in other cases they do not have words at their disposal to describe their mental problems.

The psychological meaning of a traumatic experience The discussion about protective factors proceeds from the assumption that a given traumatic experience does not necessarily have the same psychological consequences for different victims. The consequences also depend on the coping capacities of the individual and protective factors in his personal environment. By the same token, one may assume that the consequences of traumatic experiences are related to the particular vulnerabilities of the individual and additional stress factors he has to deal with incidentally. To put it another way: a traumatic experience has a psychological meaning which is specific for the individual. Whether the traumatic experience results in mental problems or not, is dependent on this psychological meaning.

Three phases

The way in which traumatization and uprooting were discussed may have given the impression that refugees are people who have experienced one or two traumatic events during a limited period in their life and that, to make matters worse, they have also been uprooted from their social and cultural environment, but that they are free and safe today. However, this picture does not reflect reality, and it would be more adequate to view refugees as people who have been subjected to a process of traumatization that extended over many years, which reached a climax in certain specific traumatizing events and the subsequent flight into exile, and that still continues in exile.

The idea that traumatization through organized violence is a process that often extends over many years was first elaborated by Keilson (1979) in his study of the vicissitudes of Jewish children during and after the Second World War. He distinguishes three phases in the process of traumatization that these children experienced:

- A first phase, characterized by an increase in repression and persecution of Jews in general
- A second phase, in which the child underwent various frightening and dangerous experiences, and was separated from his mother
- A third phase, in which the child either stayed with non-Jewish foster parents (with all the problems related to this condition) or returned to his traumatized Jewish environment

Following this description of a sequence of phases, the traumatization process that refugees have to deal with can be characterized as follows:

- *The first phase*: an increase in repression and persecution in their native country. This phase includes the social and political changes preceding the most extreme traumatic experiences in the life of the refugee, his involvement in these changes, and the consequences they had for his personal life.

- *The second phase*: the period in which the refugee personally became a victim of torture, terror, battlefield experiences, deprivations during escape, etc.

- *The third phase*: life in exile, which includes continuing involvement in what is happening back home, the painful after-effects of the traumatic experiences of the preceding phases, the uncertainty and insecurity the refugee inevitably experiences until he is officially granted political asylum, the never-ending problems of adaptation to a different culture and the recurring experiences of racism and xenophobia. In this third phase new stress may arise when, as a result of political changes, returning to the home country becomes a possibility. This possibility calls up memories of traumatic events, raising old feelings of loss and grief. It also confronts the refugee with an extraordinarily difficult and painful decision. He must choose between giving up the new life he has built in exile, or giving up the illusion of going home (Santini, 1985a).

In what follows, these phases will be illustrated with a number of examples, and will take a closer look at the lasting effects of the experiences of refugees which were summed up above. Also the special psychological meaning that a particular experience may have for the individual will be stressed.

The first phase: increasing political repression

In the period preceding the most traumatic events, refugees have often undergone various experiences which, although less directly injurious, were nonetheless painful and had an enduring effect.

A.B. comes from an Asian country. As a 23-year-old student, he got mixed up in a tumult while on his way to the university one morning. The tumult had started on a square where two prominent members of the party with which A.B. sympathized were being hanged. A.B. became very emotional when, four years later, he recounted these executions to the therapist. Those who had been executed were not friends of his but he had looked up to them as leaders, and their deaths had signified a turning point in his life. This experience had radically changed his world view and destroyed his imagined future. 'That day', A.B. said, 'I decided to give up my study and concentrate on political activities.' A year later he was arrested and tortured.

During the first interview, B.B., a refugee from Africa, told the therapist that he should be preparing for an exam, but that he could not bring himself to study. He spent the whole day in his room, brooding and worrying. The therapist decided not to delve into the reasons for this worrying, but rather asked B.B. whether he ever went out, to participate in sport, for example. B.B. then told the therapist that fellow students had, on several occasions, invited him to join them in a game of soccer, but that he had refused. He then said that when he was back home he used to like playing soccer with the boys in the neighbourhood. However, he had developed an aversion to one of these boys because, on one occasion, he had stolen their ball. Then one day, about a month before he was arrested and tortured, B.B. went out to the market to buy some fruit. There he saw a poster containing photographs of 'heroes who had died for their country', that is, boys who had died in combat after being forced to join the government army. The boy he disliked was among them.

'That night', B.B. said, 'the boys played soccer as usual. I joined them as I often did. But this time I could not move my legs. I kept thinking of that nasty little boy. Since then I never played any kind of ball game again.'

The second phase: major traumatic experiences

It is impossible to give a complete overview of all the kinds of major traumatic experience described to us by refugees, the emotional meaning these experiences had for them and the influence these experiences have on their daily life and behaviour many years later. First a description will be given of some of the lasting effects of detention, specific kinds of torture, the disappearance of relatives and friends, and hardships during escape. Then some emotions will be discussed that may stem from both detention, torture, combat experience and terror: like guilt, disgust, mortal fear, bereavement, the feeling of having been deceived, and anger. In some cases, these emotions have become transformed to a general attitude towards life, without the refugee being completely aware of this process. In other cases, these emotions have been repressed, but they suddenly may overwhelm the refugee, even years after the traumatic experiences occurred.

Detention   Some of the complaints of refugees who have been detained become more understandable when one is aware of the circumstances in which they were detained.

C.B., a 25-year-old refugee from the Middle East, often awoke in the middle of the night feeling very scared. This usually happened when he heard the neighbours coming home. He also got scared during the day whenever he heard the sound of keys rattling or footsteps on the stairs. When he entered a block of flats he became so tense that he was unable to visit friends who lived in a flat.

C.B. had been detained in a relatively modern prison, which had been made of concrete. It became clear that he associated blocks of flats with this prison. During his detention C.B. and his companions were regularly taken from their cells to be tortured. The sound of keys rattling and footsteps on stairs had become associated with the fear that overcame him when the prison guards climbed the stairs of the gallery and rattled their keys while opening the cell doors to take the prisoners to be tortured. He said that hearing these sounds and waiting to see whether he himself would be taken for torture was almost as bad as the torture itself.

C.B. always arrived at the therapist's office at exactly the appointed time, because he did not like to spend time in the waiting room.

Specific forms of torture   Some refugees have only undergone brutal forms of torture, others also experienced more selectively applied violence. In the latter case, it is often clear that those who carried out torture deliberately sought out the 'weak spots' in their victim's personality. In this connection, Vladár Rivero (1986) describes the case of a refugee who was uncertain about his sexual identity and virility. This refugee had been tortured during his detention by the application of electric shocks to his genitals. The following example also demonstrates the malicious cunning of some torturers.

D.B., a young refugee from Latin America, told the following story. 'I was beaten for a long time while I was hung to a bar by my hands and feet. I was blindfolded. The guards took turns in beating me. They wanted to see me cry, but I didn't. I lost consciousness. When I awoke they put me in a chair. One guard removed the bandage from my eyes, gave me a cigarette and started talking with a soft and friendly voice. Suddenly he slapped me in the face. Then I started to cry, and I could not stop. I guess it reminded me of a teacher I had in primary school, he used to hit me that way, and I had no defence. From that day on the guards started to slap me in the face whenever they wanted to humiliate me, and I could not help crying. That is why I don't want to come here sometimes. You are friendly and give me tea ... you know?'

It sometimes happens that the torturer is a relative or acquaintance of the victim. This experience can deliver a tremendous blow to the victim's faith in other people (Santini, 1986b) and thus become an obstacle to the establishment of relationships based on mutual trust later on.

E.B., who spent three years in prison, expressed this as follows. 'The second interrogator was a boy I knew, we had been at primary school together. He sometimes accompanied me home after school, and on a few occasions he stayed for dinner. He recognized me immediately, although we hadn't seen each other for years. I thought he would be a bit gentle with me, and that he would inform my family about my arrest. He did not. He beat me more severely than any other interrogator.' One of E.B.'s most serious problems was that he felt very lonely. He had not learnt to speak the language of the country of exile yet, and he avoided contact with compatriots, because he did not dare to trust any of them.

Sexual torture may in some cases lead to later sexual dysfunction. For instance during sexual activity the refugee may experience flashbacks in which the present partner is perceived as a rapist. Sexual contact may trigger intrusive memories when the partner behaves in a way that even remotely resemble a form of sexual torture.

F.B. had been raped several times by prison guards. Several years later in the country of exile he entered into an intimate relationship. He reported that he was sometimes afraid to have sexual contact, because it might suddenly revive bad memories. This happened on one occasion when his friend touched his nipples —something that had also happened the first time he was raped.

Torture entails by definition that the victim is helpless in the presence of people who abuse their power. For most refugees feelings of powerlessness and anger at the humiliation and pain they have had to undergo are emotions that can easily be relived if they are confronted with people who indeed have power; especially if their appearance and behaviour reminds them in some way of their torturers and interrogators.

G.B. told the therapist that her most important problem was that she had to report to the police every week to get her temporary visa stamped. 'I am so scared that one day I will lose control. Most of the officers behave correctly, but the way they walk in their boots, it's just like the police in my country. One of them always talks in a loud voice, he reminds me of the cop who beat my little brother. You know, they forced me to look when they beat him. Then there's another one who always says: they've forgotten again to kick you out of the country, and then he smiles as if he had just told a funny joke. He knows he is offending me, but what can I do?'

Torture is often combined with interrogation, and for that reason some refugees get very upset or even become almost frozen with fear, in situations in which they feel they are being questioned.

Although one could tell from his face that the aforementioned E.B. desperately sought help, he did not seem to be very cooperative during the first interview. He did not answer the therapist's questions with more than one or two words. The therapist, who knew that E.B. had been tortured, asked him whether the situation reminded him of the interrogations in prison. E.B. confirmed this and became a bit less tense.

This disappearance of relatives or friends   Not knowing what has happened to a missing person can be a torment for relatives and friends. They sometimes suffer from frightening fantasies about torture and ill treatment.

The father of H.B., a boy of 12 years, disappeared 10 years ago. He was probably killed by the government army, but this was never verified, and H.B. and his mother left the country four months later.

H.B.'s mother requested assistance for her son, because his school achievements were far below the expected level. H.B. seemed unable to concentrate at school. He often had nightmares about his father being tortured.

The uncertainty about the fate of a missing person sometimes seems to result in inner conflicts (cf. L'Hoste, 1986; Spolyar, 1974; Benson et al., 1974).

H.B.'s mother also suffered from nightmares, of which she could remember nothing, except that she was in a dark, scary place, and that there was something dangerous behind her which she could not identify. The nightmares had become worse two years ago, at about the time she had started going out with a friend. He now wanted to marry her, but she was trying to postpone a decision. In order to marry in the country of exile she would need a certificate from the authorities in her native country to prove that she was unmarried. This could only be obtained if she took legal action to get a divorce from her missing husband, or if she obtained a declaration from these authorities which confirmed that her husband had been killed.

Some people seem to protect themselves from disturbing thoughts about missing friends or relatives by not speaking about them and removing anything that reminds them of the missing person.

I.B., a boy of 13 suffered from concentration problems and nightmares about the death of his missing father. He had never seen a picture of his father because his mother had locked them all away in a suitcase and he never asked her about him because he thought that would make her nervous.

Hardships suffered in refugee camps or during escape   Sometimes a clear picture of the hardships and dangers which the refugee had to face during his escape or his stay in a refugee camp make it easier to understand his behaviour and evaluate the meaning of these events against the background of his personality development. In relation to this topic one should realize that refugee camps often are not peaceful and quiet places, and that the living conditions there are often rather unhealthy and primitive. One must also keep in mind that some refugees have the experience of being transferred like parcels from one camp to another, without having the opportunity to make a decision about their next destination.

J.B., an adolescent refugee from Africa, had been imprisoned when he was 14. In prison he had some very unpleasant experiences. With regard to his personal history it was known that his father had died when he was six years old and that he had a problematic relation with his stepfather.

J.B. was very ambivalent about therapy. Sometimes he telephoned and wanted to make an appointment for the same day and sometimes he claimed that he did not need any assistance at all.

He wanted to be reminded of his past as little as possible. Sometimes he behaved like a normal, energetic adolescent, but he could also be very depressive. He kept getting into financial difficulties, as a result of which he was sometimes unable to buy groceries for a week. He was also coercive in the way he demanded help from the adults in his environment.

After many 'forgotten' appointments and as many new invitations by the therapist, a therapeutic relationship developed. During the 14th interview J.B. broke down and cried as he related how he had made a 20-hour journey on foot through the desert before arriving, hungry and exhausted, on the other side of the border. Halfway, he had been helped by a border guard who felt sorry for him, had given him some food and water, and shown him which way to go. The guard was there to prevent refugees from escaping, and had put his own life in danger by helping J.B.

It is tempting to speculate that J.B.'s personality development had been affected by the loss of his father, and that he had ambivalent feelings toward the therapist because he viewed him as a father figure to whom it would be better not to become attached. In that case, the border guard possibly satisfied not only a need for food and water, but also a need for fatherly support. Should the constant creation of financial problems then be understood as an unconscious effort to re-enact the trauma in order to evoke the comfort in which it resulted?

Guilt   For some refugees, a feeling of guilt is the dominant affect in their life. This may occur if the refugee was forced to divulge information under torture. It may also be related to the fact that he survived detention or other violent experiences while friends, companions or relatives did not.

K.B., was a refugee from an African country. She was 16 at the time of her arrest. During detention she had been forced to witness the execution of her brother. She was haunted by the thought that her brother might still be alive if she had told her interrogators everything she knew.

However, feelings of guilt can have a variety of backgrounds. For instance, some refugees feel guilty because they have been forced, by their torturers or in order to escape, to carry out violent acts themselves, and they feel guilty about this. Others are combat veterans who feel guilty about what they did to the 'enemy' or about the pleasant excitement some of them felt while they were engaged in violent actions (cf. Solursh, 1989). In some cases they are not initially aware of any feelings of guilt; the guilt becomes conscious during therapy (cf. Schwartz, 1984b).

Self-blame can also be interpreted as an effort by the traumatized person to restore a sense of control over his fate and to maintain the illusion that the re-occurrence of traumatic events can be prevented. Or it may be considered as an attempt by the refugee to protect himself against overwhelming affects like helplessness or rage (cf. Roth & Lebowitz, 1988).

Incidentally, feelings of guilt can, of course, also be associated with many other factors which are not directly related to traumatic incidents. There are refugees who feel guilty all day because they are unable to help the friends and relatives they had to leave behind, or because they do not have the energy to continue their political involvement, and so on.

Mortal fear One form of psychological torture is bringing the subject in a situation which causes mortal fear. The result is that some refugees worry a lot about death: either their own death or that of still surviving relatives. This preoccupation is often understandable given their experiences.

L.B., a girl of 20, fled with her mother from an African country. She often had nightmares in which her mother died, and during the day she could not put the fear of her mother's death out of her mind. Sometimes she woke up thinking that she herself was dead.

L.B. had been detained for several months for political reasons. Once she had been forced to undergo a sham execution, in which some of her companions were really executed.

Mortal fear can of course also have been caused by experiences related to terror or combat. Moreover, it may become disguised as phobic behaviour.

M.B. asked assistance, ten years after he had been participating as a guerrilla in a liberation war in the Middle East. His complaints were that he became very tense and nervous if he had to use public transport. Therefore he had interrupted most of his recreational activities. He continued working, but all day he was afraid that his colleagues might guess that he was mad. The symptoms had started one day after the war broke out in the Persian Gulf. He had watched the news on television, which had made him very upset.

While he was discussing his fears with the therapist, he remembered how once he was sent from the guerrilla base on a mission to a city that was full of soldiers and checkpoints. M.B. had reached the city by bus. He described that he had been alert all the time, especially for people who looked at him with more than casual interest. M.B. said he had not felt any fear at that time, although he was aware all the time that he was in mortal danger.

Disgust Torture sometimes involves situations which cause disgust, like sexual abuse, or being confronted with people that are seriously wounded, mauled or dead. Experiences of terror, for example watching how police abuse defenceless people, being confronted with the results of terrorism, or being forced by intimidation to watch public executions, may also result in feelings of disgust. This disgust may become directed to certain things (e.g. uncooked meat), an individual to whom the refugee has close affective relationship, or oneself.

N.B. had been detained in prison for two years, where he was tortured. After his release he was forced to go into military service. One of the nightmares that haunted him was about the battlefield: he saw the mutilated corpses of dead soldiers, and black dogs eating their flesh. When he awoke he felt sick. He said: 'Even when I was awake I smelled those rotten bodies. It is as if it sticks to my body. Sometimes I feel that others can smell it on me.'

Bereavement In the cases of some refugees, traumatic experiences are concentrated around the loss of a person with whom they had an affective relationship, such as a partner, close relative, intimate friend or buddy in their prison cell or combat unit. Such specific traumatic experiences seem to result in a series of personal problems in which unassimilated grief, which hinders their entering into new affective relationships, is central.

O.B. requested help because of somatic complaints. He related these to the problems he had in making contact with other people. After a few interviews with the therapist it became clear that these problems occurred mainly in situations in which women were present. He was not only shy towards women, but also became very nervous when he saw other boys having a pleasant conversation with a girl. It reminded him of the happy times he had spent with his own girlfriend, who had died as a result of political violence.

Some refugees have very painful memories of their escape because they were unable to say goodbye to friends and loved ones (cf. Grimberg & Grimberg, 1984). When escape has entailed the sudden rupture of important relationships, the refugee may be very reserved when it comes to establishing new contacts.

P.B., a girl of 21, fled with her mother from an Asian country. She was referred because of depressive complaints. During the interviews the therapist noticed that she was unusually strongly oriented towards her mother for her age. She hardly seemed to be interested in associating with her peers. It seemed as if her personality development had been arrested in that respect. This did not seem to be the result of a possessive or overprotective attitude on the part of the mother, and it also did not fit in with the picture that she presented of herself as someone who used to have a lot of friends back home.

When P.B.'s escape was discussed, it became apparent that, for reasons of security, she had not told any of her friends that she was leaving. She had not even been able to say goodbye to her fiancé, and had not written to him after her escape for fear of endangering his life.

Some refugees, especially those who have suffered a traumatic loss during adolescence, have the feeling that they do not have any control over their destiny. This observation is in line with Van der Kolk's (1985) description of the feelings of Vietnam veterans who had lost a buddy under traumatic circumstances.

Q.B. was referred because of depressive complaints and extreme passivity, which was becoming annoying for the volunteers who tried to help him. He reacted with complete indifference to any friendly approach. Q.B. himself said that he felt lonely, it seemed to him that people just did not like him. He did not understand why, but he was sure that this would never change.

During the first interview Q.B. told the therapist that he sometimes encountered a black car and that the driver tried to run him over. He was convinced that someone wanted to murder him, and was obsessed by the question why, without thinking of ways of defending himself.

Q.B. had never been arrested or undergone political violence himself. His parents had begged him to leave his country after soldiers had killed his brother, with whom he had a very close relationship. This had happened when the soldiers had come to arrest Q.B.

The feeling of having been deceived   Many refugees had their most traumatic experiences as a result of their participation in activities, the possible consequences of which they were not fully aware at the time. Some of them were deceived by political leaders who gave the instructions while minimizing the danger, and let them do the dangerous work while they kept out of harm's way.

R.B., who was 13 at the time, had agreed to distribute a political pamphlet. His nephew, who was 25, and the local leader of an oppositional group, had assured him that this was absolutely safe. 'He was the son of my uncle, he was much older than I was, how could I refuse? How could I know he was telling me lies?', R.B. said.

While he was distributing the pamphlets, R.B. was arrested. He was severely tortured and imprisoned for five years. 'My nephew cheated me', R.B. said. 'He left the country after I was arrested, he lives in Europe and he is a rich man now. When I had escaped, he did not offer any money to get me out of the country. He knows where I live, but he did not even come to ask me how I was doing.'

Anger   Becoming a victim of organized violence implies that the victim is confronted with a lot of aggression. This may cause direct aggressive reactions in the refugee, which usually, at least partly, have to be suppressed because the refugee is defenceless against the perpetrators of the violence. This unexpressed aggression can also become repressed from the conscious of the refugee.

According to psychodynamic theory, it is also possible that the victim or the witness of aggression identifies with the aggressor. The result is that he will show behaviour that seems to be an imitation of the behaviour of the perpetrator, and is prone to experience aggressive impulses. Be this as it may, working with traumatized refugees means meeting people with a lot of anger inside. This anger may immediately be obvious.

S.B., a refugee from a Middle East country who had gone through a long-lasting ordeal of physical and psychological torture, was referred to a psychotherapist because he could not control his aggression. If he became upset for some reason (for instance after hearing news from his country) he usually became very angry, and hit his housemate. Afterwards he always regretted this and felt very ashamed.

During therapy it became clear that, when he was upset, he experienced anybody that came near to him as a torturer.

In other cases, the aggression seems to be more repressed.

T.B., a refugee from South East Asia, requested assistance because of phobic complaints and hyperventilation. He had left his country after being abducted and severely abused by secret police. Before he left his country, he had lived hidden, in complete isolation, for three months.

It took two years of therapy before the anxiety-related complaints were under control. Then T.B., who impressed as a very gentle, even sub-assertive person, started to ventilate his anger: he described in which cruel way he wanted to treat the dictator of his country, using exactly those forms of violence he had experienced or witnessed himself. After doing this, he felt rather ashamed and guilty.

The third phase: bad news, adjustment problems and social isolation

When living in exile, a refugee often continues to be very much involved in what his happening in his native country, with regard to both the political situation and the weal and woe of family and friends he had to leave behind. The refugee has become physically separated from what was important for him for a long time, but the emotional involvement continues. The news he hears from or about his country can remind him of his own traumatic experiences, fill him with worry, or just be extraordinarily bad.

U.B., a refugee from an African country, had witnessed a lot of organized violence, but never had become a direct victim. He had left his country, after the army had come to his village and abducted and killed most boys in his village. A year later he came to know that his elderly father and his younger brother had been murdered by the military. U.B. did a suicide attempt. After hospitalization he was referred for therapy. In the conversations with U.B. what happened in the third phase of traumatization—the traumatic loss of two of his relatives—was the most important theme. U.B. felt both helpless and guilty about the death of his father and brother.

During exile, a refugee may experience a lot of stress which is not directly traumatic but adds to stress related to traumatic experiences. For one thing, refugees encounter physical conditions (climate and landscape) and social and cultural conditions (norms and customs) which are different from those they were used to in their own country. This may lead to adjustment problems. The specific content of these adjustment problems depends, among other things, on the cultural background of the refugee.

For example, in tropical countries people spend much of their time outdoors. The chances of being involuntarily alone are therefore limited. In Western Europe and North America this is different, and a refugee who comes from a tropical country has to acquire a new set of social skills in order to find company, and learn to deal with being alone more often than he was used to.

To give some more examples: the way in which European girls associate with boys is quite different from what is considered proper in Iran and Sri Lanka; in Chile guests are received very differently than in Holland; the way in which Europeans and Americans treat their dogs and pets is considered quite crazy and unhygienic by most people from the Middle East; in Vietnam ones tries to avoid contradicting other people, especially in public, rather than being assertive; and the way in which Europeans and Americans discuss personal matters on television is embarrassing for anyone who used to live to the east of these areas.

Cultural differences can cause serious confusion for refugees who are not yet used to them. Misunderstandings and embarrassing situations can occur between such refugees and the inhabitants of the host country. How to behave in normal everyday situations can therefore become a problem to the refugee: it is something he has to think about and this requires some energy. Refugees who, for various reasons, are not very energetic, are tempted to restrict their contacts with the host population to a minimum.

Moreover, refugees are not always treated with respect in Western countries. From time to time they are confronted with racial prejudice, xenophobia (see the Anne Frank Foundation, 1987, for a description of these phenomena) and an image that portrays them as thankless profiteers of the social security system who are too lazy to work but, paradoxically, also the cause of unemployment because they steal the jobs of the indigenous population. They find that many people consider their native country to be backward and them to be less civilized. Such unpleasant experiences sometimes cause new emotions which are difficult to assimilate.

The language barrier makes contact with the indigenous population difficult, and this contributes to the social isolation of the refugee. On the other hand, the refugee himself may shy away from new emotional relationships—and this applies to the therapeutic relationship as well—for less obvious, intra-psychic reasons. He may, for example, experience the establishment of a new friendship or relationship of trust as disloyalty to friends and relatives who have remained behind, or to the political cause for which they were persecuted.

The average West European or North American is unaware of the details of the situation in the countries from which refugees come, and will hardly take the trouble to find out more. This does not stimulate refugees to seek contact with inhabitants of the host country. Some of them experience this lack of knowledge and interest as particularly offensive, or become embarrassed when people ask them 'stupid' questions.

Friendship with other refugees from the same country may be strained because of political differences. For example, among the refugees from Iran there are monarchists, stalinists, maoists and various groups of so called islamic marxists. Refugees who belong to certain political groups sometimes find that their political friends do not understand their problems and demand more effort from them for political activities than they are capable of. They therefore feel emotionally abandoned by their friends. Others do at first receive emotional support from their comrades but become isolated when they adjust their political views as a result of their experiences and education in the host country. Still others maintain their political views and their militancy but feel terribly frustrated because there are not many possibilities for political action; they are deprived of an important source of inspiration in their lives (cf. Cienfuegos & Monelli, 1983). Meeting political friends then becomes a depressing event and increases feelings of loneliness.

Most refugees come from a cultural background in which talking to outsiders about traumatic experiences or emotional problems is just *not done*, and this attitude is not very helpful in overcoming their problems through seeking social support. The resulting feeling of loneliness and the fear of having a mental disorder may also have a traumatizing effect (Brown, 1986).

Moreover, some refugees are afraid—and sometimes they have good reason—that agents of their native country's secret police may have infiltrated their social circle and that what they do or say could have consequences for relatives and comrades back home. Finally, a refugee may have an ambivalent attitude towards contacts with other refugees because they remind him of painful experiences with which he has not yet come to grips.

V.B. had periods of dejection and sometimes felt very lonely. He came from an Asian country and had been detained for a long period for political reasons while he was still very young. He did not want to be reminded of the past in any way and therefore avoided listening to music from his native country or watching the news on television. For the same reasons he preferred not to associate with compatriots. He seemed to adjust fairly well in his contacts with peers in the country of exile, but these contacts remained superficial, partly because of the language barrier, but also because he refused to talk about himself, especially about his past.

One may suppose that V.B. tried to put the past out of his mind and therefore denied the roots of his personal identity. For this reason he held back in establishing more intimate contacts with peers, and had to do without the emotional support of an intimate friendship.

W.B., a 20-year-old refugee from Latin America, complained about depressions and disturbed concentration. She had hardly any contact with peers. This was partly a result of the language barrier and partly because she found the youngsters in the country of exile apolitical, bourgeois and aloof. She also did not feel at ease with peers from Latin America who had been in exile longer: she thought that they had conformed too much to the way of life of the 'capitalists' and did not do enough for their native country.

Here one may suppose that the loyalty to her friends in Latin America, who were living under very difficult conditions, prevented her from establishing new relationships with peers. As a result adaptation to exile was impeded.

The third phase: uncertainty related to the request for asylum

In addition to the factors mentioned above, government policy relating to granting asylum to refugees may also cause or aggravate psychological problems (Van der Veer, 1987b, 1987c; Santini, Groenenberg & Vladár Rivero, 1987). In various countries it may take a long time—a number of years— before the decision to grant asylum is made. Uncertainty about the criteria does not make waiting any easier.

The refugee is uncertain about his future until the decision is made. Not being able to make any real plans for the future may lead to serious psychological problems. Uncertainty about the outcome of the request for asylum can also contribute to social isolation: why establish emotional ties when there is a real risk that they will have to be broken off if the decision is negative? Moreover, the procedures involved in making a request for asylum may aggravate the psychological problems caused by traumatic experiences before or during the flight into exile. Refugees have to relate traumatic events to officials, and in doing so they re-experience them, but in the absence of those conditions which would make this re-experiencing liberating.

In this connection it should be noted that some refugees remain silent about their traumatic experiences in such situations because they are unable to discuss them with someone with whom they do not have a relationship based on mutual trust. Sometimes they feel intimidated or humiliated by the official who is questioning them or the interpreter. The interpreter may make mistakes in translating information which is relevant for the request. Unpleasant experiences with officials in the native country can also interfere with communication in these interviews. For example, Iranian refugees have discovered, often with painful consequences, that Iranian government officials are not to be trusted in any way, and that it is dangerous to tell them the truth. This influences the way they react to officials in the country in which they have requested asylum, particularly if they wear a uniform, are impatient, or give the impression that they do not believe the refugee's story in the first place. As a result they do not tell the truth, or the whole truth, when providing information which could be important in the decision to grant them asylum.

X.B. only mentioned that he had been tortured after his request for asylum had been turned down. It was in the sixth interview with the therapist that he was able, with much emotion, to talk about his traumatic experiences during detention. Shocking battlefield experiences, which were also relevant for his request, were only discussed during therapy months later.

The feelings related to the stress that results from applying for asylum are comparable to those that result from traumatic experiences like imprisonment, torture and so on. Complications in the asylum procedure also cause feelings of powerlessness and anger, because they are experienced as humiliating and painful and can only be endured. The unpleasant aspects of the application for asylum therefore often remind the refugees of traumatic experiences with which they could not cope, and they intensify the problem of unassimilated traumatic experiences. They increase the chance that feelings of powerlessness and anger will come to dominate the refugee's whole attitude to life.

Y.B. had been tortured for a short period before he went into exile. After psychotherapeutic interviews his complaints reduced significantly. He no longer had nightmares, he slept well, was more cheerful and could concentrate on his studies. He also had more contact with his compatriots. Then he was informed that his request for asylum had been turned down. He appealed against the decision, but his nightmares and insomnia returned and he became depressed. He neglected his appearance and said he doubted whether further treatment would be useful.

In this connection Keilson's study of the different phases of traumatization gives interesting starting points. His research was concerned with the significance of the experiences during each of these phases for the development of psychological problems in Jewish children in the Netherlands who were separated from their parents during the Second World War. According to Keilson (1979) what happened in the third phase was crucial for the subsequent mental functioning of the children concerned. Those who experienced a relatively favourable second phase and an unfavourable third phase were found to have a less satisfactory adaptation 25 years later than those who experienced an unfavourable second but a favourable third phase.

Generalizing from these results it can be assumed that the experiences in the third phase of the traumatization process really make a difference, and that they influence the subsequent psychological functioning of refugees to a significant degree. And this presents an interesting challenge to professionals and others who are responsible for the admission and well-being of refugees in our society.

2 Traumatization and uprooting: five theoretical approaches

The preceding chapter was about the painful and intruding experiences of refugees, and presented examples that show the subjective meaning these experiences have for some of them and the way these experiences may influence later psychological functioning. Apart from some unavoidable and somewhat flippant psychodynamic speculation about the possible interaction between personality development and traumatic experiences, and the use of simple descriptive labels such as traumatization, uprooting and the phases of traumatization, in presenting the examples above, the discussion was restricted to ordinary language an commonsense analysis.

In the next section the same phenomena will be approached from the theoretical viewpoint of modern psychiatry.

The psychiatric approach

Some basic concepts and assumptions

Complaints, signs and symptoms   These terms generally refer to the observable behaviour and characteristics of people who seek psychiatric help or present themselves for psychiatric examination. Complaints are statements of an individual concerning what it is that is bothering him or makes him suffer. Signs are objective manifestations of a pathological condition, that can be observed by an examiner even if the individual does not report them himself. The word symptom refers to any manifestation of a pathological condition, including both subjective complaints and objective signs.

Disorders   A basic assumption of the psychiatric approach is that complaints and symptoms can in some cases be related to psychiatric disorders. The central idea of this approach is that there exist certain groups of symptoms, like typical complaints, characteristic behaviour, disabilities (impairments in one or more important areas of functioning) and other phenomena, that form a specific pattern. This pattern of phenomena, which is sometimes called a syndrome, is considered to be characteristic for a certain type of psychiatric disorder. This disorder is thought to be related to particular etiological factors. A psychiatric disorder is associated with present distress or a significantly increased risk of suffering death, pain, disability or an important loss of freedom. An important characteristic of a disorder is that this psychological pattern is not merely a predictable response to a particular event, but can be currently considered as a manifestation of behavioural, psychological or biological dysfunction.

In order to decide whether a person has a psychiatric disorder, and if so, to describe the type of disorder, this approach uses a classification system of diagnostic categories. The most commonly used classification-system nowadays is the DSM-III-R (APA, 1987).

The consequences of traumatization and uprooting

In principle, refugees can suffer from any psychiatric disorder that is found among human beings.

It is possible that they had some psychiatric disorder before they were traumatized or before they were forced to leave their homeland and that traumatization and uprooting did not really change the quality of this disorder. For instance, a schizophrenic person will still be diagnosed as schizophrenic after traumatization or uprooting; the same goes for someone who is mentally retarded. In these cases, neither traumatization nor uprooting is an etiological factor.

Besides this, it is possible that traumatization or uprooting is an etiological factor indeed, but only one of secondary importance. For instance, an individual may function on a level that cannot be considered as optimal, but that is sufficiently adequate to be labelled as a variation of normal functioning. One may think that he behaves a bit odd or unadjusted, or that he is rather unhappy. His behaviour may remind us of a particular psychiatric disorder, but it is not deviant enough to justify a diagnosis. However, psychosocial stress, like the stress related to traumatization and uprooting, may overburden this individual or remove the protective factors that impeded him from becoming worse. In this way, he may be pushed over the edge, so that he develops more symptoms which justify the diagnosis of the psychiatric disorder to which this individual seemed to have a predisposition.

Within the psychiatric approach it is thought that a traumatic experience can result in a specific kind of disorder, called post-traumatic stress disorder. The symptoms and other characteristics of this disorder are listed in the DSM–III–R (APA, 1987; reproduced by permission of the American Psychiatric Association) as follows:

A.   The person has experienced an event which is outside the range of usual human experience and that would be markedly distressing to almost anyone, e.g., serious threat to one's life or physical integrity; serious threat or harm to one's children, spouse or other close relatives and friends; sudden destruction of one's home or community; seeing another person who has recently been, or is being, seriously injured or killed as the result of an accident or physical violence.

B.   The traumatic event is persistently re-experienced in at least one of the following ways:

(1)   recurrent and intrusive distressing recollections of the event (in young children, repetitive play in which themes or aspects of the trauma are expressed)

(2)   recurrent distressing dreams of the event

(3)   sudden acting or feeling as if the traumatic event were recurring (including a sense of reliving the experience, illusions, hallucinations, and dissociative (flash-back) episodes, even those that occur upon awakening or when intoxicated

(4)   intense psychological distress at exposure to events that symbolize or resemble an aspect of the traumatic event, including anniversaries of the trauma

C.   Persistent avoidance of stimuli associated with the trauma or numbing of general responsiveness (not present before the trauma), as indicated by at least three of the following:

(1)   efforts to avoid thoughts or feelings associated with the trauma

(2)   efforts to avoid activities or situations that arouse recollections of the trauma

(3)   inability to recall an important aspect of the trauma (psychogenic amnesia)

(4)   markedly diminished interest in significant activities (in young children, loss of recently acquired development skills such as toilet training or language skills)

(5)   feeling of detachment or estrangement from others

(6)   restricted range of affect, e.g., unable to have loving feelings

(7)   sense of foreshortened future, e.g., does not expect to have a career, marriage or children, or a long life

D.   Persistent symptoms of increased arousal (not present before the trauma), as indicated by at least two of the following:

(1)   difficulty falling or staying asleep

(2)   irritability or outbursts of anger

(3)   difficulty concentrating

(4)   hypervigilance

(5)   exaggerated startle response

(6)   physiologic reactivity upon exposure to events that symbolize or resemble an aspect of the traumatic experience, (e.g., a woman who was raped in an elevator breaks out in cold sweat when entering any elevator).

E.   Duration of the disturbance (symptoms in B, C and D) of at least one month.

A fourth edition of the Diagnostic and Statistic Manual of Mental Disorders is expected to be published in 1992. In this new edition (DSM–IV), some changes can be expected with regard to the description of the post-traumatic stress disorder. The discussions on these changes concentrate on, among other things, the way in which the various symptoms are clustered. For example, it has been proposed to position the present criterion D6 (physiological hyperarousal on exposure to a reminder of the trauma) as one of the phasic, intrusive criteria in Criterion B (Davidson & Foa, 1991).

Sometimes the symptoms of post-traumatic stress disorder are manifested almost immediately (within six months) after the traumatic experiences. Such cases are referred to as acute post-traumatic stress disorder. But the complaints may only appear much later, and then they are referred to as delayed post-traumatic stress disorder. In the case of some war victims, the disorder manifests itself both as an acute reaction (shortly, on average five years, after the war) and a second reaction which manifests itself after a period of 15 to 25 years during which the victim did not have any complaints (Op den Velde, 1989).

Various investigators have concluded that the diagnosis of post-traumatic stress disorder is often applicable to refugees who present mental problems (Glassman, 1988; Kinzie et al., 1984). However, among refugees, the symptoms of post-traumatic stress disorder may be accompanied by the symptoms of major depression (Mollica, Wyshak & Lavell, 1987a). The most important symptoms of major depression are a depressed mood and loss of interest and pleasure in most activities, almost all day every day; as well as the presence of delusions or hallucinations whose content may or may not be consistent with the typical depressive themes of personal inadequacy, guilt, disease, death, nihilism or deserved punishment.

When one places the criteria of post-traumatic stress disturbance and major depression next to each other the resemblance is striking (Vladár Rivero, 1989). In the case of refugees the use of both diagnostic descriptions at the same time is often appropriate.

In addition to this, refugees who have the symptoms of the post-traumatic stress disorder sometimes also have auditory hallucinations, which are not necessarily accompanied by other psychotic symptoms (cf. Mueser & Butler, 1987). In other, less frequent cases, the symptoms of post-traumatic stress disorder may be accompanied by bizarre behaviour with a delusional and paranoid content, or by visual hallucinations that may be related to the trauma but cannot be considered as flashbacks (Kinzie & Boehnlein, 1989). In addition to this, tactile and bodily hallucinations with a fright-inducing content (e.g. sensation of being bitten) have been reported (Bailly, Jaffe & Pagella, 1989). Both depressive symptoms and symptoms like hallucinations and delusions may conceal symptoms related to the persistent re-experiencing of traumatic events, avoidance of trauma-related stimuli, and symptoms of increased arousal.

With regard to the consequences of traumatization, one should keep in mind that some kinds of torture may result in physical damage which may become the cause of some organic mental syndrome or disorder, like an organic mood syndrome, or an organic personality syndrome.

An organic mood syndrome is diagnosed when a person has a prominently and persistently depressed, elevated or expansive mood, while there is evidence from history, physical examination or laboratory tests of a specific organic factor (or factors) judged to be etiologically related to the disturbance.

An organic personality syndrome can be diagnosed in relation to traumatization when a person has undergone a persistent personality disturbance, representing a change or accentuation of a previously characteristic trait, involving at least one of the following: affective instability, recurrent outbursts of aggression that are grossly out of proportion to any precipitating psychosocial stressors, markedly impaired social judgement, marked apathy and indifference, or suspiciousness or paranoid ideation; while there is evidence from history, physical examination or laboratory tests of a specific organic factor (or factors) judged to be etiologically related to the disturbance.

The DSM-III-R does not mention disorders which are specifically related to cultural uprooting. It does mention a condition called adjustment disorder, which is defined as a maladaptive reaction to an identifiable psychosocial stressor, or stressors, such as divorce, marital problems, business difficulties, and so on. The diagnostic criteria of this disorder are not easily applicable to the complaints and symptoms of refugees, although uprooting certainly is an identifiable psychosocial stressor. One of these criteria is that the maladaptive reaction must occur within three months after the occurrence of the stressor and it must be indicated by either an impairment in occupational (including school) functioning or in usual social activities, or symptoms that are in excess of a normal and anticipated reaction to the stressor(s). But how can one decide whether there has been an impairment of occupational (or school) functioning in the case of refugees who have not found a job in the country of exile within three months after their flight, or who underachieve at school due to language problems? And what is an anticipated reaction to the stress of having to adapt in a new cultural environment, after forced separation from family, friends and familiar cultural environment?

Another criterion for the diagnosis of this disorder is that the maladaptive reaction must have persisted for no longer than six months: if the symptoms persist for more than six months, the diagnosis should be changed to some other mental disorder. Most refugees to whom the author attended and who seemed to have maladaptive reactions, needed more than six months in the country of exile simply to become informed about the existence of an institute to which they could apply for assistance.

It therefore seems appropriate to apply the diagnostic label adjustment disorder only to the effect of psychosocial stressors that occur some time after arrival in the country of exile, and not the effects of cultural uprooting as such.

Nevertheless, it appears that the stress of acculturation, the failure to acculturate despite several years in the resettlement country, or both of these factors, contribute to an ongoing condition associated with a decreased level of coping and an increased self-report of symptoms. Westermeyer (1988) therefore proposes the use of the label chronic acculturation syndrome. He suggests the following criteria:

1. Onset of the symptoms following refugee flight
2. The presence of symptoms falling across several diagnostic entities (e.g., depression, obsessive worry, low self-esteem, and suspiciousness)
3. Continuation of the symptoms for years after the original stressful event
4. The absence of symptom remission even with time and, in some cases, a new adaptational level

Complaints and symptoms of refugees during the first interview

What refugees tell us, spontaneously or supported by a few open-ended questions, during the initial interview may stand for what they themselves consider to be most relevant. But it is also possible that they give priority to what they think the professional helper wants to hear. What they say certainly is limited to what they want to entrust to a complete stranger.

Refugees who consult a psychologist or psychiatrist have usually been referred by family doctors, specialists, social workers or volunteers who help them with various practical matters. So when the psychologist or psychiatrist asks the refugee why he has requested assistance he also has to view the answer against the background of these prior contacts. Moreover, the psychologist or psychiatrist cannot assume that the refugee is fully aware of the kind of assistance he has to offer.

Refugees often initially only present somatic complaints. These somatic complaints have to be taken very seriously, of course. Even when it seems obvious that they are the result of psychosocial stress, a thorough medical examination by a doctor who is aware of the consequences of torture and other forms of organized violence, and familiar with cultural differences in verbalizing somatic complaints, is often necessary. If a physical cause for the somatic complaints cannot be determined, and this is patiently explained to the refugee, he may feel reassured and regain confidence in his own body. He may also be more open to suggestions about the possible psychological causes of his complaints.

Sometimes the refugee is already more or less aware of the relation between his complaints and psychological problems, but not able to express the latter. It is only after some questioning that psychological problems, relating to the client's experiences and his position as refugee, are mentioned.

A.C. was 21 years old when his family doctor referred him to a therapist. He reported the following complaints: pain in his stomach, insomnia, headaches and shortness of breath. When the therapist asked him some questions, it became clear that the shortness of breath could very well be the result of hyperventilation, that A.C. also had nightmares, worried a lot, felt lonely because he found it difficult to make contacts, and that he had problems in concentrating on his language studies.

A.C. told the therapist that he came from a large African city and had initially not been interested in politics. When he was 19 he had been apprehended and searched by a policeman who found a cassette tape of Western pop music in his bag. This was interpreted as a sign of rebellion against the regime and he was arrested and detained for several days. He was tortured and subsequently forced, against his will, into military service. The unit in which he had to serve was deployed against an ethnic minority, and he disagreed with this. During a long siege his best friend in the unit was killed before his eyes. He deserted and managed to escape from the country after many hardships. A.C. confirmed that he often had intrusive memories about his experiences in prison and during combat.

B.C. was 35 years old and a father of four when he visited the therapist. He had also been referred by his family doctor, because he could not sleep for more than three hours a night, had nightmares, could not concentrate and had very little appetite. He suffered from headaches and could not manage to get anything done. He just spent the whole day worrying and was haunted by memories of the painful experiences he had a few days before he left his country.

He had been active in a fundamentalist protestant church and had never been involved in politics. He had a government job in a small town in a Latin American dictatorship. One day he received instructions, together with a colleague, to escort a prisoner who was being transferred. The prisoner, an opposition politician, escaped and when B.C. reported this to his superiors they suspected him of complicity. He was arrested by the military police and so maltreated during interrogation that he ended up in hospital. There he discovered that his colleague had been executed because of the escape.

He managed to run away from hospital and left Latin America via a neighbouring country as a stowaway.

C.C. was 34 years old, married and the father of four children. A few months after his arrival in exile he was referred to a psychiatrist because of marital problems. He suffered from headaches, felt depressed and listless. He had difficulty falling asleep and reported having frequent nightmares and flashbacks of his experiences in prison.

He had been active in a human rights committee in a big city in Asia. Because of these activities he had been arrested and detained for a number of months. During his detention he was tortured to such an extent that he was left with permanent physical injury.

He felt unhappy because he was unable to work, and because he was afraid that his request for political asylum would be turned down. He reproached his wife that she did not understand what he had gone through and that she was jealous if he spoke to other women at meetings of compatriot refugees. His wife accompanied C.C. to the first interview. She complained that she was nervous. She worried about the children: the oldest, a girl of 14, was rebellious at home and had problems making contacts at school. The youngest, who was one year old, demanded a lot of attention. Referring to her husband Mrs C.C. said: 'It is often difficult to talk to him. Sometimes he does not say a thing for days on end.' She reproached him for not understanding what she had gone through when he was in prison and she was forced to manage on her own. A church organization had helped the family to leave the country, without additional difficulties.

The people in the examples above come from very different backgrounds. A.C. comes from Africa, B.C. from Latin America and C.C. from Asia. They differ in the extent to which they were involved in political opposition: A.C. was hardly politically conscious at all, B.C. belonged to an apolitical, but conservative group, C.C. belonged to a moderate oppositional group. Their present situation also differs: A.C. and B.C. are alone in exile, C.C. lives with his wife and children. They are in different phases of life: A.C. is an adolescent or young adult, B.C. and C.C. are adult husbands and fathers. Finally, they left their country in different ways: A.C. and B.C. suffered many hardships, C.C. and his family travelled without much difficulty.

In spite of all these differences, there are also similarities in the physical and mental states in which these three refugees found themselves when they requested assistance. They all had the following complaints in common: dejection, worry, insomnia, nightmares, intrusive memories of painful experiences, headaches and other somatic complaints, listlessness and trouble concentrating.

In all three examples presented above the refugee had suffered traumatic experiences which are related to post-traumatic stress disorder (category A) in the form of serious threats to the person's life or physical integrity; A.C. also witnessed serious harm to a friend and saw many people who were seriously injured or dead as part of his battlefield experiences.

These three refugees also mentioned characteristics of category B: the reliving of traumatic experiences in nightmares or recurrent distressing dreams and intrusive memories while being awake.

They had some of the symptoms related to category C. All three of them seemed to avoid stimuli associated with the trauma: they reported that they tried hard not to think of what had happened during their detention. All three could be considered as manifesting a numbing of general responsiveness, through diminished interest in significant activities (C.C. complained about listlessness, A.C. and B.C. seemed exhausted). Their worrying certainly meant a restriction of their affective life. C.C.'s tendency not to talk to his wife for days could also be interpreted as a form of numbing.

All three had symptoms from category D (increased arousal): difficulty in falling or staying asleep, and difficulty in concentrating.

Finally, all three had these complaints for some months. They had started before or soon after arriving in the country of exile. However, in the case of these three refugees one should not be satisfied if the label post-traumatic stress disorder can be applied. With regard to the patients discussed in this paragraph, one should remember that part of their symptoms (e.g. dejection, worry, listlessness) also fit into the diagnostic criteria for 'chronic acculturation syndrome' (Westermeyer, 1988). Moreover, patients A.C., B.C. and C.C. said that most of their symptoms had started or become worse after they left their country.

The next example illustrates that the complaints which point to a post-traumatic stress disorder sometimes only become visible after many years.

When D.C. made a request for assistance he had been in exile for more than ten years. He had fled from a Latin American country with his family after having been detained for two years and tortured for political reasons.

D.C. had been managing quite well in exile and there had been no problems in the family for which assistance was necessary. This all changed when he retired. He hardly had anything to do and just sat brooding. He considered returning to his native country, where his mother still lived, but his wife was not keen on the idea. The arrival of a nephew, who had recently had to leave his country after becoming a victim of political violence, brought a lot of emotions to the surface. Since then D.C. did not sleep very well, he frequently had nightmares about his experiences in prison, was easily irritated and afraid to lose control over his aggressive impulses, and he had difficulty in concentrating: he could hardly read a newspaper. He thought there was a connection between his nightmares and having seen riots on television news broadcasts, and he subsequently avoided watching television. He also said that he was having marital problems, and that he felt that his daughter was taking the side of his wife.

In summary, the diagnosis post-traumatic stress disorder is applicable to refugees in at least some cases. The author found this label appropriate for summing up the problems of 50% of the refugees who requested his assistance. In some cases, this label had to be combined with other labels, like chronic acculturation syndrome and organic personality syndrome. The majority of the remaining 50% requested assistance for conditions not attributable to a mental disorder, such as marital problems, parent-child conflicts, uncomplicated bereavement or adult anti-social behaviour, often in combination with problems related to adaptation to the country of exile. About 5% was appraised as having divergent disorders as mood disorders, psychoactive substance abuse, schizophrenia, sexual disorders and personality disorders.

Utility and limitations of the psychiatric approach

The psychiatric approach offers a useful first characterization of the problems of many refugees who request assistance. It supplies the therapist with lists of symptoms about which he can question a refugee in order to help him to express his complaints. The therapist will then also convey to the refugee that his problem is in some way 'familiar' to him, the therapist, and that treatment is possible. This usually has a reassuring effect.

E.C. presented his problem as follows: 'I cannot sleep, and I am afraid I am going mad.' He illustrated this by mentioning that he had lost all interest in his hobbies, felt alienated from his former friends, and had the feeling of being trapped in a cage from which he would never escape. He also said that he was unable to read a newspaper or watch television, because he could not concentrate for more than a few minutes. The therapist asked E.C. if he was having nightmares, which he confirmed. Talking about the content of these nightmares it became clear that they were related to the traumatic experiences (months of torture) which had forced him to leave his country.

The therapist concluded that post-traumatic stress disturbance was a useful provisional diagnosis. He decided to explain to E.C. that he understood his complaints as a result of his traumatic experiences, that he did not consider E.C.'s symptoms to be a sign of madness, but an understandable reaction, to be expected after months of torture. He also told E.C. that he had been right in seeking help, that he thought that E.C.'s problem was indeed serious, and that he was thinking of various methods of treatment that would help to alleviate E.C.'s symptoms.

In this way he offered E.C. a first explanation for his symptoms, and hope that he might overcome them in the future.

The psychiatric approach, especially the concept of post-traumatic stress disturbance, can help us to explain to the refugee what is happening to him. It also helps us to exclude the possibility that the refugee suffers from some other type of psychiatric disorder. What he experiences as madness or extreme weakness, or what his environment may have been interpreting as hysteria or malingering becomes understandable as a 'normal' and thus respectable reaction to extremely sad or painful experiences.

A limitation of this approach is that it does not yet offer us satisfactory and generally acceptable descriptions of the possible pathological consequences of uprooting. Moreover, the DSM-III-R manual states that this psychiatric classification system must be used with caution when evaluating the psychological functioning of persons from different ethnic or cultural backgrounds. Symptoms of distress can be very culture-specific, and behaviour that seems pathological in a Western context may be common and adaptive in the original cultural environment of the refugee. For instance, when one works with refugees it is not unusual to see a patient who feels possessed or troubled by a spirit, while this can be understood as a normal sign of cultural bereavement (Eisenbruch, 1989).

It also is the experience of the author that refugees from non-Western countries sometimes show behaviour that impresses as fitting in the picture of avoidant personality disorder (like: being reticent in social situations because of fear of saying something inappropriate or foolish, or being unable to answer a question) but that is perfectly understandable as a way of dealing with a chronic acculturation syndrome. In this case, it is important to get information about the onset of the behaviour in question: long before or after the flight. Behaviour that is associated with the histrionic personality disorder (like: expresses emotion with inappropriate exaggeration) might not be considered deviant within the culture of the refugee, because this culture uses other standards about what is exaggerated and what isn't. If one wants to apply this diagnostic label to a refugee, one should actually have a hetero-anamnesis which is evaluated by a person from the same cultural background.

A similar point can make with regard to the possibility to misinterpret more or less adequate coping behaviour of refugees as signs of a personality disorder, or the other way round. Organized violence may cause decent, gentle and conscientious people to do things one considers at first sight to be indicative of an antisocial personality disorder; while people who had an antisocial personality disorder in the first place, may later be traumatized by organized violence and manifest the symptoms of a post-traumatic stress disorder. Also, behaviour that in some cases refers to a paranoid personality disorder (like: reads hidden demeaning or threatening meanings into benign remarks or events) may be perfectly understandable as adequate coping in a situation of terror.

Another limitation of the psychiatric approach is that it does not pretend to offer as much of an explanation about the psychological mechanisms that are responsible for the development of psychological problems as a consequence of traumatic experiences. However, some research has been directed to the biological and physiological causes of the symptoms of post-traumatic stress disorder. It has been shown, for example, that the autonomous nervous system of patients with post-traumatic stress disorder does not function normally (Van der Kolk et al., 1985a,b). This type of research belongs to a long tradition in which post-traumatic symptoms are related to factors such as the physical effects of protracted malnutrition during detention or brain damage as a result of blows to the head. Van der Kolk's research on the physiological effects of pain and fear is a modern variation on this approach. However useful the results of this research may become or already are for the psychiatrist considering the prescription of psychotropic medication, they do not offer clearly visible points of application for psychotherapeutic techniques.

The DSM–III–R is not only an instrument assisting the diagnosis of disorders; it also contains a scale for assessing the severity of psychosocial stressors and a scale for the global assessment of psychological, social and occupational functioning. Nevertheless DSM–III–R does not pretend to represent anything more than an initial step in a comprehensive evaluation leading to the formulation of a treatment plan (cf. Lansen, 1988). For the construction of a detailed treatment plan, psychological approaches that provide causal explanations of the problems of refugees are needed. These approaches help to describe individual differences in the way the psychological consequences of traumatization and uprooting are manifested, and that provide concepts and a theoretical framework for understanding and evaluating the 'healthy' aspects of psychological functioning. These 'healthy' aspects, as it were, provide the basis for the application of psychological treatment methods.

The psychodynamic approach

Some basic concepts and assumptions

In the previous section it was concluded that, in order to find points of application for psychotherapeutic techniques, a theoretical approach is needed that explains the problems of refugees in general and also provides a framework for understanding individual differences between refugees. The psychodynamic approach meets these requirements to a considerable degree. The term 'psychodynamic approach' refers here to the classic psychoanalytical theories of Sigmund Freud and his followers, and more recent theories that are based, in some respects, on Freud's ideas, though they also deviate from his approach (Lerner, 1987). This label is used for the basic ideas which a large group of related, though in some respects competing, psychological theories, have in common.

Inner conflict and personality structure The psychodynamic approach focuses on the individual's inner life. Its central theme is that every individual experiences inner conflicts, between impulses on the one hand and the restrictions that reality imposes on the other. The way in which the individual handles these conflicts becomes characteristic for him, and is referred to as his personality. The concept of personality thus implies that the psychological functioning of each individual manifests a certain degree of coherence or structure.

Defence and coping In order to describe the psychological functioning of the individual the psychodynamic approach uses the concepts of defence and coping.

The concept of *defence* refers to the phenomenon that an individual can actively remove parts of reality from his conscious experience, in order to reduce both the fear of real danger and the anxiety related to inner conflicts. Anxiety is reduced through the use of various so called defence mechanisms. The most important defence mechanisms are denial and repression, which render the anxiety provoking conflict or perceptions unconscious. In some stages of personality development, certain defence mechanisms are used in relation to the specific type of inner conflicts that are characteristic for that stage. For instance, a defence mechanism called asceticism is associated with inner conflicts in adolescence due to a sudden upheaval of aggressive and sexual impulses (cf. Freud, 1958).

Coping refers to mental activities which have a more conscious character and serve adaptation to the external environment, or are aimed at overcoming painful events and finding realistic solutions to the conflicts that a person experiences (cf. Murphy, 1960; Lerner, 1987). Coping mechanisms are strategies for problem solving or dealing with conflicts, and/or for avoiding the unpleasant emotions that are related to conflicts. As a result, inner conflicts or unpleasant situations can be experienced as less painful, though they remain conscious. Coping skills are flexible and can be adjusted to specific situations, while defence mechanisms usually result in rigid patterns of reaction.

Personality development   A basic assumption of the psychodynamic approach is that, as a result of biological developments and psychosocial factors that are related to these biological developments, each individual goes through a process of personality development. The term development refers to the assumption that the psychological functioning, due to a constant interaction between individual dispositions and environmental determinants, shows qualitative changes which are related to the process of growing older and that these changes appear in a fixed, irreversible sequence. It is thought that the individual passes through a sequences of stages; in each of these stages he has to cope with specific types of conflicts.

According to the psychodynamic approach, the course of personality development in early childhood is very important for personality development later on. For instance, the inner strategies a child has developed for dealing with stressful, anxiety-provoking events in childhood, may influence the way he deals with traumatic experiences in his later life.

Disturbance of personality development   Another central hypothesis in the psychodynamic approach is that personality development can become disturbed. Such a disturbance can be caused by the inadequate use of defence mechanisms or a shortage of adequate coping skills. This occurs when:

1.   The use of defences has grown so excessive that the individual loses his grasp on reality, which is manifested in problematic or inadequate behaviour. This can be the consequence of prolonged exposure to traumatic experience.
2.   The individual rigidly uses one type of defence for a long time, so that his interactions with the environment become stereotyped and further personality development is therefore hindered. This can also occur as a result of a prolonged experience of traumatic conditions.
3.   A more or less balanced system of defences breaks down, as a result of an extreme traumatic incident, physical illness, the use of psychotropic substances or a combination of such factors.
4.   Coping mechanisms that were useful in the past are not applicable to a new situation with new conflicts. This can occur because of a sudden and radical change of environment.

In order to understand the psychological problems of refugees in the context of a psychodynamic approach, they have to be considered against the background of personality development. The therapist is therefore not only interested in their present complaints and symptoms, and the traumatic experiences they have recently undergone, but also in information about personality development from their earliest childhood, through adolescence, right up to the present. He will also need to analyse the psychological functioning of the refugee in terms of defence and coping mechanisms.

Psychosocial functioning It is characteristic for the classical psychodynamic approach that it concentrates on the inner experiences, feelings and conflicts of the individual. Its main domain is intra-psychic development. For a long time the psychodynamic approach did not devote much attention to the development of social relations. More recent contributions to this approach stress the importance of psychosocial functioning (the way a person feels and behaves in personal relationships and socially) as an aspect of personality development. Erikson (1968, 1982), for instance, has discussed the stages of personality development of classical psychoanalytic theory and reformulated these in terms of the specific psychosocial tasks that have to be fulfilled in each stage. In his opinion social experiences are processed so that the individual develops attitudes which determine much of his behaviour and thinking about himself and other people.

If one adopts this point of view, attention should be devoted to the refugee's history in terms of his psychosocial development, the way he handled the psychosocial tasks of the various developmental stages, and the attitudes he developed.

In summary, from a psychodynamic point of view the complaints and symptoms which the refugee presents will have to be evaluated against the background of his personality structure. Information about this personality structure can be gathered by talking about the way he has experienced his personal history. But it will also become apparent during the interaction between the therapist and the refugee: personality structure manifests itself in the refugee's attitude towards the person who tries to help him and the way in which he expresses his problems. The therapist can learn something about this attitude by experiencing it during the process of therapy.

The psychological problems a refugee experiences and the way he presents these can then be interpreted as the result of interaction between the following factors: underlying disturbances in personality development that result from a more recent process of traumatization, conflicts that are specific for the refugee's stage of life; and coping styles and psychosocial attitudes developed in the past and during the process of traumatization.

The consequences of traumatization: damage and repair

Within the psychodynamic approach the traumatic experience is seen as a confrontation between the individual and his environment, in which he encounters 'unbearable stimuli' and experiences 'overwhelming affects'. The usual coping skills and defence mechanisms are unable to deal with this situation. The individual's affective responses produce an unbearable psychic state which threatens to disorganize all psychic functions and damage the personality structure. He experiences helplessness and surrenders, which means that he becomes totally passive and inhibited (cf. Baranger, Baranger & Mom, 1988; Krystal, 1978). The processes of defence and coping become disorganized. This can result in the disappearance of affective reactions, apathy or depersonalization. These effects may continue for some time (Furman, 1986).

From the psychodynamic point of view, a traumatic experience has two consequences: damage and a process of reparation. The after-effects of a traumatic experience can therefore be seen either as a result of damage, or as the side-effects of a necessary and useful process of reparation. The repeated reliving of traumatic experiences in nightmares or wakeful imagination can, for instance be seen as part of a process in which the emotions that occurred during traumatization become assimilated. This process can be described as a sequence of phases (Horowitz, 1976, 1986).

In the first, short, phase (a few hours to a few days after the experience), which may sometimes be skipped, the emotions stimulated by the traumatic experience are expressed violently. Horowitz calls this the *outcry* phase.

Then there is a phase in which the emotions are repressed: the *denial* phase. The individual pretends that nothing special has happened, or that the events have not touched him. He appears to function normally, but tries nevertheless to avoid situations which could remind him of his traumatic experiences. His reactions are shallow and unemotional.

This second phase alternates with a third phase in which memories of the traumatic event and the painful feelings associated with it come forcefully to the surface. In this *intrusive* phase the person has nightmares and it does not take much to remind him of the shocking events which he has experienced.

The alternation of the second and third phase can, according to Horowitz, be seen as a gradual assimilation of the endured emotions. In the third phase these emotions are made conscious so that they can be assimilated. If they become so intense that the person is in danger of being overwhelmed, then the defence mechanisms will be engaged and he will revert to functioning as in the 'denial' phase. After a while, when he has calmed down and had new experiences which enhance his capacity for coping, he will admit more of these emotions into his consciousness so that they can become assimilated. Eventually, the intensity of the feelings that are related to the traumatic experiences will decrease and the alternation between the intrusive and denial phases will cease.

After this there is a fourth phase: the phase of *working through*. In this phase the traumatic episodes become an important part of the person's experience. They are not denied as in the second phase, but they are not dominant either, as in the 'intrusive' phase. During this phase the person learns to live with his experiences and to fit them into his world view and his self-image.

A.D., a 16-year-old refugee from Latin America, visited the therapist four months after he had been tortured by the secret police. He began the interview by saying that he wanted to tell his story. And so he did, in a session of two and a half hours. His behaviour reminded the therapist of Horowitz's description of the 'outcry' phase, although it occurred much later than a few days after the trauma. It was only at the end of the interview that the therapist found the opportunity to ask A.D. about his complaints and symptoms. A.D. then told the therapist that he had been having frequent nightmares lately, as is to be expected in the 'intrusive' phase. In later interviews the most frequent topics of discussion were A.D.'s adaptation to the country of exile, the problems of his parents and the political situation in his native country. The latter subject brought back memories of torture, but without much emotional upheaval, as in the 'working through' phase. The nightmares had disappeared after the first interview, and had not returned a year later. Other symptoms (lack of concentration, nervousness) also disappeared gradually within four months.

It is the author's experience that Horowitz's descriptions offer many points of recognition. However, the behaviour of refugees often does not conform to the sequence of distinct phases which Horowitz postulated. For instance, after 'working through' one traumatic experience, intrusive memories of a second traumatic experience may occur.

In addition to the foregoing relativizing thoughts about Horowitz's contribution, the following critical remarks can be added.

Firstly, it should be noted that according to the literature concerning emotional responses to undesirable life events, human beings show considerable variability in their post-traumatic behaviour. This variability manifests itself in the particular emotional responses that are demonstrated. It is also a fact that some individuals do not exhibit any emotional reaction at all (cf. Silver & Wortman, 1980). Given this variability, it is not surprising that empirical research does not generally support the hypothesis that emotional responses to life crises usually follow some fixed sequence of behaviour patterns which manifest clear qualitative differences. Horowitz's descriptions should therefore be evaluated as clinical impressions and not as proven empirical facts.

Secondly, Horowitz's observations that some individuals skip the first phase, and that they may move back and forth between the second and third phases, shows that his concept of 'phase' has a meaning that differs fundamentally from the concept of 'stage' as part of an invariable sequence, as it is used in developmental psychology.

This means that however enlightening Horowitz's descriptions may be in many cases, they should not be referred to as normative. If an individual reacts to a traumatic experience in a way that deviates from Horowitz's typification then this does not mean that his reactions are therefore abnormal, inadequate of pathological, or that his personality development is disturbed.

Finally, Horowitz's descriptions might suggest that a person generally recovers spontaneously from traumatic experiences. The empirical evidence suggests, however, that such an assumption is inapplicable to at least a sizeable minority of the population (Silver & Wortman, 1980).

The consequences of traumatization: impetus for inner conflict

The psychodynamic approach offers various other ideas that may contribute to understanding the fact that many people continually relive their traumatic experiences during a certain period of time. In this paragraph the ideas of Freud (1955) and of Grinker & Spiegel (see Brett & Ostroff, 1985) will be discussed. In their approaches, the concept of inner conflict plays an important part.

Freud was intrigued by the continual re-living of traumatic experiences during nightmares. He became acquainted with this phenomenon through his contact with First World War front-line soldiers. Freud saw their nightmares as a primitive (by primitive he means only adequate for very young children) defence mechanism against being overwhelmed by emotions: compulsive repetition. Freud assumed that, in a certain sense, the organism actively recalled the traumatic experiences into consciousness. This occurred in order to re-experience, or more correctly experience, the anxiety that was originally absent at the time of the traumatic event. This active recollection of very painful experiences which had been passively and helplessly endured, contributed, slowly but surely, to the emotional assimilation of the trauma.

Freud therefore thought that the individual actually tried to remember his traumatic experiences. But the memories evoked so many negative emotions that the individual simultaneously brought other defence mechanisms into action in order to avoid becoming conscious of them. There is thus an inner conflict between defences: repetition-compulsion as a defence against an overwhelming feeling of passive powerlessness which results in re-experiencing on the one hand, and defences such as denial or repression on the other hand. This inner conflict tends to frustrate the process of assimilation. Recent research has shown that one of these defences may be dominant: re-experiencing seems to be dominant in those who have witnessed violence, while among those who have physically experienced or participated in violence, re-experiencing appears to be warded off by denial (Laufer, Brett & Gallops, 1985); although appreciable overlap between these two groups also was found (Eth, 1986).

Freud claimed that traumatic experiences also have cognitive consequences: the traumatized person comes to know aspects of life, human nature, his own personality and other persons, that were unknown to him before the traumatic experiences. This new knowledge becomes very important. The person may also discover that what he has learned in the course of his traumatic events is incompatible with his former world view and self-image. The conclusions he was forced to draw from his traumatic experiences may be incompatible with what he always believed. This causes fear, which is why some memories of the experience are repressed.

The repression of certain kinds of knowledge is also part of the inner conflict mentioned above. The person knows something he would rather not know and which he would like to forget; but at the same time he realizes that what he has learned from his traumatic experiences can be useful in avoiding similar occurrences in the future. In more abstract terms: the inner conflict also tends to frustrate cognitive coping processes.

In his 50th psychotherapeutic encounter B.D. became aware that he had been an unwanted child, that his unmarried mother had always had extremely ambivalent feelings towards him, and that these factors still unintentionally influenced the way in which he associated with other people. A week later he described an experience which had occurred just before he fled into exile. It was an experience about which he still sometimes had very unpleasant dreams and which he had never talked to the therapist about.

It occurred when he was eight years old. One morning, on his way to school, he saw dozens of bodies piled up on a piece of wasteland behind a shed. 'I remember now the thought which occurred to me at that moment', B.D. said. 'It was: my mother won't protect me.'

Freud's contributions serve to direct the therapist's attention to the inner conflict related to talking or even thinking about traumatic experiences. Grinker & Spiegel (1945; see Brett and Ostroff, 1985) also relate the occurrence of nightmares to inner conflict, though in a different way. Their hypothesis is that nightmares about traumatic experiences can be understood as a form of self-punishment. These authors focus on the interaction which can develop between present inner conflicts and traumatic experiences from the past.

C.D. had a nightmare in which she re-experienced the pursuit which preceded her arrest. She dreamed that she appealed to her parents for help but that they sent her away. In reality her parents had always helped her—they had helped her to flee the country. In the talk which followed she said that she had recently started having a relationship with a married man. She suspected that her parents would disapprove and was not sure whether she would write and tell them.

The consequences of traumatization and personality structure

Coping style According to the psychodynamic approach, an individual's reaction to traumatic experiences depends on the quality of his personality structure. One factor that is thought to be important is the quality of his coping repertoire, which in turn depends on the vicissitudes of the personality development that preceded the traumatic experiences. In a retrospective study of the coping behaviour of victims of the nazi concentration camps of Treblinka and Sobibor, Schumacher (1982) distinguishes three groups of victims by the types of coping they applied: regression, adaptive defence and progressive coping. The victims who survived by regression described their behaviour in the concentration camp as passive and apathetic; they said they tried to avoid perceiving what happened around them. The victims who survived by adaptive defence did continue to perceive reality and attempted to adapt to it by submissive behaviour, keeping the relationship with their guards as good as possible, and by considering themselves lucky to be alive. Those who survived by progressive coping, tried to analyse their situation, to recognize possible danger before it became reality, to take adequate action to protect themselves from it, to make use of every possibility to improve their situation, and so on. The behaviour of these victims was determined by the aim of getting one of them out of the camp alive, so that he could tell the world what was happening inside.

About the personality development of these three groups, Schumacher concludes that the survivors who used regression were children of good, strong and protective mothers, and that this experience had given them the trust that eventually everything would turn out right. The victims who used adaptive defence had weak and helpless parents, from whom they had learned to survive by submissive adaptation. They had developed little self-esteem, but a great determination to survive. The victims who used progressive coping had strong, successful fathers who were supported by quiet but confident mothers. The relationship with their parents had enabled them to acquire self-confidence.

The three groups also differed with respect to the consequences they ascribed to their experiences in the concentration camp. Those who had used regressive coping, that is to say, adopted a passive attitude and warded off the bitter reality, seemed to have forgotten most of their traumatic experiences. In court cases against war criminals they could not give much evidence. However, they did not show signs of psychological damage. So Rutter's (1987) conclusion that cognitive mechanisms to protect oneself against stressful life experiences are probably only effective when they lead to active coping and not just passive acceptance, seems to be open to discussion. People may be able to survive and keep relatively healthy in a psychological sense by ignoring as much as they can. In that case they are also unable to describe their traumatic experiences—which may be a handicap for a refugee who requests political asylum.

Returning to Schumacher's study of concentration camp victims: most psychological damage was found in the group that used adaptive defence: they suffered from fears, nightmares, depression and so on. Those who had used progressive coping did not seem to have much psychological damage, they could also remember what had happened to them very well.

There are refugees who have experiences that in some ways resemble those of the victims of Treblinka and Sobibor, for instance refugees from Cambodia and some refugees from Iran who spent a long time in prison under the constant threat of being tortured or executed. The author has experience with the latter group. Among them, he saw nobody who seemed to have survived exclusively by way of regressive coping. This is in line with Schumacher's conclusion that those who use this coping style do not show signs of psychological damage. A few of the Iranian refugees who discussed their prison experience in detail, seemed to have used adaptive defence as a coping style, at least in some situations; sometimes in combination with regressive coping. In relation to prison experiences, they often mentioned fear and helplessness as overwhelming emotions. They had, in line with Schumacher's conclusions, problematic relations with their parents, although it would be too simple to describe these parents, as Schumacher does, as weak and helpless. These refugees also had a rather vulnerable self-concept.

Another group of Iranian refugees, described their prison experiences above all in terms of what they had seen the guards do to other people. The feeling they described most as overwhelming, was a feeling of intense powerlessness at times when they wanted to protect other prisoners. The coping style of these prisoners seemed to be comparable to progressive coping, but, in contrast to Schumacher's subjects, they certainly had psychological damage.

The presence of disturbances in personality development A second important factor which is thought to determine an individual's reaction to traumatic experiences is the presence of disturbances in personality development—which may or may not have resulted in manifest symptoms—before traumatization. The traumatic experiences may either become articulated to existing, manifest problems, or potentiate and reactivate emotional problems that had been hidden for a long time (cf. Kramer, Schoen & Kinney, 1987).

D.D. requested assistance because she had phobic complaints. She was also very depressed and haunted by terrible nightmares. Talking about the nightmares, it became apparent that D.D. had been seriously abused by her parents during early childhood. As a child she had serious depressions and problems making social contacts. As an adolescent she had been detained for political reasons and maltreated but, as she said, not extremely in comparison to what happened to some of her friends. Nevertheless, she found it very difficult to discuss her experiences in prison. Talking about this recent traumatic past evoked a lot of intense emotions she could hardly verbalize. These seemed to be related to the abuse in her early childhood. The therapist concluded that the recent traumatic experiences had reactivated a latent emotional problem, which it was better not to uncover. He therefore focused on the way in which she had coped with her recent traumatic experiences, which (in Schumacher's terminology) could be described as a mixture of adaptive defence and progressive coping. This had a supportive effect, and D.D. regained some of her self-confidence and became less depressed.

E.D. requested assistance for complaints which were similar to those of D.D. His recent traumatic experiences seemed much more severe. He had reacted to the first of these—the destruction of his house and murder of his parents by the government army—through progressive coping, by joining a resistance organization. After another traumatic event—a buddy was killed before his eyes—he had made a serious attempt to kill himself. When the therapist asked him some routine questions about his family background he became very sad. He remembered the close relationship he used to have with his parents, and mentioned the confidence they had in him. E.D. did not seem to have assimilated the loss of his parents. The death of his buddy, five years later, was a trauma in itself, but also seemed to have reactivated the emotional problem E.D. had with regard to the loss of his parents.

E.D. was able to talk about his parents, and therapy became an opportunity for mourning.

The consequences of traumatization: related to stage of life

From a psychodynamic point of view it almost goes without saying that the way in which an individual adapts to traumatic experiences or post-traumatic symptoms depends on his level of personality development. Keilson (1979) illustrates this hypothesis in his study of the psychological functioning, during adulthood, of Jewish children who had been traumatized in many ways, including separation from their mother, during the Second World War. For the youngest of them, the traumatic experiences seemed to have resulted in a personality disorder. Among those who were traumatized during pre-adolescence, he found anxiety disorders. Among those traumatized during adolescence, chronic reactive depressions were dominant.

The possible interaction between developmental processes and traumatization will be discussed in more detail in the chapters on children and adolescents in part III of this study.

The consequences of uprooting

Erikson's contributions on the relationship between psychological development and cultural factors make it possible to present some psychodynamic hypotheses about the effects of cultural uprooting. Erikson (1968) concluded that the course of identity development is closely related to the norms and values of a particular society, and the kind of ideology and future perspective that this society offers. He also observed that when the cultural pillars of identity in a society collapse, young people may suffer severe identity confusion. This psychological state may cause them to withdraw into apathy and tempt them to self-destructive behaviour like the abuse of alcohol and drugs.

It can be supposed that because the refugee has had to live under the kind of anomic repression and violence that forces people to flee, and that he was subsequently forced to leave his familiar cultural environment, this can result in identity problems. These may manifest themselves as a sense of confusion about norms and values, irresolution even in trivial matters, ideological doubts, loss of future perspective; and may result in apathy and self-destructive behaviour. Perhaps the complaints, symptoms and behaviour of refugees become more understandable when these are evaluated against the background of identity problems, and the therapist talks with them about such topics as norms, values, political ideals and the future.

F.D., a 24-year-old refugee from the Middle East who belonged to a left-wing political group, became very confused when he realized that his ideas about politics were not very sophisticated and that some of the achievements of capitalist society were very tempting. He started to visit bars, which led to conflicts with his political friends. His opinion about them changed: 'If they came to power, they would become the new torturers', he confided to the therapist. After he had received a positive answer to his request for political asylum and was admitted to a university, he could not feel relieved. He felt alienated and was uncertain when it came to making decisions. For example, he had registered for a study which he thought would be useful if he could return to his country. But he was not sure whether to stick to his original plan, choose another subject that would give him more chance of getting a good job in Europe, or follow what he called 'an impulse' to study art-history.

Utility and limitations of the psychodynamic approach

The psychodynamic approach offers many useful hypothesis with regard to the individual differences in the way that individual refugees deal with traumatic experiences and uprooting, the way they think about their problems, and their attitude towards people who want to help them. Moreover, it draws attention to the fact that psychological problems that are the consequence of traumatic experiences mingle and interact with normal phase-specific problems, and can evoke developmental disturbances that have remained hidden for a long time. Finally, it presents interesting thoughts about inner processes in relation to traumatization and uprooting of which most refugees are hardly aware themselves but nevertheless may have decisive importance for their behaviour.

The term psychodynamic approach refers to a complex field of theoretical contributions, which can offer insight into the complex nature and interconnectedness of psychological problems. But most of these theoretical contributions lack coherence. The concepts they use are often not very clearly defined, and certainly not easy to operationalize. They cannot offer a simple list of questions to ask or symptoms to check, as in the psychiatric approach. Understanding the problems a refugee presents in terms of the psychodynamic approach is not a matter of a few structured interviews. For diagnosis the therapist needs time, and he has to enter into a therapeutic relationship with the refugee.

The family therapy approach

Some basic concepts and assumptions

In this section theoretical approaches from very different backgrounds are brought together. What they have in common is that they focus their attention upon the relations and interaction processes that exist between individuals in their primary life environment, and that the quality of these relations and interaction processes are seen as important determinants of individual behaviour.

Circular interaction   A basic assumption of this approach is that an individual's family (or the people who surround him as a primary social environment) forms an important factor in his well-being. The interaction with his family can produce a lot of practical and emotional support for the individual, which makes him less vulnerable to stress from the wider environment. But this interaction is not always supportive, and it can also make the individual more vulnerable to environmental stress or it may itself be the cause of the individual's mental problems.

If an individual has a mental problem, this has to be evaluated against the background of the interaction processes within the family.

Another important assumption is that the interactions between people have a circular character (Haley, 1963). The behaviour of all the individuals who take part in dysfunctional interaction, tends to complement the continuation or escalation of the dysfunctional quality of that interaction. This means that, in the case of inadequate patterns of social interaction, it is impossible to say which individual is the cause of dysfunction. For example, in a married couple one may observe that the husband is a bit peevish, which causes the wife to react with irritation, which does not make the husband less peevish at all. The wife may comment that her husband is always moody, the husband that his wife only nags him, and neither of them seems completely mistaken.

Communication Some representatives of the family-therapy approach state that inadequate family interaction can be seen as the result of disturbances in communication between members (Watzlawick, Beauvin & Jackson, 1967). In this interaction information is exchanged, by means of verbal statements and behaviour. This information has two aspects: a message with a certain content, and an expression of emotions which concern the relation between the persons involved in the exchange. In this sense the meaning of everything which is said has two levels, and can thus become ambiguous. Misunderstanding can arise when one of the persons involved in the interaction does not notice or understand both aspects of the message. This may happen when the individual who says or does something to another member of the family is not aware of the emotions he simultaneously expresses; or when an individual tends to interpret ambiguous messages in a rigid, stereotyped way.

Moreover, one misunderstanding leads to the other, thus causing conflicts and estrangement within the family.

Communication in a family can also become disturbed when some members share a secret concerning a very important issue about which the other members of the family are not informed. These secrets usually concern topics like birth, sex or death (Van de Lande, 1980). For instance, the circumstances under which a member of the family died, the fact that one of the children was born out of wedlock, or the traumatic experiences of one of the parents can be kept secret.

Secrets in the family are kept on the basis of the fear that disclosure of the secret might result in the break-up of the family. Sometimes secrets are kept in order to protect certain moral values embraced by the family. By keeping something secret, the informed members of the family try to escape feelings of guilt, or the fear and grief related to an imminent loss (Pincus & Dare, 1978). Under circumstances of extreme repression, some traumatic experience of a family member may be kept a secret from a part of the family in order to prevent the family from becoming a victim of more traumatic events. In this case, keeping the secret may be (or have been for some time) an adequate form of coping (cf. Sluzki, 1990).

Usually it is the parents who keep a secret from the children. What they keep secret are things they believe the child would not be able to handle, or would make him overly anxious or excited.

A.E. a 21-year-old man who had left his Latin American homeland after some very traumatic experiences, told the therapist he was very nervous because his father had not written to him. Instead he had received a letter from his sister, informing him that his father had twisted his right arm and therefore was not able to write properly. When asked why this made him so nervous, A.E. responded that he was afraid that this meant that his father had died. A.E.'s mother had died two years before, but the family had not dared to inform him and had decided to prepare him slowly for the loss. First they had written to him to say that his mother was in hospital with an illness. Later they informed him that the illness was a heart problem. Then A.E. received a message that his mother's condition was serious. Finally an uncle arrived in person to inform him that his mother had died. When he received this news, his mother had already been buried six months. So now A.E. took the news of his father's twisted arm very seriously.

Secrets in the family can become a burden for vulnerable children, especially if the secret activates fearful fantasies. It then can result in disturbed behaviour or symptoms by the child. An open discussion within the family, on a level that is understandable for the child, usually leads to a diminishing of symptoms and problematic behaviour (Dare, 1980).

Family structure   Another way of analysing the interaction within a family is aimed at assessing patterns of transactions. In this way, one gets information about the way in which interaction is structured (Minuchin & Fishman, 1981). In this approach the family is seen as a system in which the parents, children, grandparents as well as each individual member can form distinct subsystems. The family is thought to function adequately when these subsystems are related to the roles of the various members, and form a functional hierarchy. Inadequate family functioning is thought to occur when *coalitions* develop which deviate from the aforementioned subsystems. These coalitions then interfere with the normal hierarchy and come into conflict with each other (for example, the grandmother and the eldest grandson form a coalition which comes into conflict with another coalition consisting of the mother and her new companion).

The forming of a coalition often means that one family member is burdened with a role which is slightly beyond his capacity. This may occur when one of the children has to assume the responsibilities of one of the parents, a phenomenon that is called *parentification*.

According to Minuchin families also differ with regard to the rigidity or flexibility in the way the subsystems fulfil their roles, and thus in the degree in which they are able to adapt to situations which demand a change in responsibilities. For example, a family in which the father takes all the decisions and allows the other members little responsibility in contacts with the environment may be quite helpless for some time when the father is suddenly absent.

Trans-generational phenomena Some family therapists (Boszormenyi-Nagy & Spark, 1973, Stierlin et al., 1980) focus their attention on the history of the family and the phenomena that can be observed through the sequence of generations. Nagy states that each individual in a family has an existential feeling of *loyalty* to his parents and other members of the family, which influences his decisions in daily life. Parents give their children *legacies*, in the form of expectations about the way in which they will lead their lives. The individual is not always aware of these loyalties and the legacies that are connected with them, but he nevertheless behaves as if he felt the obligation to make decisions in a way which concurs with the expectations, orders or wishes of the parents. This means that the individual sometimes makes decisions that are against his own interests, feels guilty about decisions which are contrary to the wishes of his parents, or seems to be unable to make a choice. For example, a parent may order the child to achieve a high status in society, which then leads the child to choose a study that goes beyond his intellectual capacities, so that he experiences failure after failure.

The legacy of a parent may also take the form of a certain attitude or feeling towards life, or people in general, which the parents developed during their lifetime as a result of their own experiences, and which is transferred to the child. For example, an individual may feel depressed for a long time without understanding why, until he realizes that his mother always seemed to be melancholic after the death of her husband.

The consequences of traumatization

It is obvious that when an individual has traumatic experiences, he needs more emotional support from his social environment. It therefore makes a lot of difference whether the traumatized individual belongs to a family that can give this support or not. The capacity to support depends on the quality of the interactions and the communication within the family, and the structural qualities of the family as a system. Moreover, after traumatization transgenerational phenomena may play an important role.

In the case of refugees, the following phenomena can be observed with regard to their primary social environment:

1. Physical separation of (parts of) the original system
2. Overburdening of one family member
3. Avoidance of open communication through over-protectiveness
4. Disruption of communication through irritation caused by external factors

5.   Disruption of communication through fear or related feelings
6.   Trans-generational traumatization
7.   Parentification

Physical separation of (parts of) the original system   Often a refugee is separated completely from his family, or is unable to maintain contact with important subsystems (for example, when the refugee is an adolescent and his parents have remained behind). In this situation the refugee has to find a new supportive system. Without the presence of at least some informal relations which the refugee experiences as supportive, therapy directed at the working through of traumatic experiences becomes a very hazardous enterprise.

Overburdening one member of the family   When a traumatized refugee is living with one or two members of his family, it may occur that his need for emotional support after traumatization becomes so intense that one of the members becomes overburdened.

B.E. was 17 when he was arrested on suspicion of being a socialist. He was held in custody for three days and tortured. After that he fled to Europe, where he joined his father, who had left the country two years earlier after becoming the victim of extreme abuse while in jail as a political prisoner. B.E. consulted the therapist because he had nightmares and was very nervous. It soon became clear that he had been able to overcome his own traumatic experiences, but could not cope with his father's need for emotional support. The therapist suggested that B.E. could bring his father along, but B.E. preferred individual contacts, which continued for about three months. Then B.E. said he felt strong enough to interrupt therapy; he had taken a job and also started dating. After a month his father called the therapist because he wanted to discuss his own problems.

Avoidance of open communication through over-protectiveness   There is some empirical evidence for the hypothesis that traumatic experiences can result in the avoidance of open communication about emotions related to traumatic experiences. For instance, after a traumatic event, the discussion of feelings of fear and sadness may be avoided. This will occur when the traumatized individual thinks that some members of the family might not be able to cope with the reality, when he is afraid that he might become a burden for his family (cf. Figley, 1988), or when he feels ashamed of what he calls his 'weakness' and so on. The effects of fear on families are described by Becker & Weinstein (1986). Their study is based on experiences during the military dictatorship in Chile, and concur with what the author observed in the families of refugees. According to Becker & Weinstein, frightening and threatening events often are not discussed, even when they are not just incidents, but a part of everyday life. They are kept secret and the emotions which are related to these events are not shared. An emotional distance develops between the members and each feels alone and not understood.

In addition, the way in which family members associate with each other becomes less flexible (see also Dare, 1980). Their roles become rigid: for example the father acts tough, the mother plays weak, the son is always aggressive and the daughter cries for nothing. But at the same time they hide other feelings and impulses. The father wants to cry but is afraid it will disturb the children; the son has received another threatening telephone call but does not mention it so that his mother will not worry: she is aware that her son feels threatened and is very worried, but she pretends not to notice because she does not want her husband to get concerned. To put it more abstractly: because they are unable to protect each other from external violence a form of overprotection develops which impedes communication and mutual emotional support. It seems as though the family is falling apart, but in reality it is an artificial distancing which stems from mutual concern.

Disruption of communication through irritation caused by external factors   Another consequence of fear and threats in everyday life is that family members become more aggressive in their behaviour towards one another. They are easily irritated and conflicts and rows develop, but they hardly speak about the threats from outside.

C.E., a Turkish girl of 16, had received a residence permit for humanitarian reasons shortly after she joined her mother who had arrived in the Netherlands a year earlier. Her mother, who was a victim of torture, was still waiting for an answer to her request for political asylum after three years. So was her brother of 17. C.E. told the therapist about the daily quarrels in the family. She also said that she was afraid that her mother might be sent back to Turkey, especially since a political friend of the family had been ordered to leave Holland after waiting four years for an answer to his request for asylum. This incident, she said, had never been discussed in the family. Her mother had not shown any reaction when she heard the news.

Disruption of communication through fear   Sometimes victims of trauma are just not able to verbalize the feelings of fear related to their experiences. Nevertheless, their daily interaction with other people in their primary environment is coloured or disturbed by these feelings.

D.E., a refugee of 21 years had been severely tortured while he was detained for political reasons. He often had sudden spells of fear, especially at places like restaurants, discos and cinemas. D.E. was not able to discuss this fear with his girlfriend. He usually became angry when his girlfriend asked him why he wanted to leave suddenly. The girl therefore thought he was angry at her every time he suddenly wanted leave a place.

During therapy, it became clear that the fears were related to flashbacks. D.E. then started to talk about his flashbacks with his girlfriend. She gave him considerable support in overcoming them.

Trans-generational traumatization   When a parent is unable to face certain feelings related to a traumatic event, he may nonetheless still express them and transfer them to the children (Reinoso, 1985).

E.E.'s father died in prison when E.E. was two years old. He had been detained for political reasons, after he had been separated from E.E.'s mother and before E.E. was born. E.E. had never seen his father. His mother, who consulted the therapist because she could not handle E.E.'s problematic behaviour, seemed to have ambivalent feelings about her ex-husband but described him to her son as a saint. E.E.'s behaviour had become disruptive at home since his mother had found a boyfriend. But he also sometimes became aggressive at school when his peers boasted about their fathers.

Parentification   Sometimes the consequence of a traumatic experience is that the traumatized individual is treated as a victim by the members of his family, or more or less willingly accepts the role of the victim who is unable to take normal responsibilities and therefore no longer taken seriously. When the traumatized person is a parent, who behaves like or is treated like a victim this disrupts the hierarchical organization of the family and may result in parentification.

After returning from prison, where he had some very traumatic experiences, F.E. had a lot of invalidating somatic complaints. His wife and his eldest son took charge of most of the problems the family faced. F.E. felt offended that a lot of decisions were taken without him being consulted. He also blamed his son for not achieving at school. The boy, who was 12, seemed to be rather intelligent. He learned to speak Dutch in less than a year and acted as an interpreter for the family. He seemed to have concentration problems at school.

The consequences of uprooting

The consequences of uprooting can, from the point of view of the family-therapy approach, be summarized as follows:

1. Continuation of existing problematic interactions
2. Additional stress as a result of adjustment problems and communication problems related to differences in the tempo of adaptation between the family members
3. Loss of contact with supportive subsystems
4. The formation of new, bi-cultural primary social systems, together with all the problems that are related to this

Continuation of existing problematic interaction   Uprooting often does not end existing forms of dysfunctional interaction within families. When a refugee goes into exile without his family, that does not mean that he is independent of his family. For example, the parentification of an oldest son may continue.

G.E. saved some money each month to call his mother who lived in Africa. After the call he was always very depressed: his mother never asked him much about himself, but only complained about her husband and his family.

Another aspect of a refugee's dependence on his family can be illustrated with the term legacy.

In order to pay for his journey to the West, H.E.'s parents had to sell their house. H.E. felt very guilty about this. He hoped to become a doctor, because that was his father's wish. When his achievements at university fell short of his expectations he became very depressed.

Additional stress as a result of adjustment problems and communication problems related to differences in tempo of adaptation between the family members Uprooting brings stress, and therefore more need for mutual emotional support within the family. The capacity of family members to support one another depends on the quality of the communication in the family and the structure of the family system. When the interaction within the family was dysfunctional before uprooting, the stress related to uprooting will often make things worse.

But, according to the author's observations, even in families that were functioning well before uprooting, new communication problems may develop as a result of differences in the tempo of adaptation to the situation of exile. Conflicts may be related to the fact that one of the family members begins to deviate from the cultural traditions all of them used to adhere to in the past.

I.E. was referred to the therapist because he had difficulty sleeping. He was a refugee from Africa, and he and his wife arrived in the Netherlands together. I.E. had trouble learning the language because of his concentration problems, while his wife mastered it in a year and went on to university. She made friends with other female students, and embraced some of their ideas about the position of women in society. I.E. felt threatened by these ideas, and the couple started to have serious disagreements.

The adaptation of a family to exile may also be hindered by rigidity of the system as a whole.

J.E. came to the Netherlands from the Middle East with his wife and four children. His oldest son soon made Dutch friends, and when he reached adolescence, he started behaving like a Dutch adolescent. J.E.'s wife tolerated her son wearing torn jeans, but did not dare to discuss it with her husband because that did not concur with her view about the behaviour of a decent wife. J.E. himself considered his son's behaviour to be outrageous, and tried to assert his traditional authority with physical punishment. The boy ran away from home.

Losing contact with supportive subsystems The effectiveness of a family system in solving problems may deteriorate because communication between subsystems has become difficult or impossible.

When K.E. had quarrelled with his wife, he usually did not speak to her for some days. He was used to reacting in this way and had done so since their wedding day. He told the therapist that his father did the same thing when he had a disagreement with his mother. In their family, marital problems were usually solved through the intervention of older brothers or grandparents who played an intermediary role and tried to invent some solution that prevented the husband from losing face. Because his brothers and parents were far away, he had to do without their interventions, and was afraid to lose face if he admitted to his wife that there might be some sense in her point of view.

The formation of new, bi-cultural primary social systems and the problems that are attached to this Finally, when a refugee starts a relationship, a bi-cultural system may come into existence. If a family has its roots in different cultures, it will sometimes be necessary to discuss differences in value systems, ideas about the education of children and loyalty to the cultures one wants to transfer to the children. This may become a problem when the family of one of the partners intervenes.

L.E., a refugee from the Middle East, and his wife, a refugee from Africa, had some problems from the beginning of their marriage. The problems escalated when L.E.'s parents came to visit them at the time L.E.'s wife was expecting her first child. The parents stressed that the grandson (they would not consider the possibility of the child being a girl) should receive an islamic name.

Utility and limitations of the family-therapy approach

The family-therapy approach stimulates us to evaluate the complaints and symptoms of a refugee against the background of the interactions he has with his primary social environment, in the first place his family but also associates from his political organization or room mates and friends who became close to him in the country of exile. It makes us sensitive to rigid patterns in the refugee's interaction with the people close to him, and draws the attention to matters about which there is no, or only inadequate, communication.

Unfortunately, the construction of a theory about the consequences of trauma and uprooting based on this approach has only just started. A therapist who wants to use the therapeutic tools offered by this approach, is often handicapped because an important part of the family lives far away, in a physical sense or in a psychological sense, or in every respect.

The learning-theory approach

Some basic concepts and assumptions

The various theoretical frameworks that are brought together in this section have in common that they depart from the assumption that behaviour can be learned and that the environment plays an important part in this. Various principles of learning can be described. According to this approach, the problems of any individual can be described in terms of behaviour that has been acquired as a result of one or a combination of several of these learning principles, and more adequate psychological functioning can be brought about by therapeutic interventions based on the same principles.

Four principles of learning can be distinguished: classical conditioning, operant conditioning (also called instrumental learning), learning through self-control and observational learning.

The theory of *classical conditioning* (Pavlov, 1960) deals with autonomous, involuntary or reflex behaviour that is the 'natural consequence' of some stimulus. Classical conditioning means that this reflex behaviour is linked to another stimulus.

The theory of *operant conditioning* (Skinner, 1974) or instrumental learning accentuates the importance of the consequences that follow certain behaviours. According to this theory, behaviour is learned through the reinforcement that follows after certain behaviour that originally occurred by coincidence. The reinforcement is called positive whenever the consequence of the behaviour is some kind of reward; as a result of this reinforcement the occurrence of the same behaviour in the future becomes more probable. Reinforcement is called negative when the consequence of the behaviour is the removal of some aversive stimulus. Negative reinforcement has, according to this theory, also the effect that the behaviour in question becomes more probable. When behaviour is followed by negative reinforcement, it is sometimes called *avoidance behaviour* (a term which suggests that the behaviour in question is determined by an assessment of danger in a certain situation, and therefore has a cognitive character). When behaviour is not followed by reinforcement, it is less likely to be repeated. This phenomenon is called extinction.

When behaviour is followed by an aversive stimulus (punishment), it will not be reinforced so that extinction is expected. Moreover, the aversive stimulus may provoke activity which leads to the removal of this stimulus and therefore results in the learning of avoidance behaviour.

According to social-learning theory (Bandura, 1977; Gross & Levin, 1987) positive reinforcement, negative reinforcement and punishment can all have a social character. For example, if a person's action is praised by others then this can function as a positive social reinforcement, if it has the effect that another person stops looking angry it may be a negative reinforcement, and if, as a consequence of that action, another person starts to shout angrily then that action will not be reinforced. Whether the consequences of a certain action are reinforcement or punishment is thus thought to depend on the cognitive interpretation of these consequences by the actor. When a person's behaviour is praised and he interprets the praise as genuine, this is a positive reinforcement. But when he interprets praise as not genuine, it may not reinforce the antecedent behaviour.

Behaviour can also be reinforced by the way in which a person reacts to his own behaviour. This is called learning through *self-control*. A person's reactions to his own behaviour are related to the demands he makes of himself. If his behaviour conforms to his own standards, it is reinforced. If this is not the case, the behaviour—even if, in the eyes of a bystander, it leads in some degree to the desired result—will not be reinforced and is less likely to recur. However, a person's standards are also the result of a learning process, and can therefore be altered.

Finally, according to social learning theory, behaviour can also be learned, without reinforcement, through the *observation* of other people's behaviour.

Learning theory focuses the attention on the way in which refugees' problems can be understood as the result of learning processes. Traumatic experiences can be analysed in terms of the learning processes that occurred during or after traumatization. Special attention might also be given to current processes of social learning in a new cultural situation, and especially the cognitive interpretation of the social consequences of behaviour as positive reinforcement, negative reinforcement and punishment. The theory of learning through self-control leads us to speculate on the standards against which the refugee compares his current behaviour, and to what extent he can be helped by teaching him different standards, which provide more scope for reinforcing adaptive behaviour. Finally, the concept of observational learning may inspire the development of therapeutic methods focused on helping the refugee to acquire a behavioural repertoire that is adaptive in the new cultural situation in which he finds himself, as a member of a not very popular and sometimes discriminated minority group.

The consequences of traumatic experiences as learned behaviour

The consequences of traumatic experiences—the re-living of these experiences, avoidance of certain situations or activities that arouse recollections of the trauma, the physiological reactivity upon exposure to events that symbolize or resemble a part of the traumatic events—can be seen as the result of learning processes. For example, the repeated re-living of traumatic experiences can be explained in terms of conditioning (see for example Lyons & Keane, 1989; Kolb, 1984; Van der Kolk et al., 1985b: Brett & Ostroff, 1985; Pallmeyer, Blanchard & Kolb, 1986). During traumatic events conditioning processes are activated as a result of which neutral stimuli become associated with the negative emotions and physiological effects that were a natural reaction to the traumatic experiences. If one of these stimuli happens to occur in a new situation, then the painful emotions will immediately be relived and the physiological effects that occurred during the traumatic experiences will reappear. Sometimes the original traumatic experiences are also instantly re-experienced.

A.F. was a refugee from Latin America. He had been tortured, after having been arrested by uniformed policemen who had forced their way into his house. Years later he became very confused when a uniformed postman called to deliver a parcel. When he told the therapist about this incident, he started sweating profusely.

The confrontation with neutral stimuli that have been conditioned to the traumatic experiences generally causes feelings of fear and fear-related physiological reactions, like sweating, hyperventilation, accelerated heartbeat, and so on. Some of these physiological reactions can cause new fears (of choking or getting a heart attack, for example). Moreover, the sensations that come with the physiological reactions during traumatization can also form stimuli that can become conditioned to the traumatic events.

For B.F. any sport or exercise could bring back memories of being tortured. The smell of his own sweat seemed to be the stimulus that had become conditioned to the experience of pain and fear while he was tortured.

When the refugee is able to realize that, in spite of his feelings of fear, there is no real danger, it becomes easier for him to cope with the fear, through the use of conscious relaxation, for instance.

According to learning theory, a traumatized person tends to avoid stimuli which have become associated with the trauma. This can be seen as a natural reaction. This avoidance behaviour may be adaptive, especially if there is real danger. In such cases it may prevent new traumatic experiences.

This kind of avoidance behaviour can also be adaptive for some time if it prevents the person from having more frightening memories than he can handle. The situations he thus avoids would have overwhelmed him instead of enabling him to realize that there is no real danger.

Avoidance behaviour can, however, also eliminate all possibility of extinguishing conditioned fear reactions. This may occur if avoidance behaviour becomes a routine through new conditioning. The avoidance of fear then works as (negative) reinforcement, and the 'natural' avoidance reactions to specific stimuli develop into a broad repertoire of avoidance behaviour that becomes a problem in itself.

C.F. became very upset when uniformed inspectors checked his ticket in the subway. Their intimidating and derogatory behaviour reminded him of his arrest and subsequent maltreatment, and he became very anxious.

After the incident in the subway he was afraid to use public transport. He could not face another encounter with inspectors, because he thought he might lose control of himself. He started avoiding all activities for which he had to travel. This led to a reduction in his social contacts, and he became more lonely and depressed than before the incident.

In his native country C.F. had, for obvious reasons, learned to hide as soon as he saw a uniform, and to avoid situations in which he might be checked by the police or the military. This behaviour had not continued after his arrival in Europe. It was the behaviour of the inspectors that triggered his fear.

On the basis of the learning approach it can be assumed that post-traumatic symptoms are the result of a conditioning process. The maladaptive effects of these conditioning processes can be diminished by exposure of the traumatized person to the stimuli that have become associated with the traumatic experience in a non-traumatic situation. This exposure can be accomplished by various behaviour therapeutic techniques, such as flooding in imagination or other kinds of therapeutically controlled visual imagery (cf. Fairbank & Nicholson, 1987; Grigsby, 1987).

Learned helplessness

The principles of conditioning may also be used to explain passivity, apathy and the attitude of helplessness that the victims of traumatic experiences sometimes manifest. In this context, reference can be made to Seligman's experiments with dogs that had been caged and tormented with electric shocks (see Seligman, 1975, or Gielis, 1982, for a detailed description of these experiments).

These unfortunate animals were subsequently more prone to illness than dogs which had not been made helpless and exposed to pain. They also behaved differently from other dogs: they were less socially enduring than the average member of their species. When these traumatized dogs were returned to the cage for more electric shocks, but provided with the possibility of escape by climbing over a barrier to the other side of the cage, their behaviour differed dramatically from that of their non-traumatized fellows. The latter became active and quickly learned to avoid the electric shocks by moving to the other side of the cage. The traumatized dogs remained passive, simply lying down and whining.

Seligman describes this behaviour as 'learned helplessness'. It can be unlearned if the dogs are shown that they can avoid torment by dragging them to the other side of the cage. This has to be repeated many times, however (Seligman, Maier & Geer 1968).

In similar experiments with humans, in which less painful forms of torment were used, similar reactions were observed (Gielis, 1982).

According to Seligman's theory, learned helplessness goes together with the following four effects:

1. Reduced motivation to react actively. Helpless people tend to adopt a passive attitude. Their reactions are slow and their thinking is sluggish. This is related to their expectation that whatever they do, it will not have any effect on the unpleasant situation in which they find themselves.
2. Reduced capacity to learn that their actions can lead to the desired results.
3. Negative feelings such as fear, depressiveness, emptiness, absence of desires.
4. Self-reproach and reduced self-esteem.

In order to unlearn helplessness, the human victims of traumatic experiences should be given the therapeutic equivalent of 'dragging them over the barrier' as occurred with the dogs in Seligman's experiment (Van der Kolk et al., 1985a). This is, of course, easier said than done.

Seligman's observations can be summarized by stating that traumatization often results in the passivity of the traumatized individual in certain situations. This passivity may be understood as the result of extinction processes which occurred during the traumatic experiences because none of the individual's actions in the traumatic situation were followed by positive or negative reinforcement. It may manifest itself in situations that in some way resemble the traumatic situation (for example, an initial interview in which the helping professional tries to gather diagnostic information may, in some respects, resemble police interrogation).

D.F. was 13 years old when he arrived in Amsterdam. His parents had put him on an aeroplane, because they feared that their son would be conscripted to a local militia. They supposed that an aunt that lived in Europe would take care of the boy, but this aunt did not show up at the airport. She seemed to have left for Canada.

D.F. was first received in a children's home, and after a few weeks placed in a foster family. He was sent to a secondary school which was attended by some compatriots. After some months, he was transferred to another school. The reason was that D.F. and his compatriots, although they had soon learned to speak the Dutch language, formed a kind of clique. Among them they spoke their own language, which was thought to be disturbing the classroom routine.

D.F. was referred to the counsellor, because of his passive attitude. He did not do anything unless he was ordered to do so. He had made no friends at the new school. He was a member of a sporting club, but during the weekly training he showed the same passivity.

In the contact with the therapist, D.F. seemed very timid. However, he slowly came out of his shell when the therapist addressed him in his native language. He pretended to be indifferent about living far away from his parents and having been moved around as a parcel, but he was able to admit that he did not like the school and considered himself to be a failure. It became clear that at this school he had to learn two foreign languages, while speaking Dutch was still quite an effort.

The therapist tried to find out what D.F. had liked or considered interesting in the time he was still with his parents, but only received evasive answers. There seemed to be an absence of desires. So he concluded that D.F.'s condition was similar to 'learned helplessness', the trauma being the sudden separation from his parents and later from his friends at school.

The consequences of uprooting

Learning theories stress the importance of the environment in which behaviour is learned. So within this framework it seems justified to assume that specific cultural situations may result in the learning of specific forms of behaviour, and that behaviour that is adequate in a particular culture may be inadequate in a different culture. This means that after uprooting, new behaviour, especially social problem-solving skills (Pellegrini, 1985), have to be acquired. It also means that some problem-solving or coping behaviour which was adequate and protective in the native culture but is inadequate in the new culture, should be restricted to certain situations (for instance meetings with compatriots), or unlearned.

E.F., a refugee from a South East Asian country, had left his country because he was a politically active member of an ethnic minority that lately had become the object of persecution. He was an extremely polite, soft-spoken person, who never contradicted anybody. This attitude had rather negative consequences. For instance, the government official that interrogated him about his request for political asylum, had said to E.F. that he supposed E.F. had never been in trouble for political reasons. E.F. politely confirmed this, although he had been detained for political reasons twice. E.F.'s request for political asylum, was therefore denied.

The social worker that was appointed to help E.F. with some practical problems, became desperate because he never could be sure whether E.F. really wanted something or just was being complaisant.

He referred E.F. to the therapist. In this discussion with the therapist it soon became clear that E.F.'s pliant attitude had been very useful for a member of an ethnic minority in his native country, and therefore had become second nature.

The complaints and symptoms of refugees might become more understandable if they are seen as learned behaviour or a result of a shortage of social skills that are adequate in their present cultural surrounding. That means that the therapist should discuss the difficulties they experience in daily social encounters, and must be aware of the possibility that his own behaviour may not be in line with the social conventions that the refugee has learned in his own culture.

Utility and limitations of the learning-theory approach

Learning theories provide us with clear concepts and formulations, which certainly help us to understand the problems of refugees as well as providing interesting points of application for psychotherapeutic techniques. In the next section it will be shown that the modern elaborations of this approach also make it applicable to such cognitive matters as the way in which refugees think about the causes of their problems.

An important limitation is, however, that these theories have not produced much to facilitate an understanding of the more complicated aspects of refugees' behaviour and inner life, such as contradictory feelings, doubts about the meaning of life, nightmares, self-destructive imagination, etc. The concept of learned helplessness introduced by Seligman can be seen as an effort to fill this gap. But by using such terms as expectation, self-reproach and reduced self-esteem, Seligman introduces a cognitive element into his explanation. The following section will show that this cognitive element becomes the backbone of a more recent reformulation of his theory. Moreover, a cognitive reformulation of his theory of classical conditioning will be discussed, which can be very helpful in understanding the psychological consequences of traumatization by political violence.

The cognitive approach

Some basic concepts and assumptions

The cognitive approach in psychology deals with the content and quality of thought processes, how knowledge is acquired and used, the way social situations are evaluated and problems are approached. The focus of this approach is on the conscious thoughts of the individual.

Information is one of the important concepts of this approach. It refers to anything that can be perceived by the senses, and then in some way is processed by the mind (Beck et al., 1979). The way in which information is processed, can be compared with the way in which a computer processes information: by working on the information when it is admitted to awareness (like working on a text that is reproduced on a monitor), by reproducing it in a different form, by classifying and by arranging the information, and by moving it between different storage locations in the mind, like from the 'working memory' to the 'long-term memory' (cf. Seifert & Hoffnung, 1987).

The way in which information is processed, depends on the *assumptions* the individual is holding and the kind of *inferences* he uses while he is evaluating his perceptions (cf. Beck et al., 1979). The term assumption refers to the basic beliefs a person adheres to, and which he rarely examines for validity. Some of these assumptions may be inadequate and result in inadequate forms of information processing and eventually in mental problems. For example: a person may have the following assumption: 'If I make a mistake, it means that I am inept.' This assumption predisposes to perfectionism and depression. The term inference refers to the way in which a person interprets what he is perceiving. Some types of inference are inadequate, like:

- *Arbitrary inference*: in this case the person draws conclusions in absence of evidence, or ignores facts that are contrary to his conclusion
- *Selective abstraction*: the person focuses on a detail he has taken out of its context, ignoring other salient features of the situation
- *Overgeneralization*: the person draws a general rule on basis of isolated incidents
- *Magnification*: the person overestimates the significance of an event
- *Minimization*: the person underestimates the significance of an event
- *Personalization*: the person tends to relate external events to himself where there is no basis for making such a connection
- *Absolutistic, dichotomous thinking*: the person has the tendency to place all experiences in one of two opposite categories, like flawless or defective, immaculate or filthy

If a person uses inadequate inferences, this results in a distorted view of himself and the world. These distorted views are reflected in his explanatory or attribution style, that is to say: in the way in which he gives causal explanations for his problems.

Traditionally, cognitive theories have devoted much attention to the relation between cognitive processes and age. One of the basic concepts in this approach is *development*, which involves a complex process of interaction between the individual's spontaneous activity and his environment. This can be seen as a process of adaptation, in which maturation, experience and the knowledge and ideas that are transmitted in the course of education in a particular culture all have their contribution.

Furthermore, different *stages* of development are distinguished, which are associated with qualitative differences in cognitive functioning. These stages are thought to have an invariant, universal order, and therefore not to be subject to cultural variations. As an individual passes through these stages, his cognitive functioning adapts to his environment and becomes more adequate. In most cognitive stage approaches, cognitive development is thought to reach completion during adolescence (De Wit & Van der Veer, 1989).

One of the main discussions within this approach concerns the way in which the functional capacity for processing can be increased, the way in which new cognitive skills and ways of cognitive representation can be acquired, and the degree to which specific training procedures and instructions can be used to promote more adequate cognitive functioning. Another point of discussion is whether the various stages of intellectual development are really universal, or do cultural factors influence the course of cognitive development?

The cognitive consequences of traumatization and uprooting

The theoretical contributions which the cognitive approach has made to understanding the consequences of traumatization and uprooting can be grouped around six concepts: disturbance in information processing, coping style, explanation or attribution style, victimization and delay or arrest in cognitive development. Moreover, cognitive concepts can be integrated in different ways into the learning approach: the cognitive behavioural approaches.

Disturbance in information processing

During the periods that a person is undergoing traumatic experiences, he is perceiving an enormous amount of very complex information. This information includes for example physical sensations of pain; emotional reactions like fear, disgust, shame and sexual excitement; physical sensations and reactions that are brought about by physiological reactions related to the aforementioned emotions; emotional reactions to the aforementioned physical sensations and reactions; perceptions of the attributes of the environment in which the person is subjected to traumatic experiences; perceptions of the characteristics of the perpetrator and possible bystanders; the thoughts of the person about himself during the traumatic experiences; the memories that were revived during the traumatic experiences and so on.

This bulk of information can easily become overwhelming, meaning that the average person's functional capacity for processing this information will fall short. This means that at least part of the information is not transformed and not stored in the long-term memory, but continues to occupy large parts of the short-term memory. The condition that information about the traumatic experience remains in the short-term memory, implies that it stays close to awareness, and may easily become aware again in the form of intrusive memories, flashbacks and nightmares. It also implies that the capacity of the short-term memory to store new information, becomes less: it is already filled with information related to the traumatic experiences. This results in disturbances in the information processing, which become apparent in such symptoms as forgetfulness and loss of concentration with regard to present-day activities.

The condition that the information related to the traumatic experiences has not been transformed, implies that, when it re-enters into awareness, it comes as vivid and intrusive as during the traumatic experiences themselves.

Departing from this position, recommendations can be made with regard to counselling trauma victims. The objective of counselling would be, from an information-theoretical viewpoint, to help the victim to transform the information about his traumatic experiences, so that it can be stored in the long-term memory, and will no longer disturb his cognitive functioning. This objective could be approached by discussing all the information that is associated with the traumatic experiences in some orderly way, so that the information can be arranged and classified. The 'testimony method', a set of psychotherapeutic techniques with victims of organized violence that is described in part II of this study, and in which the accent is on a chronological ordering of the information, is an example of a therapeutic method that is in line with this cognitive approach. Another example is the following.

A.G., a refugee from a Middle East country who had been traumatized both during combat and during captivity, over a period of seven years. One day he started the conversation with the therapist by complaining that he had had three or four nightmares every night during the last week. He added that he kept thinking of these nightmares all day. Then he remained silent.

The therapist then asked him to describe in detail the worst nightmare that came to his mind. By this question, the therapist tried, among other things, to help the refugee to structure his experiential world.

Coping styles

Coping refers to cognitive activities that are elicited by psychosocial stress and aimed at adaptation. Traumatization and uprooting are both forms of psychosocial stress and will therefore activate coping activity.

The concept of coping was already introduced in the section on the psychodynamic approach, in which it refers to an intra-psychic process and the effects of this process on behaviour and cognitive functioning. It was also briefly mentioned in the context of the discussion of learning theory, in which it primarily refers to problem-solving behaviour.

In psychological studies coping can therefore refer to concrete activities, such as discussing problems with others, consciously trying to stop thinking about certain experiences, consciously trying to 'get over' certain negative feelings, seeking professional assistance, doing yoga or other relaxing exercises, taking medicine, drugs or alcohol, seeking diversion in various activities, or looking at the funny side of problematic situations.

Many researchers assume that there are different *styles* of coping. In the section on the psychodynamic approach Schumacher's (1982) descriptions of regressive coping (which, because it includes the avoidance of perceiving traumatic circumstances, is partly described in cognitive terms), coping by adaptive defence, and adaptive progressive coping, were already mentioned. A distinction can also be made between people who, when in extreme circumstances, try to influence the situation in which they find themselves, those who direct their energy to controlling their own emotional reactions, and those who—in cognitive terms—come to view their painful experiences differently, thus reducing the influence of these experiences (Miller et al., 1985). Another categorization (Folkman & Lazarus, 1988) is even more cognitive in its terminology, and it integrates some of the foregoing descriptions.

According to Folkman & Lazarus the following dimensions of coping style can be identified:

1. Coping by the deployment of attention. This refers to coping activity that diverts attention from the source of distress (avoidance strategies) or directs attention to it (vigilant strategies).
2. Coping by changing the subjective meaning or significance of a person-environment transaction, by transforming a threat into a challenge, denying its existence, emphasizing the positive aspects of the situation or distancing (making jokes about it). Distancing may be very adaptive in situations where nothing can be done.
3. Coping by changing the actual terms of the person–environment relationship, through 'confrontive coping' (an assertive or even somewhat aggressive interpersonal form in which the individual defends his rights or makes clear what he wants, and which may generate negative emotions in the

person who is being confronted), or by 'planned problem-solving' (a strategy of using rational problem-solving while at the same time inviting others to provide emotional support).

It can be useful to assess the ways in which a refugee is coping with his problems and stimulate him to explore alternative ways of coping.

B.G. suffered from intrusive memories of his experiences during captivity. He said he actively tried to put the images of the past out of his mind, but was not able to do so. The therapist concluded that B.G. used coping by deployment of attention in the form of an avoidance strategy. He recommended B.G. to make brief notes or make a quick drawing of the content of the intrusive memories, before he tried to put them out of his mind.

The notes and drawings became a subject for discussion during therapy, and the intrusive memories soon became less frequent and less disturbing.

C.G. requested assistance because he had outbursts of anger which he was not able to control. He had beaten his girlfriend during one of these outbursts. He felt very ashamed about this. The therapist at first interpreted these aggressive outbursts as a post-traumatic symptom of increased arousal. C.G. had been severely traumatized during the years he was detained and tortured. Later, when he had heard more about C.G.'s behaviour in prison, he concluded that C.G.'s behaviour might also be interpreted as a form of confrontive coping he used whenever he was suspicious.

This became clear when the therapist had the opportunity to bring C.G. the news that he had received a residence permit for humanitarian reasons. C.G. was not able to concentrate on the rather complicated juridical facts the therapist had to explain, became very suspicious, anxious, and at last aggressive. It was the fear the therapist perceived in C.G.'s reaction that made the therapist think that aggression might be a way of coping with fear, in this case the fear of being cheated and eventually being sent back to his torturers.

In the next session, C.G. excused himself. The therapist asked him if he had ever felt the same as he felt during the last session. C.G. then described some prison experiences and explained that aggression for him had been the only way to prevent himself from giving information to the prison guards, especially if they seemed nice and patient. This form of confrontive coping was useful in prison, but became obsolete during exile.

Explanation or attribution styles

The thoughts about explanation and attribution styles of traumatized people presented in this paragraph, are based on laboratory research of the reactions of human beings to pain and stressful experiences they couldn't control (see Wortman, 1983, for an overview of this kind of research). They ought to be preceded by a relativizing remark about the possibilities of applying the generalizations of this research to clinical work with refugees. The stressful experiences one can inflict on a person in a laboratory situation differ very much in intensity, quality, diversity and duration from the traumatic experiences that some refugees have undergone (for example sexual torture or the 'disappearance' of a relative after he was arrested by the secret police).

The laboratory research on explanation styles started as a trial to show that Seligman's theory of 'learned helplessness' in dogs was useful in explaining the occurrence of chronic depressive symptoms in human beings, and led eventually to a reformulation of Seligman's theory in cognitive terms (Peterson & Seligman, 1984). This revised theory focuses on the way in which people attribute causal explanations to painful experiences they cannot control. It can be summarized as follows.

When people have experienced painful events that they could not control, they usually wonder why the events happened. Their answer, i.e. the cause to which they attribute the events, determines, or is representative of, the way in which they react to difficult situations.

It is possible to distinguish three explanatory dimensions in people's answers to the question 'Why did it happen to me?' Firstly, the individual can see himself as the cause of the calamity (internal attribution), or attribute it to the situation in which he found himself (external explanation). Secondly, the causal factor may be described as transient and alterable or persistent and unalterable. Finally, the cause may be limited to the event (specific explanation) or may effect a whole variety of outcomes (global explanation) (Peterson & Seligman, 1984).

D.G., E.G., F.G. and G.G. all had the same complaints: they started having nightmares again: 'It's because I stopped taking my sleeping tablets, I wasn't really ready to stop completely', was D.G.'s explanation. This explanation implied that by changing only one clearly defined aspect of his behaviour—taking his sleeping tablets—his complaints would be alleviated. He explained his complaints in terms of a cause which he experienced as internal, specific and transient. E.G., remarked: 'Since I began to consider returning to my native country things have not been going well.' In this explanation he gives the impression that he is the cause of the recurrence of his nightmares, and that they are not his only problem. He has an internal, global and transient explanation. In connection with her nightmares F.G. said 'It's so cold here. It's never as cold as this in the country where I come from. When it's so cold everything goes wrong.' She refers to an external, transient cause—the weather. Because she said that everything went wrong her explanation is global. G.G. gave the following explanation: 'This weekend I saw a film in which people were tortured and as a result painful memories surfaced.' He refers to an external, specific, transient cause.

H.G., I.G., J.G. and K.G. felt lonely and depressed. H.G. said: 'It's because I have an egocentric character; everything I do goes wrong.' He experiences the cause as persistent, internal and global. I.G. gave the following explanation: 'It's because the people here are so cold. You are never welcome. I'll never feel at home here.' He perceives the cause as persistent, external and global. J.G. remarked: 'It's because I can't learn the language, it's just too difficult for me. That's why I don't have any friends and feel lousy.' Here the cause is experienced as internal, persistent and global. K.G. said: 'My girlfriend broke off our relationship because she doesn't want to have children. I miss her terribly, I cannot live without her.' This is a specific, external, persistent cause.

According to Seligman, the modes of explanation which an individual uses to account for unpleasant experiences are not (or at least only to a limited extent) related to the events in question. They tend, rather, to conform to a personal cognitive style.

People who tend to explain unpleasant experiences in terms of internal, persistent and global causes are more likely to react with depression and helplessness. Because they see the cause of their problems as persistent they do not see any possibility of changing their situation for the better, and because they see it as global they think it will continue to cause new problems, which is, of course, a depressing thought.

Because they view the cause of their problems as internal they tend to feel guilty or inferior. Of course, psychotherapists will add that reflecting on one's own role in causing the problems need not necessarily lead to feelings of guilt, and can be seen as positive when it results in a change of behaviour.

According to Seligman, a mode of explanation which accounts for experiences in terms of external, transient and specific causes offers more scope for the adequate assimilation of painful events.

This theory has been supported by laboratory and other research, using diverse empirical methods and very different samples. Moreover, it has been argued that a maladaptive explanatory style could be shaped by a catastrophic, traumatic experience as well as by a series of mild stressors, for example by receiving during childhood, over and over again, the parental message that one is personally inept and to blame for the difficulties encountered in life (McCormick, Taber & Kruedelbach, 1989). It has also been shown that psychotherapeutic techniques can bring about changes in the mode of explanation used to account for negative experiences.

In practice, it is often noted that refugees direct their attention mainly to factors that they cannot influence. Powerlessness (and the accompanying feelings of anger and sorrow) is then the dominant emotion. Seligman's theory provides a conceptual framework which the therapist can use to analyse the mode of explanation which a particular refugee applies to his problems. Following Gielis (1982) it can be added, however, that attributing a problem to a persistent cause and concluding that it is unsolvable, may be realistic. When refugees consider the losses they have suffered by going into exile as persistent and unalterable they are sometimes right. Coping with the emotions related to this observation plus learning to differentiate between what is really unalterable and what may change over time then becomes vitally important.

By analysing the way in which a refugee explains his problems, the therapist can attempt to direct his attention to aspects of his situation which force him to alter his explanation, thereby offering a point of departure for beneficial behavioral changes, and perhaps even for a change in his general explanatory style.

For example, the therapist can try to replace a global mode of explanation with a specific mode, which would help to give the refugee a more balanced view of his situation and stimulate a more realistic and adaptive self-image.

H.G. explained his problems in terms of his egocentric character. The therapist knew from H.G.'s life history that he had been very active in a human rights organization. He asked H.G. whether he thought that these activities had also stemmed from his egocentrism. A discussion ensued, as a result of which H.G. concluded that he did indeed have egocentric traits, and that he was no different from anyone else in that respect, but that he was also capable of displaying less egocentric characteristics as well.

Similarly, an internal mode of explanation can be replaced by an external mode.

I.G. initially explained his depression and loneliness in terms of the cold and impassive character of the people in his country of exile. It soon became clear that he was using this to repress another explanation which was on his mind: 'It's because I'm mad,' which he found plausible because he was consulting a psychotherapist. The therapist suggested that his problems may be related to events which he had experienced a few years earlier, because these events had been so terrible that they would cause anyone with a normal emotional life to have depressions for some time after. He asked whether I.G. had nightmares. As a result, in subsequent interviews, I.G.'s terrible combat experiences were discussed, and he no longer seemed to be troubled by the idea that he was mad. He also became less ashamed of the emotions which talking about the past evoked.

Sometimes the prospect for improvement is increased if attention can be shifted from unalterable external causes to an internal cause, and the refugee begins to reflect on his problems.

J.G. was dissatisfied with her life. She felt that her boyfriend was hindering her political activities. They both had the same nationality but they had met when already in exile. The therapist observed that, in spite of her political involvement, she had chosen from among her many compatriots, one who no longer wanted to be politically active. He pointed out her responsibility for her own situation. Perhaps she was ambivalent about her political activities? The interview continued and she expressed doubts about the political views for which she had been active for so long.

Finally, the refugee may explain his problems on different levels simultaneously:

K.G. explained his depressions by the fact that he had been waiting to be granted refugee status for two years. He had a global, external, alterable explanation for his depressions. Interviews with the therapist stimulated self-reflection and after a while it appeared that he could also trace his sombre moods to internal causes. His first attempt to give an internal explanation comes down to the following: another important cause of my problems is that I had to flee and go into exile, and that was because I didn't listen to my parents and went and got involved in politics.

The cognitive reformulation of Seligman's theory about 'learned helplessness' has provoked a lot of critical comments. For instance, it has been argued that explanatory styles are not sufficient to describe a helpless attitude. Such an attitude usually goes together with a much more complex pattern of discouraging cognitions and inadequate problem solving strategies (cf. Dweck & Wortman, 1982). When facing some problem-solving task, people with a helpless attitude tend to manifest more task-irrelevant behaviour. They also tend to direct their attention to themselves, especially to the personality characteristics which they consider to be negative. This means that they do not concentrate fully on the task before them, which increases the probability that they will fail. They make less effort and give themselves less positive instructions. They also seem to consider earlier successful experiences to be less relevant. The attributional styles they use to explain failure are not identical to the attributional styles they use to explain success. For instance, they usually ascribe failure to a stable cause, but consider success to the result of sheer coincidence (Dweck & Wortman, 1982).

Victimization theories

Victimization theories (Janoff-Bulman & Frieze, 1983) are based on the central concept of the victim. In everyday usage the term may suggest passivity, pathos or weakness. In this study the term victim is used as an abstract concept, without its everyday negative connotations.

Victimization theories are concerned with the victims of various kinds of traumatic experience, from natural disasters to rape and cancer surgery. They are particularly concerned with the victim's cognitions, especially his world view and his self-image, and the way in which he integrates his traumatic experiences into these. They are formulated in such general terms that they enable the therapist to develop hypotheses about his client's psychological problems and the relevant coping skills.

But the generality of these theories also has disadvantages. 'Normal' rape probably does not always have exactly the same psychological meaning for the victim as being arrested and sexually tortured in a context of political violence; and losing all one's possessions in a natural disaster may evoke very different feelings to having them confiscated by the state. Therefore caution is indicated if one wants to use victimization theories in order to evaluate the psychological functioning of refugees.

World view and self-image The most important assumption in victimization theories is that people who become victims have undergone an experience which, even if they were aware of the dangers, they did not imagine could happen to themselves. They have experienced mortal danger and this alters their world view. They experience the world as threatening, feel less safe than before and tend to interpret various natural phenomena as heralding danger. Their self-image also changes, to the extent that they feel powerless in the face of these perceived dangers.

L.G., a refugee from an Asian country who had been waiting for a decision on his request for political asylum for a year and a half, was informed by immigration officials that it was no longer necessary for him to have his temporary visa stamped every month. He did not understand why and started to panic. He expected to be deported at any minute. In spite of the fact that he had, by force of circumstance, become something of an expert on the laws relating to the right of asylum, he felt totally helpless. It did not occur to him that he could find out the reasons through his lawyer and, if necessary, take legal steps.

Janoff-Bulman & Frieze (1983) claim that the circumstances which turn a person into a victim shatter the fundamental assumptions on which most people's lives are based. They reason as follows: most people live their daily lives believing that nothing really unpleasant can happen to them. When a person gets into his car he does not usually expect to be involved in a motor accident which will leave him crippled, even though he may be aware that many people get injured in traffic accidents every day. People are generally not constantly worried about potential dangers, even though they may be real. They live in a pleasant illusion of personal invulnerability, and as a result may fail to take adequate precautions: for example, they drive without a seat belt. In general, however, the illusion of invulnerability is the cornerstone of mental health: it protects people from much anxiety and stress. In those who have become victims the illusion of safety disappears and is replaced by the fear that the disaster may recur at any moment and that they will be even less able to withstand it.

According to Janoff-Bulman & Frieze the illusion of invulnerability is based on the assumption that what happens in the world is basically meaningful and just, and that misfortune can be prevented by being sufficiently cautious and behaving decently. For victims this assumption is an illusion. What they have undergone does not fit into their world view and they are left with the question: Why did this happen? Why did it happen to me? The victim asks himself the latter question at a time when his self-image is not all that positive. After what has happened to them victims often consider themselves to be weak, helpless, useless and scared. They sometimes feel that they do not have themselves under control or that they are doomed to suffer more catastrophes.

When the liberation movement to which he belonged split into two factions M.G., a refugee from Latin America, started to have the psychological problems for which he was to request help five years later in exile. In an armed encounter between the factions one of his friends was killed. This was a traumatic experience which caused his world to collapse. M.G., who as a guerrilla had fearlessly carried out very dangerous missions, was now afraid to leave his house. He felt like a weakling.

Processing information about traumatic experiences into world view and self-image The traumatic experiences which make an individual into a victim alter his world view and self-image. In order to be able to function properly again the victim has to integrate his traumatic experiences into a new world view and self-image. His encounters with malevolence, meaninglessness and personal failure have to be assimilated (Janoff-Bulman, 1989). In this connection the repeated reliving of traumatic experiences can be seen as a cognitive process: an attempt to process the new information provided by the traumatic experiences. Janoff-Bulman & Frieze claim that people tend to view these experiences in such a way that their original world view and self-image remain intact as far as possible.

Tailor, Wood & Lichtman (1983) have noted in this connection that victims often minimize or even trivialize what has happened to them. They apparently want to avoid constantly having the impression that the world is unsafe. They do not want to seem pathetic or in need of help, either to themselves or to others, and they do not want people to treat them as such or to look down on them or reject them. To put it more abstractly: by minimizing traumatic experiences the individual protects his world view and self-image, while at the same time relativizing the feeling that he has lost something important or his life has changed fundamentally.

According to Tailor, Wood & Lichtman (1983), there are various ways in which victims try to minimize their traumatic experiences in an attempt to avoid seeing themselves as victims. For example, victims may hide their experiences, or talk about them in a calm and humorous way. Some think of other, much more serious, things which could have happened to them and are thankful that they were spared. There are also victims who focus on the positive side of their experiences, on what they have learned from them. They interpret their trauma as a blessing in disguise. Others compare their situation with those who are much worse off and who are less capable of coping with their traumatic experiences. Compared to them they feel privileged and strong. They conclude that, given the situation, they are coping very well. Victims who are unable to cope with certain aspects of their life may selectively focus their attention on those aspects with which they can cope successfully.

M.G., the Latin American refugee already mentioned in the previous case, was tormented by fear. During his first interview he told the therapist somewhat proudly that, unlike his friends, he had not taken to drink to repress his fears.

Minimizing traumatic experiences is not the same as denial in the psychoanalytical sense of defence mechanism. Denial means that something which was conscious, or could have been conscious, becomes or remains unconscious. When experiences are minimized they remain, together with the associated emotions, conscious. The negative side of the emotional meaning of the experience is relativized rather than simply denied.

The question may be raised whether it is beneficial for an individual to minimize the meaning of his traumatic experiences, as it may prevent him from seeking support from others.

It is useful to take into account here that the victim's social environment usually encourages him to relativize his experiences and look on the bright side of things.

Giving traumatic experiences a 'positive meaning' is, according to Janoff-Bulman & Frieze, also a way of minimizing their negative side. The victim thinks that his experience was useful, that it was necessary, in order to do well later.

N.G. fled his native country after being imprisoned for a few years for distributing political pamphlets. He was a member of a sectarian political group. His political ideas were based on his study of the only critical book he could find in his country. Once in exile he read a lot about political ideology and his views became more sophisticated. 'It's a good thing that I had to go into exile', he said, 'if I had continued I would have become a terrorist and caused more trouble in my country than there is already.'

According to Janoff-Bulman & Frieze seeking emotional support from others is an important coping skill. They cite publications which show that those who have problems and appeal for help cannot always depend on understanding and support from others. Victims are often blamed for what has happened to them, or are avoided because they are miserable or unhappy. This phenomenon also can be explained in cognitive terms: if a person really listens to what a victim tells about his traumatic experiences, he will be confronted with information that cannot easily be processed because it does not fit into his general beliefs about the world and humanity.

Rejection by people in his social environment will not help the victim to adapt his world view in a balanced way and tends to strengthen the negative aspects of his self-image. Receiving emotional support has the opposite effect. If a victim receives emotional support from people in his social environment this will have a positive influence on his functioning, because he will feel a bit more free to talk about his traumatic experiences, and talking may contribute to the processing of information.

From a cognitive approach, counselling refugees may mean discussing the way in which their view of the world and themselves has changed as a result of traumatic events and experiences related to the problems they faced and are facing during exile. The counsellor can be on the lookout for possible inadequate assumptions and inadequate inferences which have coloured the way in which the information about aforementioned events and experiences was processed, and resulted in a distorted world view and self-image.

Delay or arrest in cognitive development

The theories about cognitive development have not produced very sophisticated hypotheses about the consequences of traumatic experiences for the developmental process. The same applies to the consequences of leaving one's familiar cultural environment. One may of course expect positive effects from the fact that both traumatic experiences and leaving one's country are new experiences, and new experiences will stimulate cognitive development. On the other hand clinical experience suggests that the reverse often occurs. For example, after stress or trauma the intellectual achievement of children in school often drops significantly, which seems to be the consequence of a delay in or disruption of cognitive development. This phenomenon can be easily explained within a psychodynamic framework, but it remains an enigma as long as one sticks rigidly to cognitive terminology.

However, in relation to the consequences of traumatization and uprooting, the cognitive approach does provide us with some interesting questions. Can the complaints and symptoms of a refugee be better understood against the background of his level of cognitive functioning? Is this, from a Western point of view, the level one would expect of a person of his age? If, from a Western point of view, a refugee's cognitive development has been delayed or arrested, does this hinder his adaptation to Western society or produce breakdowns in the communication with peers?

Since many adult refugees had their first experiences with traumatic violence during adolescence, it may be interesting to compare their thinking with the descriptions of cognitive development in early and late adolescence given by Piaget (1983), Elkind (1967), Damon & Hart (1982), Selman (1980), Kohlberg & Gilligan (1972), and Adelson (1975).

According to Piaget, early adolescence is the period in which the individual starts developing the capacity for abstract thinking. He claims that pre-adolescent thinking is restricted to concrete, visible objects and relations between objects, but that adolescents develop the capacity to think about more abstract concepts. They also start thinking in sequences of hypotheses and deductions; in other words they start using if-then reasoning.

This cognitive development often goes hand in hand with the development of new areas of interest: adolescents are sometimes very interested in philosophical questions such as 'what is freedom?', in the dynamics behind global problems such as pollution, war, racial and minority group discrimination, as well as the meaning of moral categories like 'human', 'just' and 'righteous'. Adolescent cognitive development also leads to the capacity for self-reflection.

Cognitive egocentrism   Piaget (1983) states that the beginning of a new stage in cognitive development coincides with a form of 'cognitive egocentrism'. Cognitive egocentrism refers to temporary inadequacies in cognitive functioning. These come into existence when the individual starts using newly developed cognitive capacities, but can only apply them from a subjective, personal point of view. He is not yet capable of placing himself in someone else's position. During adolescence this egocentrism may manifest itself as a kind of *naive* *idealism*: the individual overestimates the significance of the solutions he himself conceived for problems in society and is incapable of realizing that there are refractory facts or practical difficulties which may form obstacles. Cognitive egocentrism may also be manifested in *thinking in absolute, 'black and white' categories* and an inability to take the various shades of reality into account. Moreover, cognitive egocentrism makes it difficult for the individual to tolerate that some people don't care to think about a topic which he himself considers vital for his own existence.

O.G. was 16 when he became politically active. He was arrested after a few months and severely tortured. When he talks about politics his reasoning is in terms of a 'black and white' distinction. For instance, he considers the dictatorial government in his country (Iran) to be bad (a view which will not meet much opposition in the United States and Europe) and the armed opposition group to which he belonged as above all criticism. He considers those who do not support this group, or are not very interested in political developments in Iran (like most of his peers at school in the country of exile), to be either bad of stupid.
O.G.'s main complaint is that he feels very lonely.

One of Piaget's followers, Elkind (1967), has observed that the cognitive egocentrism of an adolescent may result in forms of inadequate self-reflection, such as the belief that others are as preoccupied with his appearance as he himself is. The adolescent then has the feeling that other people are continously watching and evaluating him, he has an 'imaginary audience' on which he wants to make a good impression. The result is that he is often ashamed.

P.G. spent most of his adolescence in jail as a political prisoner, where he was abused in many ways. When he talks about the possibility of going back to his country, he has the fantasy of other ex-prisoners being welcomed by a big crowd, consisting of the people of his village, who are all very grateful for their sacrifices and honour them. He sees himself entering alone and unnoticed, not a hero but a cowardly refugee.
One of P.G.'s complaints is that he feels trapped: he sees no future in the country of exile, but the political situation in his country prevents him from returning.

Cognitive egocentrism may also result in the adolescent having irrational beliefs about himself, like a *personal fable* of being invulnerable. She may, for instance, have the firm conviction that she will not become pregnant after having sexual intercourse without using adequate contraception, or he may be certain that he will not have an accident while stunting with his motorbike.

Q.G., who joined an opposition group in late adolescence, said that he was aware that people in his immediate surroundings had been arrested and tortured for political reasons. He had nevertheless continued his political activities for five years, without ever feeling any fear. He was simply convinced that nothing would happen to him. After being abducted by the secret police and severely abused, he entered into a state of shock. Three years later his most important complaint is fear, and he worries constantly, in a not very adequate way, about possible dangers in the future.

According to Piaget (1983), cognitive egocentrism gradually diminishes during adolescence through corrective experiences and confrontation with the opinions of others.

The development of self-concept and social cognition   According to Piaget, the cognitive developments of adolescence include the appearance of self-reflection. Damon & Hart (1982) have concluded that this self-reflection becomes more advanced in various ways.

It is initially restricted to the individual's own behaviour and personal characteristics, but comes to include feelings, motives, purposes and opinions as topics that are relevant for his view of himself. Furthermore, he comes to ascribe more stable characteristics to himself with regard to his social behaviour, and he also tends to take more aspects of his personality into consideration simultaneously, becoming more conscious of the possibilities to change his life by changing himself.

Another achievement is that the adolescent becomes capable of looking at himself and at social interactions from the point of view of a neutral outsider (Selman, 1980). This goes hand in hand with a growing capacity for recognizing contradictory motives within himself and others. He also comes to realize that it is not always possible to be instantly aware of one's own motives and feelings.

R.G., who was arrested when he was 16, still has the physical scars of the torture he endured. He was 21 when he entered therapy. In discussing his relationship with peers, he only seems to see one type of motive behind the behaviour of his peers: to have fun. He thinks he is the only one who sometimes wants to sit quietly beside a friend without talking, or who wants to talk about his worries, or who sometimes feels ashamed or nervous.

In this sense the development of his social cognition seemed delayed. But when the therapist proposed that R.G. should talk in more detail about a particular girl he seemed to like, he became interested in speculating about her motives for seeking his company.

The development of political and moral reasoning   Cognitive developments during adolescence that are related to political ideas can be summarized as follows (Adelson, 1975): as they grow older, adolescents think more and more about political questions in terms of abstract principles and ideology. When they talk about their opinions, they use more abstract concepts and terms which refer to groups of individuals. They gradually become more interested in the possibilities for changing social institutions. Initially adolescents can hardly appreciate the idea that there may be different ways to solve a political problem, and that simple solutions that may seem 'logical' may not always work out.

Later they come to understand that the reality of politics often means trying to maintain a balance between contradictory values and interests.

During adolescence there is also growth in the capacity to evaluate political problems in the light of their historical context, as well as in the capacity to think about the long-term consequences of political decisions.

Moral development in adolescence has been described as a transition from an orientation to values, rules, conventions and traditions that are shared within a particular community, to an orientation to more universal ethical principles which may be in disagreement with the laws or convictions that are supported by the community (Kohlberg & Gilligan, 1972). Furthermore, the moral development of male and female adolescents is sometimes thought to follow different patterns. According to Gilligan (1982) female adolescents consider a moral problem as a matter in which taking care for other people within a social context is a very important dimension, while male adolescents tend to analyse moral problems in terms of rules and principles. These different forms of moral reasoning have been observed in an empirical study (Walker, 1989), but they do not coincide with a difference between the sexes.

Be that as it may, the concept of moral development incidentally may provide an eye opener for the therapist in the treatment of refugee married couples.

S.G., a 25-year-old refugee from the Middle East, had various somatic complaints which he saw as the result of marital problems. The therapist suggested that he bring his wife (T.G., aged 27) along. Their differences were then related as follows: S.G. wanted to bring their-three-year old child into contact with Dutch children and give it a Dutch education because he did not want his child to feel like an outsider. His reasoning about the education of his child thus resembled what Gilligan considers a characteristic for female adolescents. T.G., who was a member of what her husband considered a rather dogmatic political organization, thought that the child should be educated according to traditional islamic rules, and that contact with Dutch peers should be avoided. She also considered her husband's Western clothes to be 'degenerated capitalist', and admitted that she had only come to therapy reluctantly. Psychologists, she said, were mostly mad themselves; she had only come because it was her duty as an islamic woman to follow her husband. Her moral reasoning resembled that which Gilligan sees as typical for male adolescents.

Moral development can be stimulated by discussing personal experiences of choices and doubts and related moral questions (Turiel, 1983).

Looking at the cognitive development of refugees in terms like capacity for abstract thinking, cognitive egocentrism, development of self-concept, development of social cognition, development of political and moral reasoning, one must of course keep in mind that all the descriptions that are given in this section have been formulated from a Western cultural perspective. When the cognitive functioning of a refugee deviates from what is to be expected, given his age, that does not mean that his cognitive development has been delayed or arrested in reference to his own cultural background. His cognitive functioning may just have a different, culture-related quality.

Trauma and learning: a cognitive reformulation

In this section an example of a cognitive-behavioural perspective on the consequences of traumatization is presented. It is founded on four basic assumptions:

1. Behaviour is, among other things, determined by cognitive representations that can be conceptualized as inner speech or self-instructions (cf. Meichenbaum, 1979).
2. Traumatic experiences instigate conditioning processes which result in unpleasant biophysiological reactions when particular previously neutral stimuli that have become conditioned to traumatic events are presented, as well as cognitive representations of the traumatic event that may have been adequate at the time the trauma occurred, but that are inadequate in the present situation. These inadequate cognitive representations induce inadequate self-instructions which result in maladaptive behaviour (cf. Korrelboom et al., 1989).
3. Behaviour can be changed by changing the cognitive representations by which it is determined. For instance, behaviour can be changed when new self-instructions are acquired through observational learning (cf. Meichenbaum, 1979).
4. Conditioned biophysiological responses can be deconditioned through exposure of the traumatized individual to different kinds of stimuli that have become conditioned to the traumatic events, under circumstances in which the cognitive representations of the traumatic events are not proven to be adequate at this time; that is to say in a safe situation in which the individual feels protected (cf. Korrelboom et al., 1989).

In the foregoing section, classical conditioning was defined as a process in which some reflex that is the involuntary consequence of a particular stimulus becomes linked to another stimulus that is contingent with the first stimulus. The stimulus that has the reflex behaviour as a natural consequence is called unconditioned stimulus (UCS), the reflex behaviour is called unconditioned response (UCR) and the contingent stimulus that becomes linked to the reflex behaviour is called the conditioned stimulus (CS). According to the theory of classical conditioning, the CS is thought to automatically provoke a response (called: conditioned response CR).

From a cognitive point of view, classical conditioning can be seen as a process in which the organism tries, in an active way, to gain knowledge about his environment (Davey, 1989). The CS is consciously experienced by the subject as a predictor of an UCS; in the case of a traumatic UCS, as precursor for another painful experience of extreme helplessness. The habitual response that follows the CS is a preparatory response on the anticipated UCS, through which the traumatized individual tries to cope with pain and feelings of extreme helplessness. It is similar to the response he showed during and directly after the occurrence of the traumatic events.

Emanating from both the classic behaviouristic and the cognitive view of conditioning, the effect of traumatic experience can be summarized as follows:

The traumatic experience is an UCS which is contingent with a conglomerate of stimuli which can be described in simple terms (for example the sound of rattling keys or the smell of blood) or have a more complex nature (a tone of voice which suggests humiliation, being alone in a small room). All these stimuli become conditioned stimuli. The traumatic experience, as an UCS, triggers biophysiological reactions, like sweating, an acceleration of heartbeat, hyperventilation and so on.

A traumatic experience often is not a momentary presentation of a distinct stimulus, but something that may continue for hours or longer. This means that the aforementioned biophysiological reactions that are triggered when the first traumatic stimulus is perceived, become contingent with trauma-related stimuli that appear later. Therefore the bodily sensations and feelings (for instance tightness of the chest and oppression) that were generated by these biophysiological reactions, but that might also occur under different circumstances, may become conditioned stimuli.

When one of the CS that were contingent with the traumatic experience presents itself, it may, according to the classic behaviouristic approach, trigger the same kind of biophysiological reactions. According to the cognitive view on conditioning, the CS also brings the representation of the UCS to awareness, which means that a memory of the traumatic experience comes to the mind. This memory interferes with other cognitive activities (for instance, when the person is reading a book at the time the CS presents itself, the memory may disturb his concentration). Both the biophysiological reactions and the memory result in emotions (usually fear, disgust, aggression, depression or a numb feeling).

In the case of a traumatic experience the representation of the UCS is not just a memory, but also has a complex structure of thoughts related to the traumatic experience. It contains causal explanations or attributions, a complex of thoughts one may summarize with terms like self-image and world view and (usually pessimistic) ideas about voluntary action that could help to escape from a repetition of the negative sensations that accompanied the traumatic experience.

This cognitive representation of the UCS also involves thoughts about conscious, voluntary actions the individual may undertake to cope with his biophysiological reactions and the accompanying sensations and emotions. In other words: the cognitive representations include self-instructions which eventually result in some overt responses. These responses usually have been the best possible reactions in the traumatic situation, but may be not very adaptive under different circumstances.

Therapy can be focused on changing the UCS representations by discussion, explanation and relabelling. For instance, what a refugee experiences as fear, sometimes can be relabelled as understandable, legitimate rage which is not bad in itself, but has to be canalized in an adaptive way. UCS representations can also be changed by suggesting alternative self-instructions.

U.G. suffered from flashbacks about his experience in a refugee camp that was invaded by soldiers. When he had a flashback, he had the tendency to hide in his room. The therapist explained to U.G. about the phenomenon of flashbacks and their biophysiological aspects, taught him several breathing and relaxation exercises. He suggested to U.G. that, at the first sensation of fear, he should instruct himself to say: I have to counter these physical reactions by doing one of the exercises.

Utility and limitations of the cognitive approach

The cognitive approach inspires us to analyse the way in which refugees think about themselves, their problems and their social contacts, as well as political and moral questions in relation to both their traumatic experiences and their life in exile.

From the cognitive approach one can deduce that it may be useful to discuss abstract matters in relation to personal experiences in order to overcome cognitive egocentrism or other forms of inadequate reasoning. In this way the psychotherapist may prepare himself to enter tactfully into discussions with his client.

The cognitive approach has contributed much to the creation of new ideas within the psychodynamic and learning-theory approach. For example, within the psychodynamic framework it has been said that whether a person's psychological problems can be discussed with him depends on his level of cognitive development. The cognitive, introspective possibility of perceiving inner conflicts and thinking about them does not develop until adolescence (Harter, 1988). In work with refugees this means that, when dealing with young adults, one first has to check whether their cognitive development has been delayed in some way before commencing with a type of therapy in which inner conflicts may become a topic of discussion.

For learning theory, the cognitive approach stimulated an extension of the concept of behaviour. The term behaviour is no longer reserved for overt, observable action, but can also refer to thoughts, self-instructions, convictions and cognitive strategies for solving problems. This also means that the afore-mentioned cognitive categories are seen as susceptible to modification through special training instruction or education. This cognitive-behavioural perspective offers new ideas for the psychological treatment of refugees and other trauma-tized persons.

With regard to refugees, the cognitve approach also suggests that the explanations refugees give for their symptoms can become an important obstacle to their recovery, and that their explanatory style can be altered by offering them plausible alternative explanations. For instance, symptoms that the refugee evaluates as a sign of going mad, can be explained to him as the usual side-effects of a normal process of repair. When the refugee starts to recover he can, in a similar way, be prepared for relapses, for example by explaining to him that the process of recovery often follows an uneven course, best described by some variant of 'three steps forward, two steps back' (Simons et al., 1986).

Moreover, the cognitive approach could also become useful in various other ways. It focuses the attention on delays in social cognition (e.g. through lack of education or social stimulation because of protracted imprisonment) or inadequate social cognition (e.g. because the knowledge in question was acquired in a different culture). Delays or deficiencies in social cognition lead to inadequate ways of evaluating social situations or the use of inadequate cognitive strategies to solve a problem that might be modified by instruction or training procedures.

Finally, cognitive theories to date remain very vague concerning a matter that is extremely important for refugees: the processes involved in learning to speak a foreign language. The little empirical evidence that is available suggests that there may be a relation between level of cognitive development and the speed with which a new language is acquired, and that generally speaking adolescents tend to learn a new language quicker than younger children (Seifert & Hoffnung, 1987; Grosjean, 1982). Clinical experience with refugees suggests that learning to speak the language of the country of exile can be described as a sequence of stages. First the refugee translates what he wants to say in the new language from his native language. Later he may report a dream in which he is speaking the new language, or having inner dialogues in the new language. Still later he is able to express himself for a short time in the new language without having to translate from his native language. Between the different stages there are periods of transition, in which the refugee seems to fall back in his achievements and is prone to lose confidence. Systematic research on this topic is badly needed.

3 Diagnostic appraisal

Looking from a distance

The starting point for any kind of assistance to refugees is to listen carefully to the complaints the refugee presents. These complaints can initially be simply transcribed as the refugee relates them, then later amplified by the observations of the therapist or counsellor, and finally completed with the professional's interpretation of what he heard and observed in terms of the various theoretical approaches he feels comfortable with.

In the first contact with the refugee the helping professional will usually try to come to an agreement with the refugee as to the nature of his problem. He tries to summarize the complaints of the refugee in terms that are recognizable for both the refugee and the professional and which suggests the direction in which their cooperation can develop.

The articulation of the problem in terms that make sense for both parties will suggest topics about which the therapist needs to know more, in order to reach an understanding of the circumstances and processes that brought the problem into being in the first place. Talking about these subjects will also provide him with information about the necessity for assistance, and possible starting points for therapy.

The term diagnostic appraisal refers here to this process of gathering information in order to gain insight into both the problem itself and points of application for professional help (cf. De Wit & Tak, 1988). It is an effort to look from a certain distance, with as much objectivity as possible, at the problem of the refugee, and to interpret what is seen and heard in such a way that the phenomena can be related to one another in a meaningful way.

In order to find starting points for therapy, the therapist also has to make an estimation of the capacities and limitations of the refugee, in relation to his own professional capacities and limitations. This means among other things that the therapist tries to make an estimation of the motivation of the refugee to change certain aspects of his behaviour or make certain opinions a subject for discussion, and observes how the refugee reacts to tentative proposals to tackle his problems.

Diagnostic appraisal as a regulative cycle

At the end of the first interviews, diagnostic appraisal results in a series of provisional statements about the coming into existence of the problem and starting points for professional help for the individual refugee. These statements form a hypothesis. Often it is possible to look at the problem from more than one angle, and to formulate more than one hypothesis. These hypotheses may amplify one another, or be contradictory. In the latter case more information is needed to decide which of them is most credible and offers the clearest perspective for therapy.

A diagnostic statement worded or written at a certain moment does not of course have unlimited validity. It tells 'with a reasonable amount of certainty' the ins and outs of the problem, but its contents should be continuously tested in the light of all new information that becomes available in later therapeutic sessions. New data may generate new insight, which forces the therapist to adjust his approach or even change it radically. Thus diagnostic appraisal will continue just as long as the assistance process. It is a process of adjusting one's course to every new signal, in order to help as effectively as possible.

In order to avoid turning in circles, the progress of this process needs to be accounted for. It is important to give explicit descriptions of each decision that is taken during the course of the helping process, so that the therapist can justify his interventions. In making reports about these therapeutic interventions, the professional reconstructs his patterns of decision making in relation to the modifications made in the diagnostic hypotheses due to the reception of new information.

Making these reconstructions after each interview is called the 'regulative cycle'. Its components are: the complaints, the diagnostic hypotheses, the questions aimed at obtaining more information or other therapeutic interventions made on the bases of the diagnostic hypotheses, decisions made on the basis of new information, an evaluation of their effects, and reappraisal of the original diagnostic hypotheses.

A.H., a refugee from a South East Asian country, had lived through a long series of traumatic experiences, starting with the killing of his father for political reasons. After the death of his father, he fled and lost contact with his family. He was 15 at the time. In the following years he had many traumatic combat experiences. He requested political asylum at the age of 20. When he first requested psychological assistance, he was 24.

He suffered from nightmares and spells of panic and looked very depressed. He nevertheless continued his studies at a technical school, played his weekly game of volleyball and continued to have an intimate relationship with a girlfriend. The following diagnostic hypothesis was formulated: post-traumatic stress disorder, aggravated by the continuing traumatic uncertainty about his request for political asylum and the very realistic fear of being sent back to his country, in an otherwise adequately functioning young adult.

A.H. was treated at first with anxiolytic medication and supportive therapeutic techniques. After he had received a residence permit, the therapist applied techniques directed towards working through traumatic experiences by discussing his nightmares and the memories related to those nightmares. During this phase of the therapy, A.H., managed to find out where his mother was living and started to correspond with her and other relatives. After eight months A.H.'s complaints had disappeared and therapy was concluded.

Two years later, A.H. requested assistance again. This time he complained of spells of anxiety, depression and thoughts of suicide. These complaints had started after a compatriot had put pressure on him to return to his country as a guerrilla. In the meantime, A.H. was still functioning well at his work and the relationship with his girlfriend continued. The therapist failed to look at the story from the approach of family therapy and forgot to ask how his girlfriend reacted to the returning of his problems.

The therapist started treatment from the diagnostic hypothesis that A.H. had not worked through parts of his traumatic experiences, which had been brought back to his memory through the meeting with his compatriot. This hypothesis first seemed to be correct: A.H. spontaneously started to talk about some horrifying incidents which included the killing of close friends. But this time the discussions did not result in any improvement of his condition.

In the sixth interview anti-depressive medication was prescribed. This had an unforeseen effect. A.H. took the medication only once and it made him a bit drowsy. This attracted the attention of his girlfriend. She asked him what was wrong with him, and A.H. told her about things he had tried to conceal from her: his depressive feelings and his thoughts of suicide. 'After that night', A.H. said in the seventh interview, 'I decided to pull myself together. I realized I was not alone and helpless, that there are people who stood by me. I realized that I had to take care of my girlfriend, that she needs me. I do not feel suicidal any more. The fear still comes occasionally, but then I think: it will go away, and so it goes.' He also told the therapist that his girlfriend and he had decided to marry as soon as possible.

After this interview, the therapist concluded his original diagnostic hypothesis had not been proven wrong, but that part of the problem had been a disturbance in the communication between A.H. and his girlfriend (a hypothesis from the approach of family therapy). A.H. had concealed his problems, and it might prove worthwhile to know his motives for doing so. It turned out that he had been ashamed, and that the returning of his symptoms had confirmed his view that he was essentially a weak person for whom other people would have contempt. So a diagnostic hypothesis could be added in terms of the psychodynamic approach: traumatization had resulted in a negative self-image.

In the tenth interview, A.H. told the therapist that he had decided to go back to the part of his country that was under control of an anti-government group in order to visit his mother whom he had not seen since he was 15. He said that he had the feeling that his mother needed to see him. The therapist noted the coincidence between the fixing of a date for the marriage and the decision to visit his mother. He concluded that another psychodynamic diagnostic hypothesis could be added: reactivation of inner problems related to the forced separation from his mother.

Which information is needed?

What kind of information is needed for diagnostic appraisal? The answer to this question is in the first place dependent on the theoretical approach of the helping professional, and probably also not independent of less rational beliefs or stereotypical views he may have. Nevertheless most therapists who work with refugees will agree about a basic 'shopping list' which is useful in making a rough screening during the first interviews. The items on this list are:

1. The therapist's first impression of the refugee
2. Complaints and statements about problematic behaviour, the concrete situations in which both these complaints and this problematic behaviour manifest themselves, and factors or conditions that make the disturbing effect of the complaints or problematic behaviour more or less severe.
3. Information about aspects of the psychological functioning of the refugee which are not problematic, but adequate or even charming, or environmental factors that suggest points of application for professional help, like the availability of a social network, such as a family or a compatriot community, which can provide emotional support (Boman & Edwards, 1984; Figley, 1985; Wren, 1986).
4. Information about the way in which both the refugee and people in his social environment experience his problem, and their ideas about what caused or provoked the complaints or problematic behaviour.
5. Information about traumatic experiences that the refugee may have undergone.
6. Information about the course of the refugee's personality development, and the level of his development in various dimensions.
7. Information about the political field of forces to which the refugee is a subject, and other environmental factors that are burdening him, such as uncertainty about his legal status, having to live in a neighbourhood with a high incidence of delinquency, worries about relatives who have remained behind, and so on. Another example: Van Dantzig (1990) described the case of a man who had nightmares about his detention in a concentration camp. His wife was depressive, and when she had been successfully treated the man's nightmares stopped without further treatment.
8. Signals that indicate the possible presence of psychiatric symptoms, like disturbances in perception and reasoning and so on.
9. Statements about the kind of help the refugee himself asks for or explicitly rejects, in relation to experiences he possibly had with other helping professionals.

This information has of course to be evaluated against the refugee's cultural background. The therapist also has to be aware of the possibility that the setting may restrict the information he gets. For example, a refugee may not talk about sexual trauma when members of his family or an interpreter are present, and some topics might be omitted because of the sex of the therapist.

Diagnostic tools

The most important source of diagnostic information is the clinical interview with the refugee. Diagnostic interviews sometimes have to be conducted with the assistance of an interpreter. In such cases there is always the possibility of translation errors, disturbances in the refugee's reasoning, the refugee being misunderstood by the translator, or the refugee withholding relevant information because he does not trust the interpreter for political or other reasons.

Additional sources of diagnostic information are people in the direct environment of the refugee, like members of his family who are also in exile, or other people who assist the refugee. These could include, for example, his lawyer or language teacher. Sometimes, notably in the case of children, it can be useful to contact relatives in the native country.

Diagnostic questionnaires can be useful, especially if they are worded in the native language of the refugee. Standardized tasks, like projective tests or the instruction to make a drawing, can be very helpful in the contact with children.

Observation is an important diagnostic tool, both during interviews in the consulting room or in the refugee's home. For example, it can be very useful to note the frequency and quality of eye contact, signs of tension, and the refugee's general appearance.

Finally, tentative interventions are an important diagnostic tool. In a first diagnostic interview one can for example try to find out the refugee's reaction to advice by giving him advice on some minor point of his problem, and then asking him about the effects at the following meeting.

The diagnostic interview

In the diagnostic interview two things are important: to maximize the active contribution of the refugee to the conversation, and to stimulate him to give relevant information about his personal problems. With regard to these two goals the following suggestions are useful.

It is essential that the helping professional should have a 'warm' attitude, which he expresses in both words and non-verbal behaviour, and which represents his genuine care and interest. Next to this basic attitude, in the initial contact it is usually more stimulating for the refugee if one frequently reacts with short statements or asks simple questions (cf. Pope & Siegman, 1972), than just sitting back and listening—although the latter approach seems to be indicated in the occasional case.

B.H., a 17-year-old boy, hardly gave the therapist the opportunity to introduce himself before he started to talk about what had happened after his arrest in a dictatorship in the Middle East, four months earlier. He did not seem to want any interruption. The therapist's only reaction was to sit close to B.H., but without physical contact. After half an hour of talking about the torture he had undergone, he started to cry, and this was the first opportunity for the therapist to intervene verbally.

In diagnostic interviews, open-ended questions (What is your most important problem at this moment?) often result, after some hesitation, in longer answers than questions phrased in a more directive way (Did that happen in prison, or after your escape?). The answers to open-ended questions generally also contain more personal data. But when the topic of conversation is highly emotionally charged for the refugee, directive questions produce more information than open-ended questions (cf. Pope & Siegman, 1972). In the latter case, however, the answers will often not be more than a series of facts. To obtain an impression about the feelings of the refugee concerning these facts one needs to ask open-ended questions (cf. Cox & Rutter, 1985). Sometimes suggestive additions to open-ended questions (How did you feel when this happened? Didn't you become very angry? Or were you just flabbergasted?) can be stimulating, at least if they are emphatic and allow alternative answers.

The content of the first interviews

The topics for the first diagnostic interviews are of course dependent on what the refugee wants to tell the therapist. Apart from that, they are dependent on the theoretical approach(es) the therapist embraces. In commonsense terminology the content of the first interviews can be summarized with the following key-words: problem-analysis, situation-analysis, incident-exploration and position-analysis (De Wit & Van der Veer, 1989).

The term *problem-analysis* refers to a discussion of the refugee's current problems. The therapist tries to get an overview of all persons, conditions, and happenings that are related to his current problems. He asks questions about the part which the refugee himself plays in these problems. The therapist also gathers information about the role of other persons and the possible influence of rules and regulations to which the refugee is subjected when his problems develop and continue.

Situation-analysis refers to the discussion of the context of the refugee's problem, with respect to the present situation. It concerns matters which may at first sight seem unrelated to the problem, but nevertheless can make it more understandable, or help the therapist to get an impression of the levels at which the refugee is functioning adequately, and factors that might prove helpful in coping with his problems.

Situation-analysis may also refer to a situation in the past. In that case the historical background of the problems are discussed, either in relation to complaints (for example: when did you have these nightmares about prison for the first time?), or less directively, by biographic questions. Montessori (1987) states in this connection that in the case of traumatized clients it is important to acquire a detailed biographical case history: 'This should not be carried out in a formal manner. One must show interest and explain that it is necessary to know more about a person before he can be helped; it is preferable to let him speak spontaneously. The data can be ordered later, and it is not necessary that the patient be present. If anything is lacking it can be supplemented the next time.' Biographic questions may also lead to a conversation about non-problematic aspects of the refugee's personal history, and provide useful information about special strengths and capacities which the refugee possesses.

In the case of refugees, traumatic experiences often form a part of their life history. In the first interviews the therapist will also carefully ask some questions about possible traumatic experiences in order to obtain relevant information, to make it clear to the refugee that he has knowledge about the kind of things that happen during torture, combat and so on, and that he is prepared to discuss these topics if the refugee wants to.

The conversation about the context of the refugee's problem usually includes a discussion of those aspects of the political situation in both the native country and the country of exile that may be relevant.

Incident-exploration refers to the exploration of an occurrence that had great emotional impact on the refugee, usually something that happened just before the interview. The incident, for example a conflict with another person, often shows in a nutshell where the problem lies, and is in a sense representative of the way in which the refugee experiences his present situation.

Incident-exploration involves systematic questioning by the helping professional about details of the incident, until he can visualize it like a film. During the conversation both the therapist and the refugee get an overview of what happened, and an insight into the role played by the refugee and other persons who were involved. The therapist pays attention to the feelings the refugee experienced during the incident, his behaviour, and his cognitive interpretation of the behaviour of other people who were also involved.

The term *position-analysis* refers to the conversation about the respective standpoints of the refugee and the helping professional and the political field of forces in which both function. Topics for discussion would include the kind of help the refugee expects and wants from the therapist, the way in which the therapist could, and is willing to, help, and what the refugee himself can do to contribute to the solution of his problems. Sometimes it is necessary to discuss the restrictions forced upon both parties by the political reality of the day. For example, a refugee seeking asylum has nightmares about being sent back to his country. The therapist cannot provide a great deal of support because those nightmares are in fact at least partly based on a realistic judgement of the situation. The therapist might be able to give some advice about how to react to the nightmares, or even more effectively use his status as an expert in helping to obtain a residence permit for the refugee, thereby eliminating the source of his fears.

The use of various approaches

The theoretical approaches discussed in chapter 2, each give rise to their own specific diagnostic questions. The psychiatric approach leads to observations of and questions about specific signs and symptoms, in order to exclude disturbances that primarily have an organic cause, and to identify possible psychiatric disturbances. Working with refugees, one must be aware that they can be suffering from any mental disorder. However, one must be especially on the lookout for symptoms and signs of the post-traumatic stress disorder. Some refugees tend to minimize the impact of their traumatic experiences, that nightmares may be forgotten, and intrusive memories or flashbacks often remain hidden behind other complaints, like concentration problems, being distracted, headaches, alcohol abuse and forgetfulness.

The use of this approach leads to diagnostic hypotheses in terms of mental disorders. A psychiatric disorder like post-traumatic stress disorder can sometimes be treated with psychotropic medication, and therefore this approach also suggests an investigation of the refugee's attitude to medication.

The psychodynamic approach gives less specific suggestions for diagnostic interviews, but it focuses attention on the feelings of the refugee and the specific personal meaning that events may have for him.

Diagnostic appraisal from this approach means that the therapist evaluates the way in which the refugee talks about his problems in relation to questions such as:

- Is there any reason to presume that the refugee's personality development was disturbed before he left his country or before he was traumatized?
- If the refugee was traumatized by political violence, in which stage of personality development did this happen?
- Did this interfere with a developmental task?
- How can the psychological functioning of the refugee be characterized in terms of Horowitz's phases?
- Which defence mechanisms seem to be typical for the refugee?
- Why is he presumably using these defences?
- Is there any indication about the coping styles (like regression, adaptive defence, or progressive coping) the refugee was using during traumatization?

● Is his present psychological functioning understandable in relation to this coping style?

The psychodynamic approach will lead to diagnostic hypothesis in terms of inner conflicts, intra-psychic processes and their relation to social functioning.

The family-therapy approach leads to questioning the refugee about what he experiences as his primary social environment, and to arrange diagnostic interviews in which both the refugee and his primary social environment are present. If that is not feasible or possible, this approach leads to questioning the refugee about his relations to his family and to the persons that at present constitute his primary social environment. What the therapist observes and hears will then be evaluated in relation to questions such as:

● Is there physical separation from the original primary social system?
● Has the refugee found or formed a new primary social system?
● Which stereotyped, circular interaction patterns or inadequate forms of communication, that impede social support for the refugee, can be identified?
● Is there a reason to suspect that the family has some secret?
● How is the structure of the family in terms of subsystems and coalitions?
● Which members of the family have been traumatized? Has the structure of the family possibly been disrupted because of traumatic events?
● Is there a functional hierarchy? Or are there signs of parentification?
● Which loyalties may possibly influence the decisions of the refugee?
● Does the refugee have legacies that form a burden to him?
● Is one of the family members overburdened?
● Are there signs of overprotection by avoiding open communication?
● Is there reason to presume a process of trans-generational traumatization?
● Is there reason to believe that some patterns of interaction that existed for a long time, are being continued after the flight?
● Could some of the communication problems be the consequence of a difference in speed of adaptation to life in exile?
● Is the refugee part of a new, bi-cultural system?

Along these lines, the family-therapy approach may generate diagnostic hypotheses in terms of rigid interaction patterns or difficulties in communication.

The learning-theory approach suggests diagnostic questions centred around complaints and problematic behaviour and the circumstances under which they occur. The therapist can be inspired by such questions as the following:

● Do I observe behaviour that can be characterized as conditioned and is troublesome for himself or other people. Is the refugee aware of this behaviour? How is this behaviour reinforced?

- Which behaviour can be labelled as avoidance behaviour?
- Which processes of learning by self-control can be identified?
- Is the refugee setting adequate standards?
- Do I observe any behaviour that indicates learned helplessness (like a passive attitude under circumstances when activity might be useful, slow movements, sluggish thinking, querulous behaviour, self-approach)?
- Could I, with regard to the conventions in the country of exile, identify shortcomings in social skills (like: lack of assertiveness in the sense of not being able to contradict another person because that is considered improper in the native country, behaviour that in the country of exile is considered as exaggerated and theatrical, excessive expressions of gratitude that make people in the country of exile feel embarrassed, avoidance of giving direct answers to particular questions, not asking things straightforwardly, but vaguely hinting about what one is requiring, avoiding certain topics of conversation and so on)?

The learning-theory approach results in detailed diagnostic hypotheses in terms of inadequate behaviour, deficiencies in adequate behaviour, and learning processes.

The cognitive approach encourages curiosity about the way in which the refugee thinks about the causes of his problems or interprets failures and disappointing experiences.

While looking at the refugee from this approach, the therapist will be lead by such questions as:

- Are there signs that the refugee is able to summarize his traumatic experiences in some orderly way?
- Which forms of coping is he probably using: coping by deployment of attention (vigilant strategies or avoidance strategies); coping by changing subjective meanings (transforming a threat into a challenge, denying a threat, emphasizing the positive aspects of the situation, distancing); confronting by changing the relationship with the environment (confrontive coping, planned problem solving).
- Which explanatory styles is the refugee using? Is his way of explaining his situation stereotyped, or can he explain his problems on different levels? In which sense are his attributions inadequate?
- Which statements of the refugee can be interpreted as reflections of his world view and his self-image?
- Which incorrect assumptions can be identified from his reasoning? Which types of inadequate inferences, like arbitrary inference, selective abstraction, overgeneralization, magnification, personalization, absolutistic, dichotomous thinking, is he using?
- Can the refugee's cognitive functioning, viewed from a Western cultural

bias, be seen as not fully developed (in relation to concepts such as: naive idealism, thinking in absolute categories, having an imaginary audience, clinging to a personal fable, differentiation of the self-concept, development of social cognition, level of political reasoning, level of moral reasoning). If moral reasoning has developed fully, is the refugee reasoning in a principle oriented or in a social context oriented way?

- Could part of the refugee's thinking be explained in terms of 'cognitive representations of unconditioned (traumatic) stimuli' and related 'self-instructions'?

The diagnostic hypotheses that can be formed on the basis of this approach, will be realized in terms of adequate and inadequate ways of thinking or cognitive representation.

Each of the aforementioned theoretical approaches highlights some special part of reality, and ignores other parts. They also structure reality in different ways, on different levels of abstraction. In the opinion of this author, these approaches are complementary. They all provide valuable contributions to diagnostic appraisal, and suggest certain types of therapeutic intervention. From each approach one can deduct indications for treatment, in terms of both therapeutic techniques and the targets at which these techniques are directed. The therapist however has to decide which approach gives him the clearest perspectives for helping an individual refugee. For this decision his own clinical experience and the documented clinical experience of colleagues is an important factor. If he carefully records his diagnostic hypotheses and his way of weighing them and discusses his accounts with his colleagues, the knowledge he has gathered from clinical experience will gradually become more useful.

Refugees have problems that are partly based on current and real detrimental events. If that is the case, diagnosis is not an easy job and one should be very careful in deciding about therapeutic interventions.

C.H., a 21-year-old boy from a country in the Middle East, began the interview by saying that he had many problems and did not know where to start. The therapists asked him what had made him decide to come to his office. C.H. then said that he was referred by a doctor at the local medical group of Amnesty International, who had written a report on the visible sequelae of torture on his body. C.H. explained that he had hardly been able to answer the questions of that doctor about what had happened to him in jail, because he was overwhelmed by fear. He said that he had horrible nightmares, and never slept more than four hours a night. The nightmares were about his being forced to return to his country. During the day, C.H. said, he worried a lot about his request for political asylum. He could not understand why it had been refused. His lawyer had appealed, and the case was still pending.

C.H. also worried about his future. He had been in prison for five years, and felt that he had fallen behind to such an extent that he would never be able to make up. Moreover, C.H. felt guilty about being unable to support his parents who had sold almost all their belongings to pay for his flight. He often wrote to his parents, but that was also a problem because he did not want to burden them with his difficulties and therefore had to invent positive things to tell them.

In such cases therapeutic tools may alleviate some symptoms. But not every therapist will be happy to help in this way: it is like soothing a person while someone is putting a knife to his throat. In cases like this, therapeutic interventions do not alter the continuous, actual causes of suffering. It then makes more sense to try to remove the actual danger.

In the foregoing example of the first interview with C.H., every question led to the discussion of more problems, in relation to which this refugee felt completely helpless. The therapist decided to use his professional influence and contacted the ministry of justice. After a few weeks, C.H. received a residence permit. His post-traumatic symptoms continued, but he talked about them in a very different manner: he was determined to fight his symptoms in every possible way.

Sometimes the removal of a real danger is beyond the professional influence of the therapist. Then the therapist has to come to terms with his relative powerlessness in the face of a real, continuing traumatizing situation. In the case of real, continuing trauma for the refugee, the therapist should be very reserved in formulating diagnostic hypotheses. Diagnostic hypotheses that do not generate therapeutic interventions are useless, and blame the victim.

If the therapist cannot help the refugee within the ambit of his profession, he can of course see what he can do as a responsible citizen in a political situation where little attention is paid to the possible malignant effects of government policies and procedures upon the mental health of refugees.

Part II

THE USE OF PSYCHOTHERAPEUTIC TECHNIQUES

Introduction

Helping refugees confronts the mental health professional with special problems. First, when refugees request assistance, they rarely do so at the first sign that something is going wrong. Most refugees initially try to solve their problems on their own or with the help of friends or relatives, or just hope that they will go away by themselves. It often happens that a refugee only asks for assistance after minor problems have escalated over time and a major crisis occurs. The problems he then presents are usually a complicated mixture of mental problems, social problems—such as lack of adequate housing—and material problems that have all become very urgent. The refugee then needs to be helped as quickly as possible. Usually, treatment of the mental problems cannot be postponed, while on the other hand, real improvement only becomes possible after the material and social problems have been resolved, or are at least in the process of resolution.

Moreover, working with refugees often means that the helping professional or volunteer must overcome language problems and become familiar with, or adapt to, cultural differences.

Part II of this study starts with a discussion of the last mentioned problem (chapter 4). After this, the establishment of a therapeutic relationship and the various objectives of the use of psychotherapeutic techniques with refugees will be discussed (chapter 5). Chapter 6 will be devoted to therapeutic techniques aimed at limited goals: supportive techniques and techniques for dealing with nightmares and flashbacks. Therapeutic techniques with a less limited goal, like the testimony method, the techniques of uncovering psychotherapy and crisis intervention are discussed in chapter 7, along with some remarks about improvisation and guidelines for choosing therapeutic techniques. In a separate chapter (chapter 8), written by psychiatrist V. Vladár Rivero, the use of psychotropic medication will be discussed.

4 Providing assistance to refugees: overcoming cultural differences

Cultural differences

Refugees are not only individuals who have been traumatized by violence and persecution, they are also migrants in a foreign culture. Therapy with refugees therefore often entails meeting people from cultural backgrounds with which the therapist is not or less familiar. The therapist has to face the fact he cannot be sure in which way the specific cultural background of a refugee has determined his personality development, and how possible culturally determined differences in family life and child development may be reflected in specific ways of coping with stress, specific psychological problems or specific forms of transference. On the other hand, there is no reason to let oneself become intimidated by cultural differences in personality development as long as there are strong indications that, beyond any cultural differences, the needs, feelings, and vulnerabilities that we experience as people are the same the world over (cf. Alexander et al., 1981). In particular, the way people react to psychological trauma does not seem to be very much dependent on their cultural background.

Counselling refugees also means that one has to deal with the condition that, due to their cultural background, refugees may have divergent moral values as well as divergent ideas about mental problems and the way they should be treated. Everyone who seeks assistance for mental problems wants to be treated by an expert whom he can consider as trustworthy (cf. Pederson, 1981). But the criteria by which someone is considered as an expert and as trustworthy are not the same in all cultures. The same goes for specific therapeutic techniques: what is considered as useful and credible in one culture, may be thought of as stupid or immoral in a second culture. The therapist has to be attentive to these differences, and flexible in the use of therapeutic techniques. For instance, when he wants to use the discussion of dreams as a therapeutic technique, he has to inform himself about the ways in which dreams are interpreted in the refugee's cultural background.

Cultural differences between the therapist and the refugee may also result in communication problems. To overcome these problems, the therapist will have to become informed about cultural differences so that he can develop cultural empathy (Dahl, 1989). On the other hand, he has to be aware that cultural sensitivity can fall into cultural stereotyping, when the therapist underestimates the individual differences between people from the same culture.

The helping professional can inform himself about the cultural background of refugees by studying anthropological and other relevant sources about the cultures in question, or by contacting local experts. And the refugee himself can be an important informant, of course. Many refugees are aware that communication problems may come into existence, and are ready to explain things to him as soon as he shows some interest. From his side, the therapist can prevent communication problems from becoming bigger by explaining rules and norms that are common in Western society.

Communication problems based on cultural differences during counselling or therapy are part of the more general problems to which the sudden transfer to another culture gives rise, and that may contribute to the personal problems for which the refugee seeks help.

In this chapter these problems first will be discussed in terms of the concept of 'culture shock'. After this, a section will be devoted to the ways in which communication problems are manifested in contacts with the therapist. It concludes with a section about the language barrier and the use of interpreters.

Culture shock

The term 'culture shock' is used to refer to the violent emotions which can occur in people who find themselves in a strange cultural environment. The term gives a dramatic description of the emotional upheaval and identity problems that may be the consequence of cultural uprooting. A distinction can be made between the 'uncomplicated culture shock', which is the result of a more or less voluntary decision by the newcomer to a country, and the 'complicated culture shock', which is the result of a forced refugee flight (Garza-Guerrero, 1974).

Sometimes the emotions that are provoked by being in an unfamiliar cultural surrounding may be limited to amazement, as in the famous speeches of the Samoan chief Tuiavii about his meetings with Europeans (Tuiavii, 1985). According to Coelho (1982), who did research on culture shock among foreign students in the United States, these emotions often have a much more negative meaning for the individual and may be characterized by the word loss. By this he means:

1. The loss of love and respect as this was experienced in the relationship with friends and family
2. The loss of social status, which may or may not be accompanied by discrimination
3. The loss of a familiar social environment with its mutual obligations and dependencies which gave meaning to life.

It is the author's experience that refugees suffer the same kind of loss. The loss of love and respect that may, for instance, be experienced in connection with companions in distress during detention or combat, whom they had to leave behind. The loss of social status almost certainly occurs, because most refugees have to start at the bottom of society in the country of exile. The students among them sometimes also experience a decline in social status through a decline in their academic achievements due to language difficulties and the necessity to adapt to a very different educational system than the one they were used to. And many refugees who request assistance take the risk they will lose the respect of some of their compatriots, just because they are seeing a psychologist or psychiatrist.

The loss of a familiar social environment is, among other things, experienced through the ignorance and lack of interest of the people in the country of exile with regard to the situation in the refugee's country.

Moreover, directly after arrival, refugees are often directed to reception centres that are organized in a way which deprives them of the possibility to make their own decisions in many ways (cf. Marx, 1990). For some time, they are not free to decide where they want to settle and they may be prevented from moving around, working or studying. This also is a form of loss. On the other hand, the country of exile, because it is more affluent, usually provides in many other respects more opportunities for personal decisions than refugees used to have in their own country. In order to make the right decisions and impose restrictions upon themselves, a much more integrated personality structure is required than was needed for adequate adaptation in the native country (cf. Bettelheim, 1960). The gain in opportunities, comes together with a loss of clarity and security.

As a result of the loss of familiar cultural backing, the ability to integrate new experiences is reduced: familiar frames of reference cannot be applied to the flood of new experiences and impressions.

Because it is also a form of loss, culture shock and cultural uprooting can be compared to the way in which people cope with bereavement (cf. Eisenbruch, 1984). In the process of adaptation to cultural uprooting, phases of denial, anger, depression and finally acceptance can be distinguished (Lin, Masuda & Tazuma, 1982).

In the case of culture shock Hertz (1987) distinguishes between intra-psychic and interpersonal aspects of the problem. The intra-psychic aspects relate to inner conflicts about norms and values. Someone who settles in a different culture will come into contact with norms and values which deviate from those in his own culture. He will be under pressure to adopt the new norms and values and this leads to inner conflict.

Inner conflicts are often resolved through communication with others. This brings us to the interpersonal aspects of the problem: communication can be impeded by cultural differences. First, there are cultural differences in non-verbal communication. For example, a Dutch youth would be less likely to express sympathy towards a friend by holding his hand than an Iranian or Vietnamese youth. In addition, language differences can easily lead to problems in verbal communication. For example, during therapy in a language which is foreign to the refugee, various subtle expressions of emotion, affection and appreciation will be difficult or impossible to express or to understand. As a result both the therapist and the refugee may feel uncertain or even helpless.

This means that the communication which is necessary to solve inner conflicts is hindered and as a result the conflicts may linger. These communication problems can eventually become a source of preconceptions on both sides. For example, after a few unsuccessful attempts to communicate with a Cambodian refugee the European therapist may get the impression that the Cambodians are inscrutable, whereas the refugee may get the idea that Europeans do not want to or are incapable of understanding his problems.

The role of women in society exhibits great intercultural variation. Therefore, many of the experiences brought together under the heading culture shock are related to the interaction between the sexes. Culture shock may be a very different experience for men and women. For example, men from non-Western cultures are often very unfamiliar with women in managerial positions. Women are often in danger of becoming isolated because they no longer have the network of female neighbours or relatives who supported them in caring for their children. On the other hand, Western society offers them opportunities which exceed the limitations placed on them by traditional roles. Women that take these opportunities may come into conflict with their husband, who feels weakened in his position as head of the family. In many cases such problems result in divorce (Groenenberg, 1991).

Overcoming a culture shock

Hertz claims that culture shock is a temporary condition which passes through the following phases:

1. The first phase is one of euphoria: everything in the new situation is beautiful and impressive, or challenging and mysterious. One could add that refugees also experience relief because they are free from persecution.

2. Then there is a second phase of disappointment and related anger. The society in which the refugee finds himself turns out not to be so ideal and in some respects it is inaccessible. In exile the refugee is also confronted with injustice, violence, bureaucracy, human error or indifference toward the misery of their fellow-men, and so on. In this phase, some refugees strongly accentuate their cultural roots, e.g., he starts to play the traditional music of his country, while previously he considered this music as boring or primitive (cf. Garza-Guerrero, 1974).

The sequence of the first and the second phases might offer an explanation for Beiser's (1988) observation that South East Asian refugees experience high levels of depression 10 to 12 months after arrival.

3. Finally, there is a phase of adaptation, when the refugee starts to learn the language, build up a supporting social network and establish emotional relationships, without denying their own cultural heritage.

According to the author's observations, this division in phases offers useful descriptions of the different ways in which refugees may react to life in a different culture. However, these phases do not form an invariant sequence. People may go back and forth between the different phases. Moreover, the phase of adaptation may have different forms. The form Hertz describes, can be characterized with the term *adaptation and formation of a bi-cultural identity*. In a second form of this phase, to which one could refer with the term *superficial adaptation*, the refugee adapts himself to his new environment, but in an opportunistic or superficial way. For example, he learns the language and manages to mobilize citizens of the country of exile who help him to find better housing, but avoids more personal contacts with them, and strongly rejects many cultural values of the country of exile. His only friends are compatriots, and he sticks rigidly to traditional values.

A third form of adaptation can be labelled as *over-adjustment*. Some refugees adapt very quickly to the habits of the country of exile, while they strongly reject every behaviour they associate with their own cultural background. For instance, they avoid compatriots, try to conceal that they are not European, and speak about their native country in a derogatory manner. Some of these refugees seem to attach very great importance to the acquisition of material wealth, and like to possess all the paraphernalia they consider characteristic of a modern Western individual. Sometimes, they also want to change their name to make it sound more Western. From a psychodynamic point of view, it could be argued that this form of adaptation is not adequate, because the loss of the familiar environment has not been worked through (cf. Garza-Guerrero, 1974).

According to Hertz three approaches can be fruitful in providing assistance to migrants:

1. A cognitive approach, in which the migrant is provided with information so that he can orient himself more adequately
2. An affective approach in which the emphasis is on overcoming the fear of what is experienced as 'strange'
3. A behavioural approach, which is primarily aimed at re-activating those who have become passive as a result of disillusionment

It may be added here that, from a cognitive-behavioural point of view, culture shock can be seen as the result of a series of experiences in which the individual, after arriving in an unfamiliar cultural environment, was unable to use formerly effective coping skills and consequently lost self-confidence. Explaining this process to the refugee and teaching him more adaptive coping skills can be a useful therapeutic technique.

The contact with the therapist

The first contact with a Western therapist and Western attitudes toward assistance for personal problems may form part of the culture shock which the refugee experiences. What he expects from this assistance, given his knowledge of his own society, does not correspond to what a doctor or healer in a different culture has to offer (Kabela, n.d.; Kinzie, 1978). For example, the refugee may expect to be cured quickly. The idea that his complaints will disappear if he learns more about himself through a long series of talks is strange and difficult to comprehend.

Sometimes the therapist employs different norms, for example his distinction between 'madness' and 'normality' may be much less strict than that which is made in African or Asian cultures (Kortmann, 1986). Some refugees come from cultures in which visiting a psychiatrist is proof of madness.

Refugees from non-Western cultures may express their complaints in a manner which is unfamiliar to the Western therapist. Giel (1984) describes the moaning and sighing of patients in an Addis Ababa polyclinic. He initially found this behaviour theatrical but his interpreter was impressed by their suffering. Further investigation revealed that these patients were not suffering from a hysterical complaint but were really sick. Giel concluded: 'The generally reserved Ethiopian apparently loses his armour of impassivity during illness.'

Such apparently theatrical behaviour can sometimes also be observed in refugees, especially those who have not been in exile long. But such behaviour may, in some cases, also be a result of the fact that the refugee is in the first phase (crying out), of the process of assimilating his traumatic experiences.

In addition, the refugee may be used to other norms relating to what counts as morally responsible or healthy behaviour. In such cases it is useful to explore these norms (cf. Brown, 1986; Agger, 1988).

A.O., a 25-year-old refugee from the Middle East, was very worried about his younger brother, who had gone into exile with him and for whom he felt responsible. He had caught his brother masturbating and was worried about the consequences of this for his health. The therapist asked A.O. what he thought about the physical consequences of masturbation and how he viewed it morally. He also explained that research in the West had shown that masturbation was a common form of sexual behaviour, that it was seen as preparation for other forms of sexuality and that the majority of the population did not view it as morally objectionable.

There are also cultural differences in the causes people ascribe to illnesses. For instance, in Cambodian culture illness is thought to be the consequence of coming into contact with dangerous spirits, witchcraft or sorcery (Eisenbruch & Handelman, 1989). The same belief can be found in India (Srinivasa & Trivedi, 1982), in some Caribbean (Cancelmo, Millán & Vasquez, 1990) and in African cultures. This kind of explanation may occasionally be mentioned by refugees. However, traumatized refugees usually have little trouble in considering the idea that there may be a relation between their symptoms and their traumatic experiences.

Moreover, cultural differences are also present in the ideas which people have about the cause of traumatic experiences. Mollica & Son (1988) reports in this connection that Cambodian refugees who have been tortured relate this to the Buddhist concept of *karma*. They feel responsible for their suffering because of their karma. This is opposed to the Western conception that torture is something which is done to the individual for political reasons. More generally speaking it is important for the therapist to understand the cultural framework within which certain symptoms are evaluated and the causal explanations that are implicit in any cultural framework (Lee & Lu, 1989).

Another cultural difference that directly influences the contact with the therapist is the readiness to talk about personal matters with someone outside the family. Kabela (n.d.) reports that Chinese and other East Asian patients, like those from the Middle East, are not used to talking about feelings of dejection or loneliness, or sexual problems, because they feel guilty or are ashamed. In some cultures, Japan for example, personal feelings are discussed, but only through symbolic expressions derived from nature, such as 'rain', 'dark', 'misty', 'cloudy' (Kabela, n.d.). Denley (1987) notes that refugees from Indochinese cultures mask their personal suffering by politeness and smiles. Asian clients in general seem often to avoid expressing their emotions and tend to express psychic distress by physical complaints. In the first contacts, the therapist may mistakenly perceive them as passive; this passivity however should be seen as a cultural expression of respect for authority (Tsui & Schultz, 1985).

According to the author's observations, people from Middle East countries may start talking a bit tediously about trivial matters before they are ready to discuss what really is bothering them. An inexperienced or impatient therapist might therefore underestimate the seriousness of their problems.

Finally, in some cultures it seems to be normal for the client to occasionally give the therapist small gifts. Some refugees maintain this habit in their contacts with European therapists. If the latter is not in the habit of accepting gifts he will have to make this clear in a tactful manner.

Corrective feedback from the therapist can help the refugee to understand what kinds of behaviour are acceptable or unacceptable in particular situations (De Anda, 1984). In some situations however, it is desirable for the therapist to conform to the expectations of his client.

B.O., an islamic refugee, always drank a cup of coffee during the weekly therapeutic sessions. During ramadan the therapist offered him his usual cup of coffee, but he refused. The therapist asked him about the way in which he celebrated ramadan and did not offer him any more coffee that month.

It is important that the therapist is continuously aware of the communication problems that may rise as the result of cultural differences. Sometimes, he may decide to accommodate a bit to the refugee. For example, the therapist may ask himself how his clothing will be seen by refugees from various cultural backgrounds, in order to avoid under- or overdressing (cf. Vontress, 1981), or examine the covers of the magazines in his waiting room from the point of view of an orthodox moslem.

On the level of treatment techniques (cf. Sundberg, 1981), he should be careful in using a nondirective approach, because many refugees are unfamiliar with it or misinterpret it as a sign of inadequacy or lack of interest. He also should be aware of the fact that, with people from particular (e.g. Micronesian) cultures and under certain conditions, eye contact can be experienced as threatening or disrespectful. More generally, it is important that the therapist takes the time to explain again and again how his treatment works, why he is asking certain questions, what he expects from the refugee and so on. In this connection, therapist and counsellors could compare their service to that of a bank. Most refugees soon learn how to cash a cheque, although it may seem knotty at first to explain to them all the ins and outs of plastic cards and pin codes, and it usually does not make much difference whether the employee is white or black, male or female.

It is the author's experience, that the therapist cannot always recognize that a misunderstanding has arisen. The consequence may be that the refugee interrupts treatment. Any time a refugee misses an appointment, the therapist may ask himself whether some communication problem may have come into existence without him being aware of it. In those cases, the misunderstanding can sometimes be cleared up if the therapist takes the trouble to invite the refugee to come again, for example by phoning him or by writing a personal letter.

Sometimes, the refugee may have more confidence in the helping professional because the latter belongs to a different culture. He may think for instance that the professional is more objective, more trustworthy, or better educated.

Whatever the cultural background of the refugee, there is no need for the therapist to compromise his professional manner. Genuine interest, respect and tolerance for the anxiety in his client are basic conditions for counselling and therapy. Of course, the therapist has to make sure that these features are recognized by the refugee.

Finally, the importance of the cultural factor in communication problems with refugees should not be overestimated. Culture should not be seen as a complete package of meaning, which totally determines the behaviour and thinking of any individual that grew up in this culture (cf. Knudsen, 1991). The alternative is to understand cultural background as one of the factors that contributes to the process of the identity development of the individual refugee. Meeting a refugee does not mean that one meets a sort of representative of an exotic world, but an individual with a personal identity.

Language problems and misunderstanding

In the ideal therapeutic situation both therapist and client would speak the same language fluently. Fortunately, this is not always true: sometimes it is easier to discuss a private matter or a taboo in a second language than in one's native language (cf. Sundberg, 1981). However, counselling refugees often means that the therapist has to work with people who have grown up speaking very different languages. Refugees with personal problems often have difficulty concentrating or cannot remember what they have been taught. This usually has a negative effect on their efforts to learn the language of the country in which they are in exile.

In the case of refugees who do speak the therapist's language it is necessary to realize that they probably only have access to a limited vocabulary of common terms and do not know or understand many of the terms which they require to describe or express their emotions. This means that they are limited in their ability to articulate their problems, and the therapist must take care that what he says comes across in the way he intends it, and he must be constantly alert for misunderstandings which stem from the use of a language with which the refugee is not familiar. In such cases, therapeutic sessions will be slower than usual and often cannot be limited to the usual 45 minutes.

C.O., who had left Iran a year earlier, had a very limited English vocabulary. He only knew the concept of feeling in the sense of physical perception, not in the psychological sense. But he solved this problem when he said of his torturer: 'With my heart I thought: I'll kill him, but with my head I thought: You shouldn't do that.'

Even if he cannot speak it, some knowledge of syntax of the refugee's native language, will help the therapist to understand the problems which the refugee has and may help to reduce misunderstandings. The therapist can check whether the refugee has understood abstract concepts by asking him to give examples (Kortmann, 1986). The refugee can be taught concepts which facilitate communication in the same way.

Translated questionnaires, such as the Hopkins Symptom Checklist (Mollica et al., 1987), in which mental complaints and feelings are subtly articulated can help to facilitate communication and find translations in European languages for feelings which the refugee considers important.

Moreover, even if the therapist speaks the refugee's native language fluently there can still be misunderstandings if the therapist is unaware of certain customs in the refugee's culture. Swartz (1987) describes the *hlonipa* tradition among the Xhosa speaking peoples of South Africa. In this tradition it is taboo for a woman to use certain words, which include the names of her male relatives and that of her husband. Therapists who were unfamiliar with this tradition thought that the Xhosa women who came to them for help had language problems or even that they were mentally deranged.

Working with interpreters

When the language barrier between therapist and client is so great that they cannot communicate adequately then use can be made of an interpreter. This leads to an unusual situation: communication proceeds through a third person, who is usually not trained to give assistance, but who, nonetheless, makes a personal contribution to the course of the encounter. The interpreter's attitude towards the client determines the atmosphere in which the encounter takes place, and this attitude does not always conform to what the therapist considers desirable. A sympathetic, businesslike, authoritarian or patronizing attitude on the part of the interpreter may facilitate or impede the development of a relationship of mutual trust between the therapist and his client. The extent of the interpreter's knowledge of the client's culture may also facilitate the course of the encounter.

Characteristics of the interpreter's behaviour can evoke certain feelings in the client. If the interpreter is a compatriot the client may be comforted by his presence, but he may also be ashamed of problems which are considered to be a sign of madness or a cause of contempt in their common culture. Refugees sometimes distrust compatriot interpreters for political reasons. If the interpretor has the same political ideology as the client the latter will not feel free to express doubts about his political convictions.

The gender of the interpreter can also influence the client's frankness, particularly in relation to sexual problems. Various transference phenomena may also be present in the relationship with the interpreter. For example, a client who feels that the therapist does not understand his problems may direct his irritation to the interpreter and accuse him of not translating properly. Also, the therapist may vent his irritation at the client by directing it to the interpreter.

Sometimes the client places the interpreter in a difficult situation: for example, by telling him something and then asking him not to tell the therapist.

Finally, the interpreter may make translation mistakes which have a negative effect on the therapeutic process. Some of these mistakes can be attributed to words which do not have an exact translation (Sue & Sue, 1987). For example, it is difficult to find a completely satisfactory equivalent for 'disappointment' in Persian. Price (1975) has done research on the mistakes made by three hindustani interpreters working in a psychiatric practice in Australia. He found that translation mistakes very rarely led to the wrong diagnosis being made, but they do increase the time needed to make a diagnosis. According to Price, more mistakes were made when translating the patients' answers (at most 15.5%) than the doctors' questions (at most 7.4% when they were talking to psychotic patients, 4.2% when they were talking to neurotics). In translating the answers of patients who were diagnosed as acute psychotic or chronic psychotic the interpreters made more mistakes (15.5%) than with neurotic patients (5.2%).

The most common mistakes which interpreters made in translating doctors' questions were: they changed open questions into leading questions, altered the content of questions and added their own comments. Their mistakes in translating patients' answers included: leaving out part of the answer, adding something to the answer and mistakes because of their limited knowledge of English.

Various authors have made recommendations, based on their own experiences, concerning the use of interpreters in a therapeutic context that concur with the author's own experiences. Pentz-Moller et al. (1988) claim that it is important that the interpreter speaks in the first person whenever the person speaking does so. They also consider it to be of vital importance that the interpreter feels empathy towards the refugee, but this should not lead him to intervene in the treatment without the consent of the therapist. They consider it important that the interpreter has some knowledge of such relevant topics as the different forms of torture. Baker (1981) claims that it is important to inform interpreters about the basic principles on which the therapist bases his approach: for example that he assumes the client has to make decisions himself, that the topics discussed during sessions are confidential, that silence during sessions may be meaningful, etc. In addition, Baker considers it necessary that the interpreter feels involved with the client, even if he is from a different social class or background. He prefers interpreters who do not have problems themselves: they provide an adequate identification approach for the client and are less likely to lose their objectivity during sessions.

Putsch (1985) also considers neutrality and objectivity to be important characteristics of a good interpreter. The client often brings along friends or relatives to interpret. He considers them to be unsuitable. They have the advantage of being familiar with the client, but the disadvantage of not being objective, and this affects their translations. For example, they may exaggerate or minimize the client's complaints. In the case of children (who often learn the new language faster than their parents) playing the role of interpreter can disturb the existing family hierarchy. Marcos (1979) also considers relatives to be less suitable as interpreters because they often answer the therapist's questions without even putting them to the client.

Therefore, an interpreter who does not know the client but who is somewhat familiar with the procedures used by the therapist, is preferable. But even then the therapist must be aware of the possibility of wrong translations and the loss of information, for example information which points to thought disorders or covert depression (Sabin, 1975). Incidentally cultural differences can also hinder the contact between therapist and interpreter. For instance, interpreters, because of their own cultural values, may not feel very comfortable with some questions about sex (Rendon, 1989).

Another problem with interpreters is that they may have experienced traumatic events similar to those of which the refugee became a victim. If this is the case, the interpreter may avoid unhappy memories for himself by not translating accurately, avoiding certain topics, changing the subject, informing the therapist that the interview is too stressful for the refugee and so on (Westermeyer, 1989).

Finally, let us consider some of the author's own experiences. One way of maintaining the client's anonymity, and thereby increasing the chance that he will discuss his problems openly, is to use a loudspeaker telephone and the services of external interpreters. The interpreter then need not meet the refugee personally; he does not know what he looks like and need not even know his name. This method has the disadvantage that gestures and other non-verbal aspects of communication are not included in the translation and are lost.

When an unfamiliar interpreter is to be present the client's embarrassment or suspicion can be reduced if the interpreter introduces himself to the client before the session and they have the chance for an informal chat. It can also be very useful for the therapist to have a preparatory conversation with the interpreter. It can be very enlightening to check whether certain questions (e.g. about sexual behaviour) can be expressed at all in the client's language by this interpreter.

When the therapist is speaking to the client he can, in spite of the language barrier, maintain eye contact with him. This seems to facilitate the client's understanding of what is being said without the intervention of the interpreter. Keeping questions and remarks concise also helps to improve communication. Long questions mean that the therapist has to direct more of his attention to the interpreter than to the client. Sessions should be prepared beforehand, if necessary in consultation with the interpreter. Sometimes it is useful for the therapist to explain to the interpreter why he says or asks certain things.

Using an interpreter from the same culture area as the refugee has the advantage that they share not only the same language but also the same cultural background. Working regularly with the same interpreters also increases the therapist's understanding of other cultures.

The emotional reactions of interpreters during therapeutic sessions are sometimes a useful source of information. If the therapist sees that the interpreter is embarrassed, surprised, or shows some other emotional reaction he may interrupt the session to consult the interpreter about the reasons for his reaction.

Sometimes it is useful to ask the interpreter for his opinion on the client's emotions. Such interventions break the conventional boundaries of the interpreter's role and he becomes a bi-cultural co-therapist. In order to enable him to fulfil this role adequately proper training is necessary.

In the United States a lot of experience has been gained in the cooperation between American and Vietnamese or Cambodian co-therapists, and in providing special training programmes for the latter (see, for example, Teter, 1987).

5 Treatment goals and the therapeutic relationship

Various forms

The use of psychotherapeutic techniques in order to help refugees can take various forms. The form which is chosen in a particular case depends on a number of factors, such as the following:

1. The training which the psychotherapist has undergone (psychoanalytic, Rogerian, behavioural, family-oriented, etc.)
2. His experience in different work situations (private practice or multidisciplinary team, out-patient clinic or hospital)
3. His preference for working within certain social settings (individual contact with the client, family therapy, group therapy, marital counselling)

In this chapter discussions about the choice of theoretical perspective, work situation or social setting will be avoided. Giving professional help to refugees based on the achievements of modern psychology and psychiatry is such a complicated but urgent task that helping professionals cannot afford to be orthodox in any way. A flexible approach in which well-considered use is made of the achievements of various perspectives, and in which the actions of the psychotherapist are documented and therefore justifiable, is indicated.

Given the complex nature of refugees' problems, and their diverse cultural backgrounds, the working together with a team of experts with different levels of education, from different disciplines, preferably from different cultural backgrounds, but at least willing to become aware of and to subdue their ethnocentric tendencies, is necessary.

The thoughts about the use of psychotherapeutic techniques with refugees which are discussed below are based on the publications of helping professionals who described their clinical experiences. These publications make use of a predominantly psychodynamic terminology, amplified by or mixed with terms emanating from other psychological approaches. What they write about their professional work often is not very thoroughly structured and therefore difficult to render. Often the descriptions of their therapeutic interventions are not very detailed. It is therefore necessary to summarize these publications by concentrating on the objectives the authors formulate or implicitly seem to hold regarding the use of psychotherapeutic techniques with refugees or other victims of political violence.

In order to give a kind of overview about the possibilities for using psychotherapeutic techniques with refugees, the different objectives psychotherapeutic techniques can be aimed at will be discussed first.

Treatment goals

Ideally, before psychotherapeutic interventions are started, a thorough examination is made of the refugee's background and problems. This examination is meant to provide the therapist with diagnostic data on the basis of which he can determine whether there are any points of application for psychotherapeutic techniques.

Sometimes these cannot be identified, although the refugee has a mental problem. In this context one can think of, giving some examples, refugees with psychiatric disturbances such as schizophrenia, severe mental retardation, organic personality syndrome or psychoactive substance abuse. Then the therapist has to conclude that, at least at this point in time, the instruments of psychotherapy cannot contribute anything in order to alleviate the problems of a particular refugee. The professional help will then be restricted to psychiatric treatment and care, in order to stabilize the condition of the refugee and to foster the quality of his functioning as much as possible, for example, by helping him to structure his daily life.

If points of application for psychotherapeutic techniques are apparent, the therapist has to form an opinion about the question of what would be the best setting (out-patient or in-patient; individual; in a group; with the partner; or with the family). He also has to make an inventory of the general objectives the use of psychotherapeutic techniques could have in this particular case, and about more specific targets.

As far as the general objectives of the use of psychotherapeutic techniques are concerned, a basic distinction can be made between helping the refugee to change things that can be changed, and helping the refugee to accept things which cannot be changed (cf. Mikulas, 1978).

Many therapists (e.g. Bleich, Garb & Kottler, 1986) make a second basic distinction: between stimulating long-term changes in certain aspects of the client's personality, or trying to achieve more adequate functioning as quickly as possible. In the first case, therapy is aimed at promoting a re-living of emotional experiences and insight into intra-psychic processes. In the second case, therapy is aimed at the behavioural aspects of coping skills and at the cognitive components of adequate and inadequate coping mechanisms and makes use of techniques which stimulate behaviour modification or the restructuring of habitual ways of thinking.

If it is decided to promote long-term processes of emotional integration of traumatic experiences and personality change then the therapist usually attempts to get the client to re-experience emotional conflicts, so that he realizes the effect which they are having on his present situation and is then able to cope with them. The result which the therapist hopes to achieve is that the client frees himself from emotional impediments to his functioning, thus putting his life on a new course.

If the objective is a more adequate functioning in the short term, then the therapist will concentrate on achieving limited changes as rapidly as possible. He will choose this strategy if he considers far-reaching personality changes to be unnecessary, or if it seems likely that such changes will occur as part of the result of the more limited changes. A determining factor which may also play a role is that the client is not considered to be capable of dealing with the emotions which would be generated by re-experiencing conflicts which he has not yet assimilated, that there are not many people in his social environment who can provide emotional support, or that there is insufficient structure in his daily life (e.g. a job or other routine activities) from which he could derive support.

Not all psychotherapists who work with traumatized clients agree with the classification of objectives described above. Ochberg (1988) employs the following division: the first type of psychotherapy is directed at the pre-traumatic personality and the problems which were present before the trauma developed. According to Ochberg this approach suggests that the client's symptoms are partly related to weaknesses and limitations in his personality.

A second type of psychotherapy places more emphasis on recent events, on coping skills and the client's stronger characteristics, and on the mistaken but rectifiable ideas which obstruct rapid emotional assimilation.

Ochberg prefers to start with the second approach, unless the client is of the opinion that his pre-traumatic problems are at the heart of his present difficulties. He thinks that the first approach places the blame for his problems on the client himself, whereas the second approach facilitates a working relationship between therapist and client.

Ochberg's distinction is very useful in providing assistance to clients who have undergone a single traumatic experience within a limited period of time. Many refugees, however, have experienced a long and continuous process of traumatization which interacts with the normal process of personality development. The result of this could be that personality development has not been optimal, and then therapy aimed at personality changes would be desirable. This does not mean that the client is being blamed for his present problems, which are the result of a long process of traumatization.

A third distinction can be made between treatment aimed at well defined complaints and symptoms, and treatment that is not focused in this way and can be directed to the refugee's total functioning. Of course the difference between these two extremes is not absolute: in practice, treatment often begins with the use of techniques that are directed at relieving incapacitating symptoms and then expands to include wider objectives; or that the successful treatment of one symptom has an important effect on the total functioning of an individual.

For the sake of completeness it is important to mention the distinction between therapeutic techniques aimed primarily at the individual refugee and interventions aimed at the social system(s) of which the refugee is a part. Part II of this study will concentrate on the techniques that are directed to the individual refugee.

A pragmatic distinction

In this study the following pragmatic distinction will be made:

1. The use of psychotherapeutic methods aimed at limited goals. These include supportive techniques aimed at improving the refugee's psychosocial functioning in the short term, without the pretension of bringing about personality changes, which only require an intermediate level of expertise of the helping professional, and the more specialized techniques aimed at symptoms as nightmares and flashbacks.
2. The use of techniques of which the goals are less limited. These include the techniques that constitute the testimony method, the techniques of uncovering psychotherapy aimed at the long-term goal of emotional assimilation of traumatic experiences that interfered with personality development for a considerable time and which is therefore also aimed at personality change, and the techniques of crisis intervention.

In many cases it can be indicated that one should use mixtures of the aforementioned types of psychotherapeutic techniques, or to combine them with other forms of professional help. How techniques of different types can be blended in a responsible way, will be discussed in sections on improvisation and on guidelines for choosing therapeutic techniques.

Establishing a therapeutic relationship

When refugees ask for help they are usually in need of immediate assistance. Generally the therapeutic contacts will have to commence immediately after the first acquaintance has been made, even though the therapist may not yet know what exactly is required. In such cases he could, to begin with, support the client's motivation to seek assistance and attempt to build up a therapeutic relationship. Such a relationship requires that:

1. The therapist and the client have some affinity for one another
2. That they trust each other
3. That the refugee can overcome his fear of becoming in some ways dependent on the therapist
4. That in their relationship their objective is to overcome the client's mental problems
5. And—as far as is humanly possible—nothing else.

Some affinity for one another   The way in which mutual affinity between people develops has not been studied sufficiently from a scientific perspective, and perhaps it would be better if that remained so. It can be stated that some refugees can experience the presence or absence of a sincere interest on the part of the therapist through certain characteristics of the room in which they are received. If there is a map of their country of origin, reading matter in their vernacular and toys for the children in the waiting room then this will be viewed positively. If the therapist can speak a few words of the client's language then this will also be seen as a sign of sincere interest. These days refugees are not very popular in Western countries. A basic condition for providing assistance to refugees is that the therapist makes them feel welcome.

Mutual trust   Trust usually develops gradually on the basis of direct or indirect contact between therapist and client. Sometimes the client trusts the therapist right from the start because he has already heard something about him and his methods from a friend or doctor or someone else whom he trusts. Previous positive experiences with other therapists or social workers can also contribute to the ease with which trust develops in a new therapeutic relationship.

In her first interview A.I. described, without hesitation or restraint, the details of her experiences as a prisoner. During the second interview she said that she had felt secure on the previous occasion. She had the impression that the therapist knew what it was like in the prisons in her country. Moreover, shortly after her release, but before leaving the country, she had discussed her experiences on a number of occasions with a psychologist, and she had retained pleasant memories of those talks.

On the other hand, previous negative experiences with a therapist or social worker can have the opposite effect. Such experiences may occur when the therapist—usually unintentionally—arouses expectations which he cannot fulfil.

B.I. had serious depressive complaints and isolated himself from the other refugees with whom he shared an apartment. The volunteer who was counselling him was sympathetic and initially ready to help him day and night. But when the burden became too great he tried to refer B.I. to a psychologist. B.I. reacted with anger and suspicion, and the referral took place in a crisis situation, a day before the volunteer went on holiday for two weeks. B.I. let it be known that he considered a talk with a psychologist to be unnecessary. He made use of the occasion to give an exposition on the uselessness of psychology, and—B.I. speaks German— to lecture the psychologist whenever he made a grammatical mistake. In this situation a therapeutic relationship could not develop.

Overcoming fear of dependency   Refugees who have been traumatized, often have felt very powerless and dependent on the whims of other persons during traumatization. They know how horrible it can be to be dependent on somebody else. They may therefore fear to enter a therapeutic relationship, or leave this relationship when it is becoming too close.

Overcoming the client's mental problems   When refugees consult a psychologist or a psychiatrist it is often because they have been referred by a doctor whom they consulted for somatic complaints. In other cases it may be members of the family, friends or a partner who were concerned about his condition and persuaded him to seek help, while he is convinced not to have a mental problem. Conflicts with a partner can also lead to a request for assistance, and in that case the refugee sometimes is not ready to consider the possibility that his own behaviour might contribute to the conflict. Generally speaking it is not very common for refugees to say that they have a mental problem and to express the desire to discuss personal problems with a psychologist or psychiatrist, even when they are afraid of becoming insane. Admitting that they have a mental problem, seems to be identical for them with being a lunatic. When they meet a mental health professional for the first time they often adopt a wait-and-see attitude. It can take some time before they will be ready to think about their own behaviour and to reflect on what they are feeling and thinking.

C.I., a 20-year-old refugee from an Asian country, had been suffering from attacks of shortness of breath for years. His doctor had been unable to discover any physical cause, and examinations by a number of specialists had also been without result. He was told that his problem was 'mental' and sent to a psychologist.

At his first meeting with the psychologist C.I. asked for medicine for his complaint. He was prepared to answer questions about himself and the reasons for coming to this country. But he did not take up the suggestion that his physical illness might be related to the experiences which had caused him to flee from his own country, or to the problems of adjustment in exile. He indicated that he was reluctant to discuss these topics. However, he did accept the invitation to come and see the psychologist regularly, although he cancelled or 'forgot' two-thirds of the appointments.

In 10 interviews spread over eight months he generally told the psychologist that he was alright and that he did not need any help. Here mutual trust and sympathy were present, but C.I. was not motivated by the desire to overcome his mental problems. It was only in the eleventh interview that he told of his traumatic experiences after escaping from prison.

... and nothing else   One of the fundamental rules of psychotherapy is that the therapist should be as aware as possible of his own needs and desires in his relationship with his client. He has the responsibility to prevent his own feelings from obstructing the main objective of therapy: overcoming the client's mental problems. And it is just as important that the client also has only this goal in mind during therapy.

D.I. had so many complaints that he seemed to manifest the symptoms of three psychiatric syndromes simultaneously. But at the same time he functioned reasonably adequately in his day-to-day life. After the therapist had made clear to D.I. in the course of three interviews that he, the therapist, could not possibly influence the outcome of his request for political asylum, and had complimented him on the way he was managing to cope, in spite of the stress related to his request for asylum, D.I. broke off all contact with the therapist, though they did part on friendly terms. D.I. did apparently have mental problems, but was primarily concerned with avoiding deportation to the country from which he had fled.

Ambivalence

In some cases refugees have an ambivalent attitude towards requesting assistance. They seem to experience the fact that they require help from a mental health expert as humiliating. When a doctor refers them to a psychologist or psychiatrist for somatic complaints without apparent causes they sometimes feel fobbed off or insulted and may have the impression that they are not being taken seriously.

So when a refugee finally decides, sometimes after a lot of hesitation (some refugees postpone or 'forget' appointments for registration interviews a few times), to seek help, he is then confronted with a therapist who demands a lot of him. The therapist has to evaluate the problem—even if this is only to be able to estimate whether the refugee has come to the right person—and therefore cannot avoid asking a number of personal questions. This means that the therapist has to ask about exactly those things of which the client is ashamed, or those experiences which he would rather forget. On the other hand, this show of interest and concern is not without effect: it if leads to the client releasing some of his suppressed emotions then it may be difficult to stop him and there is a chance that he will regret and be ashamed of this openness afterwards. It is from this somewhat precarious position that a therapeutic relationship must be built up.

E.I., a 23-year-old refugee from Africa complained, in his first interview with a psychologist, of headaches, insomnia, nightmares and the inability to concentrate on his studies. When the therapist (suspecting traumatic experiences, given the information he had received from the referee) asked him why he had left his country E.I. replied decisively that he would prefer not to talk about that. He said that he would rather talk about his present problems with housemates and girls. He started to talk about these problems, but after two sentences went on to give an emotional account of the painful events which had led to his flight. Afterwards the therapist had the impression that he had not been sufficiently in control and that it had been a painful experience for E.I.

In a second interview, a week later, E.I. recognized his ambivalence: 'On the one hand I want to keep it all inside, and on the other hand I want to get it all out', he said. That interview and the next one were more tranquil. E.I. started the fourth interview with the statement that he wanted to terminate the therapy. The therapist listened to his reasons and asked him to sleep on it. When E.I. did not keep his appointment the following week the therapist sent him a personal letter. Two days later E.I. called in unexpectedly 'to say goodbye'. On that occasion—the fifth interview—he said that the therapist did not understand his cultural background. The therapist agreed with this and asked E.I. to explain it to him. He had the impression that E.I. was looking for excuses to keep coming without having to admit that he needed help. This interview was concluded with the agreement that E.I. would come and see the therapist the following week at the usual time and tell him more about his country. It was only in the seventh interview that he mentioned his problems again. He stated that he would only be prepared to discuss his traumatic experiences once a number of practical problems (such as housing) had been solved. The therapist agreed.

In the eighth interview E.I. spontaneously told the therapist of a nightmare which referred to his traumatic experiences. At the end of this interview he asked for sleeping tablets, but later it became apparent that he had not taken them. E.I.'s complaints about his insomnia led him to spontaneously talk about his traumatic experiences. He seemed to be relieved after the interviews and his mood improved visibly.

In the example above the client's ambivalence appears to have been determined primarily by his embarrassment at having expressed emotions and his need for assistance. This ambivalence can also be coloured by suspicion.

F.I. had asked his doctor to refer him to a psychiatrist because he was suffering from depression. The first interview took place in a pleasant atmosphere, and F.I. described how his problems were manifested in his day-to-day life. In the second interview he had a lot of questions about the institute for which the therapist worked. Because it was partly state subsidized he was afraid that there may be some contact with the embassy of the country from which he had fled. All this was discussed in a calm manner. The therapist had the impression that, given this refugee's world of experience, these fears were justified and not merely delusions. The therapist also had the impression that the client was sounding out his political views.

The development of a therapeutic relationship is a necessary condition for any type of therapy. It is, at the same time, also part of the therapy: the experience of the attention and effort of the therapist, and the regular appointments which have to be kept, provide emotional support and help to structure the client's life.

G.I. was a refugee who complained of depressions and attacks of anxiety. In the course of 10 therapeutic interviews an attempt was made to promote more adequate psychosocial functioning in the short term. But the results remained limited. G.I.'s comment on this was: 'At least there is one day in the week on which I get up at a normal time, take a shower, and get the feeling that I am treated like a human being.'

Even in its later stages the therapeutic relationship may still be fragile, and this needs to be recognized and some effort made to maintain the relationship. The establishment and maintenance of a therapeutic relationship is, in the first place, a question of time, real concern on the part of the therapist and respect for the conflicting feelings of the client. It also helps if the therapist succeeds in recognizing the nature of the client's ambivalence. Moreover, it is advisable for the therapist to ask himself whether he feels personally threatened, rejected or hurt by the behaviour of the client, and is therefore less capable of taking an open attitude to the client's conflicting feelings.

Sometimes it is useful to discuss the client's conflicting feelings immediately and convince him that his ambivalent feelings are respectable. This also applies if they are related to previous unpleasant experiences in the contact with other helping professionals or volunteers. Talking about conflicting emotions is sometimes a great relief for the client and gives him the feeling that, at least as far as that is concerned, he is understood. Moreover, it also gives the therapist the opportunity to dispel possible misunderstandings.

6 Treatment techniques aimed at limited goals

Supportive techniques

When a refugee has to some extent overcome his conflicting emotions relating to the decision to seek assistance it often becomes apparent that something must be done urgently. Depression, anxiety or stress have increased, the refugee is not calm enough to reflect and the therapist feels that something must be done immediately. Under such circumstances he may decide to direct his attention to short-term goals: trying to promote more adequate functioning on the level of ordinary, everyday behaviour and the reduction of symptoms. Sometimes this seems to be sufficient. In other cases, these therapeutic methods are used in order to prepare the refugee for other forms of therapy. By promoting more adequate functioning in everyday life the therapist tries to create favourable conditions in which to tackle those problems that cannot be solved with these relatively simple techniques.

There are various therapeutic or therapy-supporting methods which can be directed to short-term objectives and require only an intermediate level of expertise from the helping professional (see Winston, Pinsker & McCullough, 1986).

1. Discussing overpowering negative feelings and making them understandable for the refugee by relating them to everyday occurrences
2. Prescribing psychotropic medication (see chapter 7)
3. Providing the concrete assistance which is part of social casework
4. Discussing the refugee's ideas about the development of his mental problems in order to relativize feelings of helplessness and powerlessness
5. Explaining the development of refugees' mental problems in general, in order to reduce the possibility of the client developing a negative self-image, and to relativize the fear of being or going mad
6. Discussing the positive side of his functioning, to strengthen adequate coping skills

7. Analysing recent, everyday experiences of associating with other people, so that the refugee gains more insight into the way in which people socialize, and how to avoid unpleasant situations and create pleasant ones
8. Stimulate orderly thinking about the political and social aspects of human existence (see Beets, 1974), so that the refugee realizes his special position, both in relation to his native country from which he has fled and in relation to the country in which he has gone into exile.

A.J., a refugee from an African country, was referred by his doctor after he had reported wanting to commit suicide. In the waiting room he made a tense and depressed impression. But during the first interview (the day after he had seen his doctor) he opened up. Since going into exile he had been troubled by insomnia. He said that he could not sleep for more than three hours a night. He brooded a lot and spent the whole day at home watching television (he lived together with a number of compatriots). During the first interview the therapist examined the possibility of short-term changes in A.J.'s daily routine. He asked him what his daily routine had been when everything had been alright.

It appeared that he had done a lot of sport in his native country and the therapist pointed to the possibilities for doing sport with other people from a similar cultural background. He offered actual help by picking up the phone and calling a sports club, then passing the telephone to A.J., who made an appointment to go and train the next day. The therapist also introduced him to his medical colleague, who prescribed medicine for his insomnia.

A few days later, during a second interview, A.J. looked healthier and more cheerful. He had slept better, spent less time in front of the television and done some sport. During this interview he gave more details about his reasons for fleeing his country and spoke of his anxiety about relatives who had remained behind.

In a third interview he told of sometimes being overcome by fear and thinking that he was going mad. The therapist explained that this did not mean that he was going mad but that it was a normal reaction to the frightening events which he had experienced during his flight. It became clear that this fear was related to bad news about the political situation in his home country and the fact that he had not heard anything from his family.

During a fourth interview A.J. said that he was still sleeping well and had not experienced attacks of fear or depressions, even though he had stopped taking his medicine. He then spoke of his uncertain position as a refugee whose request for asylum had not yet been granted, and his disinclination to learn the language until he was certain he could stay.

The discussion then moved on to government policy relating to granting political asylum to refugees and the controversy about this in the society.

In the fifth interview A.J. said that he was feeling alright and that he was now ready to do a language course. He was disappointed that there was a waiting list. He still had difficulty with the idea that his request for asylum may be turned down. Nonetheless, he thought that he did not need any more psychological help at that moment.

In this case medication served to break a vicious circle of tension and exhaustion. In the case of some clients, relaxing exercises or martial arts can have the same effect.

The advice about his daily activities was meant to provide situations in which he would have positive experiences, thereby using existing skills—social skills in this case—to overcome problems. By contacting the sports club himself the therapist briefly intruded into the domain of social casework.

By talking about the overwhelming attacks of fear which he experienced it became easier for A.J. to understand their origin. He explained his fears as 'going mad', an explanation which is, in the terms of the cognitive approach, internal, global and persistent and thus unalterable. The therapist's questions enabled him to relate his fears to specific occurrences, like waking from a nightmare about his detention, or receiving a letter from his family. Once he saw the relation between his fears and certain specific causes then these fears no longer automatically resulted in a negative self-image. In this connection the therapist told him something about the mental problems of refugees in general. This had a calming and supportive effect, while at the same time inviting him to say more about his traumatic experiences. The discussion about the situation of refugees in general helped A.E. to feel related to those in a similar situation, and to understand his own ambivalent feelings towards the people of the country in which he was in exile.

Discussing overwhelming negative feelings

One of the first and most important things which the therapist can do is to give the refugee a chance to tell his story and express related negative feelings. This does not automatically lead to immediate behavioural changes or insights which will improve the refugee's situation, but its therapeutic value must not be underestimated.

The fact that the therapist listens to the refugee's story and is interested can give him the feeling that his emotions are justified and understandable, and that his actions are not being morally judged.

To put it differently (in Krystal's (1987) terminology): the client's tolerance for his own emotions is increased. As a result, experiencing unpleasant emotions no longer automatically leads to more or new negative emotions such as shame, fear of going mad, or of being seen as putting on airs. Instead the client can reflect on his emotions and start to integrate them.

B.J., a middle-aged Latin American refugee, had an argument with a colleague, who had made racist and discriminatory remarks about him. B.J. was angry and grieved. He remembered all the instances of discrimination which he had experienced during his seven years in exile, and concluded that the people of the country in which he had been given asylum were not to be trusted.

During the next interview B.J. thanked the therapist, a native of that country, for giving him the opportunity to express these feelings. He said that it was only now that he realized that his recurring depressions were related to the condescension with which he was sometimes treated.

However, do not expect an outpouring of emotions whenever you talk to a refugee. Some of them are numb or focused on somatic or other symptoms in an effort to avoid memories of the past (Kinzie & Fleck, 1987).

Concrete assistance

Within the context of supportive psychotherapy it does no harm for the therapist to occasionally give direct assistance, for example by contacting social organizations for the refugee, helping him to write a letter or fill in a form. But in the case of time-consuming problems, or matters which require detailed knowledge of the social system or the methods of social casework then it is advisable to bring in an expert.

C.J., a 24-year-old refugee from the Middle East, had been in exile for two years. Recently his 13-year-old brother had joined him. C.J. had difficulty caring for his brother but did not want to be separated from him. The therapist brought him into contact with an organization which was concerned with caring for young refugees.

Discussing the causes of psychological problems

Some refugees have very clear ideas about the causes of their problems. As was pointed out in chapter 2, the cognitive approach provides a point of departure for offering the refugee more adequate explanations which will make behavioural adjustment possible.

Some of the refugees who request help claim they do not know the cause of their complaints. They are aware that they behave differently or do not function as well as they used to, but are often even unable to say when these changes first started. They obviously have negative feelings about these problems, which are sometimes transformed into a negative self-image and have a patina of helplessness. This becomes apparent from expressions like 'I have become weak' or 'I no longer have the perseverance.' A detailed look at the moment when the first symptoms were manifested can be useful in stimulating the client to think about the genesis of his problems, and this may in itself lead to a reduction in feelings of helplessness and powerlessness. By doing so the therapist implicitly shows that he thinks the problems can be solved and that the client's own intellectual activity can play an important role in this. In this way feelings of helplessness can be relativized.

Explanation and information

Many refugees who ask for assistance are afraid of going mad or already being mad. This fear may be related to the fact that the refugee does not understand his own emotional reactions and personality changes (Eitinger, 1960). The same idea, but then more specifically aimed at the problems of refugees who have been tortured, can be found in the work of Genefke (1984). She claims that refugees' fear, nightmares, insomnia, headaches and concentration problems stem primarily from the fact that they do not understand why they feel and act differently since they were tortured. The changes can be spectacular: people who have always been extrovert become introvert; active, independent individuals become passive and dependent; optimists become pessimists; social altruists become egocentric.

Genefke considers it of vital importance to explain to refugees that torture is aimed at breaking the victim's personality. She points out to her patients that torturers often explicitly threaten their victims, for example by predicting that they will never be able to sleep well or have a normal sex life again. Moreover, she stresses that such personality changes are the reaction of healthy individuals to inhuman experiences. Her explanation is meant to help the refugee to accept that, as a result of torture, his personality has been partially and temporarily damaged and altered, and to use this acceptance as a basis from which to restore his identity.

The same kind of explanation can be given with regard to the refugee's integration in the country of exile. Some of the inexplicable emotions and personality changes or the deterioration of academic achievements which the refugee notices in himself can be explained by the fact that he suddenly finds himself in a very different, sometimes confusing, cultural situation. Here one can also speak of normal reactions to radical changes in an individual's situation. The aim is then to work towards restoring his identity, which has become vulnerable as a result of cultural uprooting.

Explaining the cause of symptoms and placing the client's experiences within a conceptual framework can be seen as a version of the technique which neo-behaviourist psychologists call 'cognitive restructuring'. Psychodynamically oriented therapists could consider it to be a form of supporting of the defence mechanisms against emotional memories: an approach which leads to rationalization and intellectualization. Strengthening defence mechanisms seems to be opposed to the goal of emotional assimilation or the traumatic experiences, but this is sometimes necessary to keep the client's fears down to acceptable levels (Parson, 1984; Kordon & Edelman, 1986). It therefore seems more adequate to speak of strengthening coping mechanisms in this context.

When explaining the causes of symptoms one should always be aware that the client may interpret the explanation wrongly. For example, some may see it as proof that there is no hope of recovery, and point to the fact that some of the victims of the German concentration camps still have serious mental problems after more than 40 years.

If the therapist uses professional jargon, like post-traumatic stress disorder, in his explanations then there is the possibility that some clients will go and look this up in the literature without having the proper knowledge and professional distance to determine whether what they read is applicable to their own case.

Discussing the positive aspects of the refugee's functioning

Discussing the positive aspects of a refugee's functioning is aimed at the re-examination of the refugee's negative views of himself (Boehnlein, 1987) and at increasing his self-esteem. In addition it gives some impression of the adequate coping skills which he already possesses. The therapist can make suggestions about the application of existing coping skills to new areas, thereby increasing the area of behaviour in which the client functions adequately, as well as the number of activities which contribute to his general well-being.

The refugee can make use of this repertoire of activities to structure his daily life, which improves his ability to cope with the problems he is facing.

A discussion of the positive aspects of the refugee's functioning can only develop if he has the impression that the therapist understands how serious his problems are. This means that the therapist must usually first discuss the overwhelming negative feelings with which he has to cope.

Analysing recent experiences

Analysing recent experiences in associating with other people (i.e., discussing what has happened in the last few days) is aimed at improving the refugee's insight into the way in which he functions. It may also serve to help the refugee distinguish beween the past and the present life situation. As a result he may gain insight into how to alter his behaviour in certain situations.

The D.J. family had a lot of problems. The father had somatic complaints as a result of having been tortured by government officials in the dictatorship from which he had been forced to flee. There were conflicts relating to the upbringing of the youngest children. The oldest son made a depressed impression and had difficulty making contacts with peers. In a family interview it appeared that he did associate with his classmates at school but could not hang around with them after school. He had to go straight home because the family, following the tradition of their native country, had their main meal at four. They agreed to alter this routine and have their meal at the time that was considered normal in their country of exile.

Discussion of political and social matters

Refugees generally have the experience that the political situation has a great deal of influence on their lives. They have had to leave their own society and go into exile in a very different society because of political complications. In order to be able to function in a psychologically adequate manner it is necessary to have a realistic picture of everyday reality. This includes the political and social aspects of that reality.

A refugee can achieve a better understanding of everyday reality once he realizes how the reality of life in exile differs from life back home, and how it came about that he had to exchange one everyday reality for another. For example, it is useful for the refugee to realize that he is now part of a society of which he, at least initially, did not want to become part; that this society seems strange and frightening to him; and that some members of that society consider him to be strange, frightening and unwanted. This knowledge makes his own behaviour and that of the indigenous population more understandable.

E.J., a young woman who had been in exile for 12 years, had still not learned to speak the language properly. The topic was broached when she complained of not being able to find a job. When she spoke she often purposely used a number of Spanish terms to show that she was foreign.

In the course of a number of interviews it became clear that she was resisting the necessity to learn the language properly. She experienced this necessity as a direct result of the dictatorship in her native country which had forced her to go into exile, and it was against this that her resistance was aimed.

She then realized that she was still letting the dictatorship dominate her life. The need which she felt to resist impeded her social contacts with people. She began to realize that some people interpreted it as a sign of disrespect that she kept using Spanish terms in spite of the fact that the vernacular equivalents had been explained to her.

Conclusion

The therapeutic methods which have been described in this section have been formulated in commonsense terms and occasionally have been explained in terms of various theoretical approaches. These methods are not only useful for promoting more adequate short-term functioning. They form a set of basic tools that often also have to be used when a therapist is employing therapeutic methods that require more expertise.

Lastly, all these therapeutic techniques can be adjusted to a group setting. Contact with those who have had similar experiences can contribute to more adequate functioning. The group provides emotional support, offers the opportunity of recognizing shared experiences, reduces the feeling of deviance and supports cultural group identity (cf. Barudy, 1981; Bruers, 1985; Santini, 1985b).

Especially effective are groups composed of people with a similar background (e.g. with respect to their age or cultural experience). The same can be said about groups who share the same kinds of problems (e.g. refugees who are waiting for the answer to their request for political asylum, or refugees who are considering returning to their native country after some years of exile) (cf. Santini, 1985a, 1985b).

These groups seem to mitigate the disintegrating effect of a forced separation from family and friends. They provide an environment that makes gradual psychological reorganization possible, through the sharing of common values and beliefs. They provide the opportunity to discuss traumatic events in an atmosphere of mutual understanding. The group process may result in a diminishing of feelings of guilt and helplessness, when these feelings are discussed in relation to the conditions in which they came into existence. The therapist can contribute to the effectiveness of the group by introducing interventions aimed at the reduction of the intensity and frequency of symptoms (cf. Fischman & Ross, 1990), like the ones that will be discussed in the next section.

Psychotherapeutic techniques aimed at such symptoms as nightmares and flashbacks

In this section special attention is devoted to various psychotherapeutic techniques that can be used while discussing nightmares about and intrusive memories (flashbacks) of traumatic experiences. The term nightmare here refers to any terrifying dream which results in the individual wakening with a feeling of horror. A flashback can be defined as an intrusive memory, that results in a re-experience of a traumatic situation of the past, so that the individual for a restricted period (varying from a few seconds to a few hours) partly or totally loses contact with the present reality.

Nightmares and flashbacks can be important symptoms, even when they are not reported by the refugee. This sometimes happens when a refugee is ashamed or afraid of talking about this subject.

A.K. first denied having nightmares, because he sometimes wet his bed when he had one. He also suffered frequently from flashbacks, but at first denied having them because he was afraid that the therapist would consider him to be a lunatic.

It also happens that a refugee is not aware of having a nightmare, because he forgets the content of it almost instantly after waking up. A similar process can be observed with regard to flashbacks.

B.K., had left his country after two years of obligatory military service. During this two years he had many traumatic combat experiences. In the initial interview B.K. had denied having nightmares.

During the second interview he reported that he had felt depressed and agitated since he woke up, but could not remember having a nightmare. Later during the interview, while discussing his physical sensations after waking up, he remembered that he had indeed experienced a nightmare.

C.K. had left his country after escaping from the prison where he had been detained for political reasons. In the initial interview he said that, several times during the last week, he had been sitting in a chair for an hour, with a book in his hands, but not reading one line. He could not remember what had been on his mind during that hour.

When asked how he felt after he came to himself again, he said he felt very anxious and was profusely sweating. The therapist explained to him that he possibly might have been having flashbacks from his experiences during detention.

In the next interview, C.K. reported that he had a similar experience some days after this discussion, but then became aware of having had a flashback.

In some cases, a refugee does not mention flashbacks, because he is more worried about his behavioural reactions to having a flashback.

D.K. had been referred to the therapist because he had outbursts of aggression he could not control. His unpredictable behaviour resulted in problems with the compatriots with whom he shared an apartment. D.K. at first felt that his anger was provoked by his housemates.

After some discussion, it became clear that the aggressive outbursts were reactions to flashbacks of his experiences in prison.

Why discuss nightmares and flashbacks?

The discussion of nightmares and flashbacks is an important means of helping refugees and other victims of violence, for both pragmatic and theoretical reasons.

First, these symptoms bring a lot of suffering. Therefore discussing these symptoms in detail links up with the motives of the refugee to request assistance.

Moreover, relieving these symptoms often results in other improvements. For instance the individual becomes less depressed, can concentrate better on his work, gets more patience and pleasure in the contact with other people and so on.

Discussing the contents of nightmares and flashbacks with a person who is ready to listen and does not become overburdened by the matter, diminishes the loneliness the victim is feeling with regard to his painful experiences. In that sense, it brings comfort. This is why some refugees appreciate it when one listens to their stories, even when it does not result in an immediate relief of symptoms and the therapist himself feels rather powerless about these symptoms.

Talking about nightmares and flashbacks may also help the victim to understand better why he has these symptoms, and to feel less overwhelmed by them. It results often in a diminishing of the victim's fear that he is going mad.

The above reasons are formulated in commonsense terminology. On the basis of the theoretical knowledge presented in part I of this study, the following reasons can be added.

From a psychodynamic point of view, the content of a nightmare (e.g. it is about being tortured) is very important. This content has a personal meaning for the victim (e.g. the torturer was a friend from primary school, which made the torture much more than physical pain). Discussing the personal meaning which the content of the nightmare or flashback has for the individual, includes talking about what the various ingredients of the nightmare and the original trauma to which the nightmare refers, mean for the refugee. The nightmare in some way illustrates how the traumatic experience has influenced the refugee's self-concept, his world view, his attitude towards other people and towards life in general. When these topics are discussed, this contributes, in psychodynamic terms, to emotional assimilation of traumatic experiences. After discussing a nightmare in this way, it usually does not repeat itself on the following nights.

The same things can be said about the discussion of the content of flashbacks. After discussing one flashback in detail, it often becomes easier to control later flashbacks because the emotional upheaval caused by these flashbacks has diminished.

From the theoretical approach of family therapy, it would be interesting to discuss whether family members or close friends are aware of the refugee having flashbacks and/or nightmares and how these symptoms influence the communication in the primary social system of the refugee. This discussion might produce ideas about the ways in which family and friends can support the refugee to bear up against these symptoms.

Discussing the personal meaning of the content of the nightmare or flashback results—in the terminology of the cognitive approach—in cognitive restructuring. That is to say, the victim may start to think differently about important matters, like the cause of the traumatic events, his self-image and world view, and his ideas about voluntary actions that could help him avoid or escape from traumatic events in the future. The information about the experiences that are relived during the nightmare or the flashback, can become processed and integrated in the view the person has of himself and human existence.

From the approach of learning theory, the biophysiological reactions that accompany nightmares and flashbacks can be seen as learnt responses, that have been acquired by conditioning processes. Discussing the way these symptoms came into existence and the way they are interpreted by the refugee, may produce suggestions for more adequate ways of coping with these symptoms.

Sometimes, however, talking about nightmares and flashbacks does not bring much relief. This happens when a refugee has very contradictory feelings about discussing private, emotional matters and soon feels embarrassed. In those cases the refugee is not able to speak his true mind and mentions only a part of what is on his mind during the therapeutic sessions. Afterwards he can be obsessed for hours with memories that came to his mind while he was discussing a nightmare or flashback, but that he did not dare share with the therapist.

Nightmares and flashbacks: how do they come into existence?

In discussing nightmares and flashbacks one can proceed from the assumption that their development is related to five factors, the first three of which have already been mentioned by Blitz & Greenberg (1984) in relation to nightmares.

Nightmares and flashbacks in principle have an adaptive function. From a psychodynamic point of view, it can be supposed that they develop because of the presence of strong defence mechanisms, which may have been necessary for a long time, but now impeded the integration of traumatic experiences. The refugee having a nightmare means that his resistance is decreasing and a process of integration is starting. From a cognitive point of view nightmares and flashbacks can be viewed as a form of information processing during sleep or waking life, through which the individual tries to prepare himself for situations that are just as bad or even worse than the traumatic experiences he has undergone.

A nightmare or flashback may be related to incidental, everyday events or sensations which actualize traumatic experiences. For example: receiving a letter from a family member who stayed behind, reports about the deportation of refugees or the rise of right-wing political parties in Western countries, tidings of war or violence. This phenomenon has also been described by Glover (1988), who observed that Vietnam veterans' nightmares about fighting or fleeing are often related to everyday incidents in which they feel out of their depth and desperate. This phenomenon can, as far as flashbacks are concerned, be explained within a cognitive behavioural framework (see chapter 2). The incidental, everyday events or sensations can then be seen as conditioned stimuli (CSs) that trigger conditioned biophysiological reactions and cognitive representations, including emotions, memories and self-instructions that result in some behavioural response. With regard to nightmares, a psychodynamic explanation can be given: the events that happened during the day triggered anxiety provoking memories that were repressed immediately. During sleep the defences are weaker and the anxiety provoking memories become aware.

Nightmares are partly the result of an absence of interactions which facilitate cognitive and/or emotional assimilation of the traumatic experiences during the day. To put it more concretely: the traumatized person feels that there is no one to whom he can talk about his traumatic experiences. For refugees this impression is often based on an accurate assessment of their social environment, but it can also be an inaccurate one based on communication disturbances within the family which might become a target for therapy.

The occurrence of nightmares and flashbacks may be related to social interactions which impede the process of overcoming traumatic experiences, because they trigger feelings of being overwhelmed and helpless. For example, experiences with ethnocentric prejudice and negative experiences as a result of cultural misunderstandings which are not immediately recognized as such during which the refugee felt overwhelmed and helpless, may trigger nightmares and flashbacks in which the same feelings are experienced. Or, the therapist stimulates the refugee to talk about his traumatic experiences, but is unable to structure the conversation sufficiently or to contain what the refugee is saying.

The result is that the refugee becomes overwhelmed by his emotions and feels helpless and/or misunderstood.

A social position which makes it more difficult to cope with the traumatic experience also contributes to the occurrence of nightmares. For example, the position of those seeking asylum leads to feelings of powerlessness, uncertainty, fear and, in certain respects, restricted freedom. Within a psychodynamic framework, one can say that these feelings are very similar to the emotions that are associated with the traumatic experiences. Therefore it becomes very difficult for the refugee to experience that his traumatic experiences are something from the past. This interferes with the process of emotional assimilation of traumatic experiences, and may obstruct the helping process almost completely. It is the author's experience that feelings of uncertainty, fear and powerlessness related to the request for political asylum, cause specific nightmares, in which the refugee dreams that he has been sent back to his native country and is once again being persecuted.

Giving information

It can be helpful to discuss with the refugee what is a nightmare or a flashback. In the course of various interviews the therapist can ask the opinion of the refugee about this matter. Relating to the opinions of the refugee, the therapist can give explanations with regard to the following points of view:

- That these symptoms are a normal result of abnormal experiences.
- That they are related to other symptoms like concentration problems and forgetfulness.
- That although they are disrupting daily life they have an adaptive function.
- That they mean that the person is trying to overcome his bitter experiences.
- That they are no reason for panic, but have to be observed as quietly as possible, although this sometimes may be very hard for the person concerned.
- That flashbacks are usually triggered by some perception which brings back bad memories, for instance smelling something (like the smell of blood or burning flesh when you are grilling a steak, or the smell of one's own sweat as it was smelled during torture), hearing a noise (like the sound of an alarm signal, the sound of a key in a lock), seeing something (like a uniform, a police car, a movie about war, or the news on television), reading something (like the name of a friend who was executed), having a physical sensation (like when a part of the body which was touched during torture, is touched by another person or becomes sensitive for some other reason), or having a more complex feeling (like having the feeling that one is humiliated, or having the feeling that one has to choose between two unacceptable alternatives).

- That nightmares in a sense are very like flashbacks, in the way that they often are triggered by some perception; either while the person is sleeping (for instance the siren of a passing police car), or during the previous day. For instance, a nightmare can be composed of elements from a movie one has seen on television, and memories of a prison experience. In that case the nightmare can be seen as a kind of delayed flashback.

General discussion about gaining control

To support the motivation of the refugee, the therapist can raise the matter of how therapeutic interviews can contribute to the refugee gaining control over nightmares and flashbacks. The therapist can start by asking the refugee about his expectations and/or doubts regarding this point. Reacting to these thoughts, he can advocate the following opinions:

- That control of the symptoms will come when the person, in one way or another, can face the facts to which the symptoms refer
- That gaining control is a step-by-step process which takes time
- That control can be gained as a result of thorough observation
- That gaining control is a very individual thing, for which the therapist only can offer suggestions for starting to learn by trial and error, and that watertight advice cannot be given,
- That gaining control over physical symptoms by means of exercises often precedes gaining control over disturbing thoughts
- That improvement tends to come in a spasmodic way, something like three steps ahead, one step back, three steps ahead, four steps back, which may seem like no progress at all, but has as a net result the proof that movement is possible, and one step ahead that is permanent.

Discussion about the behavioural reactions to nightmares

The conversation about nightmares may also include the refugee's reactions to his nightmares or flashbacks and the possibilities for behavioural changes.

When E.K. awoke from a nightmare he usually lay in bed for a while, petrified. The first change of behaviour which was discussed was that E.K. would try to move his right little finger and, then bit by bit the rest of his body. At the same time he would start to control his breathing (this part was rehearsed during the interview). After that E.K. would get up as soon as possible, and look out the window to verify that he was not in prison, but in his new home, in the country of exile.

The next step was that E.K. would write down what he had dreamed. He would do this in the easiest way possible: writing it down in his native language, or in English. The writing should be finished within five minutes. If the writing made him anxious,

E.K. should interrupt it by some quiet deep breathing. The therapist gave the advice that he should not read again what he had written before the next interview. Moreover, it was agreed that after writing down the content of the nightmare E.K., would drink a glass of water and, if he felt like it, have a hot shower. The result of these behavioural changes was that E.K. found it much easier to go back to sleep, without the nightmares recurring the same night.

The suggestions for behaviour change are aimed at two targets: breaking an attitude of passive helplessness, and restoring the contact with present reality. Writing down the content of a nightmare can be seen as a form of information processing. It also produces interesting material that can be discussed during therapeutic interviews. It often has a beneficial effect (cf. Delany, 1979). But a few refugees will not be able to stop ruminating their nightmares once they start to write about it. It may be helpful for them to express the feelings that seem to be related to the nightmare, for instance by writing down what is on their mind after waking up from the nightmare or by expressing their feelings in a different creative production, like a drawing.

Discussing the content of nightmares

When discussing a refugee's nightmares the therapist can ask him to describe them in as much detail as possible. After that, he can ask the refugee to describe the feelings and associations which the nightmares evoke as a whole. If he considers it necessary the therapist may ask for the associations evoked by all the details of the nightmares as well. These often relate to memories of traumatic experiences.

F.K. said that she had felt tense from the moment she got up. The therapist asked her whether she had been dreaming. She said she had a nightmare in which she met the man who had maltreated her during her detention. In her nightmare she burned him with a flame-thrower. During the discussion the memory of the moment the man had burned her face with a cigarette lighter surfaced.

Nightmares often also reflect the refugee's present emotional problems or inner conflicts.

G.K., an unmarried refugee, had nightmares in which he was married and his wife betrayed his political activities to the police. He related his dream to a traumatic experience which he had had. He had been arrested at a place only his best friends knew about, and he therefore thought one of his friends had betrayed him. During detention he had been tortured. He did not know which friend had betrayed him, and as a result was very distrustful of other people. There was also a second association. He had received a letter from his father, who was pressuring him to get married. G.K. did not yet feel ready for marriage and did not know what to write back.

It should be noted here that dreams may also reflect the denial of feelings of sadness, particularly those related to bereavement (Van Ree, 1987). Such dreams are, obviously not nightmares.

After H.K. had received a residence permit he dreamt that he was back in his native country. He was visiting a friend who was, in fact, dead. They told each other jokes and H.K. woke up laughing.

Sometimes the content of a nightmare can be interpreted as a metaphor for the refugee's fear of his own aggressive impulses.

After a long series of nightmares that were related to his traumatic experiences in prison, I.K. had two nightmares of a different kind. In the first nightmare, he was robbed of some money by a man much bigger and stronger than himself. In the second nightmare, I.K. dreamt that he had a vase of flowers on his table, which he touched by accident. As a result, the flowers pulverized. This made I.K. very afraid, and he woke up wet from sweat and with his heart beating fiercely.

If the therapist decides to discuss the possible psychodynamic interpretations of a nightmare, he has to be familiar with the specific problems that are connected with the use of techniques of uncovering psychotherapy.

The content of a nightmare sometimes may be considered as a metaphor for the self-image of the refugee.

J.K., a refugee from the Middle East, reported the following nightmare: 'I had a birthmark on my body. It was very big, it extended over most of my body. It was ugly, dark brown, and swollen. It seemed to be filled with pus. It was hurting. I noticed that my left leg was the most painful part. Then I woke up. I was covered with sweat, my heart was beating like a drum. But I did not feel pain in my leg.'
The therapist asked J.K. if he had ever seen something like this birthmark. J.K. answered that it reminded him of the way his foot-soles looked after they had been beaten with an electric cable. While discussing his thoughts about his nightmare, J.K. casually remarked that he was suffering from eczema. Although this problem was under control since he used a special cream, he had the feeling that the eczema made him very unattractive. When the therapist commented that the eczema was hardly visible, J.K. replied that his appearance wasn't attractive anyway.

In order to understand the personal meaning of a nightmare, the therapist must be aware of the fact that a particular attribute may have a symbolic meaning within the cultural background of the refugee.

The therapist asked J.K.: 'What do people in your country say about birthmarks?' J.K. then explained that a birthmark on the head was considered to be a good omen, and a birthmark on the foot-sole a bad omen. 'I dont't believe those things', he added. 'And where is your birthmark located?', the therapist asked. 'On the sole of my left foot', said J.K.

Making up a happy ending to the nightmare

In play therapy with children, progression is sometimes made when the child can think of a more happy ending to a traumatic situation he plays over and over again. A similar approach can be used during the discussion of nightmares (Strunz, 1987) and in at least some cases it results in the disappearance of a recurring nightmare.

K.K., a refugee from the Middle East, suffered a lot of turture during the time he was in custody. He had also survived very traumatic combat experiences. Several times he had had the same nightmare: he was entering the house of a friend, who in reality had been executed in prison before his eyes. In the house there were six other friends, all buddies of K.K. who had in reality been killed during combat. All these friends wore white clothes. K.K. associated these clothes with the shrouds of the dead. He was also wearing white, and therefore concluded that he too was dead. This made him very afraid.

The therapist invited K.K. to express his sadness about the death of his friends, and from that point the conversation turned to the K.K.'s fear of making new friends. 'My friends always die', he said.

Finally, the therapist asked K.K. whether there were other circumstances in which the people in his country usually wore white clothes. K.K. said that these white clothes are often used when one is sitting and having a cup of tea with friends in the evening. After this K.K. could think of a happy ending to his nightmare: he just sat with his friends like in the old days, making jokes and having tea. In different words: the scene he originally had interpreted as a sign of imminent danger, was reinterpreted as a happy memory.

After this discussion the nightmare did not return.

Discussion of the events that trigger flashbacks

When a person knows in which kind of situations he often gets flashbacks, he will become less overwhelmed when he gets into such a situation. He will be better prepared and may not panic. He may also decide to avoid the situations or events in question at moments when he feels vulnerable. Therefore, it is useful to describe the variety of events that can possibly trigger a flashback and ask him to think what might be the triggers in his case.

L.K. had been successfully treated for his flashbacks. But 13 months after the therapy was concluded, the war in the Persian Gulf broke out. L.K. started to have flashbacks again. These were triggered by pictures of combat he saw on television and the accompanying sounds. He told the therapist that he was watching television for hours, also during the night.

While discussing this, he decided to restrict himself to one broadcast of television news each day, at a time when he felt relaxed, and to practise respiration exercises while he was watching. In a second interview, L.K. reported that this way of acting had produced favourable effects, and there was no need for further therapy.

Discussion of the reactions to flashbacks

It is interesting to discuss the physical reactions a refugee experiences while he is having a flashback. Common reactions are sweating, crying, accelerated respiration or hyperventilation, headaches and an increase of tension in various groups of muscles. When the physical reactions are clear, it becomes possible to discuss behaviour (for instance exercise to cut hyperventilation and regain control over respiration; promote respiration by using the diaphragm, relaxation techniques or exercises from the martial arts) that has a relaxing effect or may diminish feelings of helplessness.

M.K., a refugee from the Middle East, was 21 when he requested assistance. At that time he lived in a student home, where he shared the kitchen with fellow students.

M.K.'s most important complaints were difficulty in concentrating on his academic work and intrusive unpleasant memories of the four years he spent in prison, where he had been tortured severely and had witnessed the killing of a friend. These memories caused accelerated heartbeat, sweating, blushing or flushing, a feeling of oppression and hyperventilation. He summarized his complaints with the words fear and panic.

Anxiolytic medication had been prescribed, but had not brought much relief.

The therapist analysed M.K.'s problems on the basis of the cognitive-behavioural approach, and departed from the hypothesis that the accelerated heartbeat and other somatic reactions were conditioned biophysiological reactions. In this case neutral stimuli, that were contingent on the traumatic events and could be considered as CS, were: the smell of blood, the smell of M.K.'s own sweat, the sensation of being humiliated, the sound of an explosion, the sound of a person crying.

M.K.'s cognitive representations of the traumatic events contained memories of the prison environment and what happened during detention, thoughts of being weak and therefore inferior, thoughts of being helpless and on the verge of going mad. These cognitive representations seemed to result in such behaviour as in the following situation: 'The fear came when I smelled the steak my friend was preparing. The smell of burning flesh reminded me of the interrogation session, when they burned by toes with a lighter. I left the kitchen, passed through the lounge—I did not stay there because I did not want the others to see that I was upset, I was ashamed—and went to my room. I closed the curtains and lay down on my bed. I tried not to think and to feel nothing. It often takes more than two hours before I can get up again.'

Therapy started by explaining the principles of conditioning. After this explanation, the therapist suggested that M.K. no longer summarize his problems as fear and panic, but as 'having to learn how to cope with unpleasant physiological reactions'. The therapist also discussed M.K.'s cognitive representations, carefully advocating the opinion that M.K.'s problem could be considered as a normal reaction to very painful experiences and not as a sign of madness or inferiority. He suggested that M.K.'s behaviour when flashbacks occurred was more or less identical to his behaviour during and directly after the original traumatic events. This was confirmed by M.K. The therapist commented that he thought that this behaviour had been most adequate at the time, but that today, under totally different circumstances, another type of reaction could possibly be more adequate. After ample discussion, he instructed M.K. to experiment with the following reaction: 'If something like this happens this week, go to your room, but leave the curtains open. Lie down on your bed, but do a relaxation exercise with the help of the cassette I gave you. Then get up, look out of the window, open the door of your room. If you don't feel too bad, proceed to the lounge to see if there is company. If there is nobody, at least go to the kitchen and make yourself a cup of tea.'

After five weeks, M.K. reported that his flashbacks had become less frequent and that he could usually control them within two or three minutes. His concentration had become much better, which resulted in better achievements at school.

The stimulus that was still giving him considerable trouble was the sound of explosions. When children played with fireworks it took five minutes before he could start to control his breathing. It reminded him of the execution of an intimate friend. The therapist instructed him to say 'I am startled' (in his native language, of course) as soon as possible after the disturbing sound, and then to try to control his breathing. This instruction resulted in a diminishing of his complaints.

Another topic for discussion is the reaction of family members, housemates or other people to the refugee having flashbacks. In relation to this, the therapist can discuss the possibilities for, and the pros and cons of, discussing parts of nightmares, flashbacks and traumatic experiences with one or more of those persons in the direct social environment. Sometimes a family member is aware sooner of the refugee having a flashback than the refugee himself. In that case it can be discussed whether it would be useful if this family member brings the refugee back to reality, and in which way that could be accomplished.

N.K. suffered from flashbacks, which brought about aggressive impulses he could hardly control. His wife could tell from his face when he had a flashback like this.
    After some discussion, he decided to ask his wife to 'wake him up' whenever she thought he had a flashback. He instructed her to call his name in a friendly way, but not to touch him. He felt that any intrusive sound or physical contact at such a moment could trigger an aggressive outburst.

Sometimes it is helpful for a refugee to write down the memories of traumatic experiences that form the content of the flashbacks (cf. Pennebaker & Klihr Beall, 1986), because it brings emotional relief. It can, of course, also be viewed as a form of information processing.

Discussion of the content of flashbacks

Another important topic is the content of flashbacks, and the personal meaning the original traumatic experiences have for the individual. After listening to what the refugee spontaneously relates about this, he can be asked, in one way or the other, what was the worst flashback he had lately, or what was the worst part of the flashback that is being discussed at the moment. A more intrusive question could be phrased as follows:
    'I understand that this is a very bitter memory, it would be bitter for me and for anybody who has human feelings. But maybe there are reasons that this experience has an extra bitter meaning for you as an individual, which I cannot instantly understand. Could you explain to me why this experience was so bitter for you personally?'
    The answer to this kind of question, may help the refugee to discuss the most important thoughts or feelings related to his traumatic experiences, for example a very distressing feeling.

O.K. had been imprisoned for political reasons while he was 16 years old. He had escaped from prison after four years. During his stay in prison he had been severely tortured. When he requested assistance, he was suffering from flashbacks (intrusive memories of traumatic events in the prison) with extreme biophysiological reactions. These flashbacks were accompanied by the feelings of having fallen backwards and hopelessness. Apart from this, O.K. suffered from nightmares, sleeping disturbances, and loss of hair.

After some months, the nightmares and sleeping disturbances had almost disappeared. The loss of hair continued, according to O.K.'s dermatologist as a result of psychological stress. The flashbacks had become less frequent, and the biophysiological reactions had disappeared. But one part of them had remained: occasionally the feelings that formerly were connected with flashbacks came to his mind. O.K. considered his feelings of hopelessness and the feeling of having insurmountable arrears to be realistic.

He mentioned three reasons for this conclusion: he had arrears in paying debts his family incurred to pay a smuggler that had helped him escape from his native country; he was just starting his studies while he sometimes met former classmates, who were already finishing their education; and the hair loss was still going on.

The therapist asked O.K. whether he remembered having felt like this earlier in his life. O.K. answered that it made him think of the hopelessness he had felt when he was in prison and had heard that he was sentenced to a term of imprisonment of 10 years. He also mentioned a childhood experience: O.K. wanted to play soccer with some neighbourhood children, but they did not want him to join because he was not very good at soccer.

In the discussion about thoughts and feelings that in some way are related to the way in which the refugee relives his traumatic experiences, the therapist can move in two directions. First, he can choose to explore the personal meaning of the traumatic experiences in relation to the personal history of the refugee. He can, to give just one randomly chosen example, explore the hypothesis that the refugee is punishing himself by reliving his traumatic memories again and again, or by focusing all the time on the dark sides of his present life. The therapist then is moving to the domain of uncovering psychotherapy aimed at promoting emotional integration and personality change, so he should ask himself if such a move is indicated.

As an alternative, the therapist may use a cognitive behavioural approach. Within this approach, the therapist will first discuss the benefits of the thoughts that are bothering the refugee. Generally this discussion will lead to the conclusion that most of the aforementioned thoughts are useless, and have unpleasant consequences. In that case the therapist can advise the refugee about methods of putting his unwholesome thoughts aside.

The author has favourable experiences with the techniques described by De Silva (1985), who presents a hierarchy of five pieces of advice. Whenever an unwanted, unwholesome cognition occurs, the client first has to try the first piece of advice, if that fails, the second, and so on. The advice can be summarized as follows:

1. Try to think of something that is opposite to or incompatible with the thought in question
2. Think of all the harmful consequences of the thought in question

3. Try some distracting activity
4. Think of what brought the thought to your awareness and try to think of ways of removing the immediate cause of the thought
5. Try forcefully to restrain and dominate your mind, concentrate on the thought in a down to earth, unsentimental way, and then push it from your mind, if necessary, 'with clenched teeth and tongue pressed hard against the palate'.

After some discussion about how the feeling of being backward in comparison to his age-mates was connected with childhood experiences, the aforementioned O.K. was able to acknowledge that the thought, that he had unsurmountable arrears, was not very productive. He realized that this thought would neither pay his debts, nor make him study any quicker, nor make his hair grow more luxuriant. So he agreed to label this thought as an irrelevant, time-consuming one, which he could try to get of his mind. The therapist then gave him some advice about managing his budget, and introduced him to the programme for thought stopping.

In relation to step 1, O.K. said that it might help if he tried to think of what he considered as his achievements: learning to speak the language of the country of exile almost fluently, having overcome most of his post-traumatic symptoms and having a relationship with a girlfriend.

Talking about step 2, he said that it might be useful to think that ruminating unproductive thoughts would interfere with his study. The therapist suggested to him to remember also that the target thought implied that he was humiliating himself, in the same way as his torturers had tried to humiliate him, and that he probably did not really want to continue along that line.

With regard to step 3, O.K. thought that it might help him to do some jogging in a wood near his house.

During the next interview, after two weeks, J.F. told the therapist that he had managed to improve his financial situation a little. He had also been quite successful in getting rid of his pessimistic thoughts. Usually the first two steps of the programme had been sufficient. One time he had to proceed to step 4. At that moment O.K. had realized that his negative thoughts often started when he saw a compatriot he considered to be successful. He then had said to himself that he did not know whether this compatriot was really happy and that he probably would not want to change his own life for that of his compatriot if he knew everything about it.

Evaluation of the results

Discussing the progress which is being made with regard to the treatment of nightmares and flashbacks also has therapeutic value. When a refugee can observe progress, this may diminish feelings of helplessness and hopelessness. And if the progress is not convincing enough for the refugee, observations of progress at least help the therapist to contain the hopeless feelings of the refugee without being overwhelmed and become hopeless himself.

Progress with regard to the therapy of nightmares and flashbacks can be deduced from the frequency, intensity and content of the dreams (Hartmann, 1984). In the case of post-traumatic nightmares one may speak of improvement if:

1. The nightmares have become less frequent: for example, once a month instead of every night.
2. They have become less intense: the refugee still has unpleasant dreams, but they are not as bad as they used to be. He is still afraid when he wakes up, but no longer wet with sweat, and he does not have much difficulty falling asleep again.
3. The content of the dreams gradually changes from a direct representation of the traumatic experiences to a more symbolic representation, to which other dream elements are added. The dreamer feels less helpless, less alone and more active. At the start of treatment the refugee's dreams are often about persecution and imprisonment, and he wakes up at the point when he can no longer escape and will be killed. Later he may dream that he has been able to escape together with others.

P.K. often dreamed that he was being pursued by soldiers and guerrillas and that he was surrounded. Sometimes he was on the edge of a ravine, so that the only escape was to jump. He was alone.

After three weeks, he dreamt that he was together with a friend and they were both being pursued. He escaped while his friend was killed. A few days later he dreamt that he had managed to escape together with others and that he had become their leader.

Q.K. had spent four years in prison after being detained for political reasons. He had escaped when the prison was bombed by the air forces of a neighbouring country.

After twenty sessions of therapy aimed at nightmares and flashbacks, Q.K. reported a dream in which he was back in his native country, arrested and brought to a prison. Until that moment the dream was fearful. But then he realized that the prison was painted in bright colours, and that there were no bars before the windows. So he opened a window, stepped outside and escaped. Then he woke up, feeling rather happy.

With regard to flashbacks, one can speak of progress:

1. When the frequency of the flashbacks, as monitored by the client, has become less
2. When the duration of flashbacks has become shorter, or in other words, the person is quicker to realize he is having one, is quicker to become aware again of the present reality, and more quickly gains control over his behaviour
3. When the flashbacks have become less terrifying or depressing, and get mixed with pleasant memories.

After six sessions of therapy focused on nightmares and flashbacks, R.K. still had intrusive memories of his experiences in prison. However, these only made him tense for one or two minutes. Sometimes the flashback ended in pleasant memories of one of his fellow inmates.

The order of the interventions

In this section several groups of topics for discussion were described that a therapist can have at the back of his mind when he talks with a refugee about nightmares and flashbacks. That does not mean that it is useful to discuss every single one of them with every refugee who is suffering from these symptoms. In bringing them up, the therapist can try to tune in to what the refugee has on his mind. This implies that no advice can be given about the order in which these subjects can be discussed best.

However, in order to give a clearer impression of the therapeutic process in which nightmares and flashbacks are the main focus, a more elaborate case example will be presented. It is about a therapy that quickly brought improvement. The success in this case was probably affected by the following favourable conditions: the patient was feeling secure because he had a residence permit, he was happily married and had just become the father of a son, he had prior experience with therapy which had brought improvement, and the psychotherapeutic process was supported by the prescription of psychotropic medication.

S.K. was a man of 36 years, he was born in the Middle East, and arrived in the country of exile after being in prison for two years. During those years he was severely tortured.

When he met the therapist for the first time, S.K. told him that he suffered from nightmares (he had them almost every night) and compulsive brooding. He did not mention anything that pointed in the direction of flashbacks. At the end of the first interview, the therapist advised S.K. to make notes of his nightmares.

In the following interviews, the therapist asked S.K. to tell about last week's nightmares. After this he asked S.K. if the nightmares were related to something that happened in prison, which was always the case. Actually, the nightmares were almost identical to incidents that happened in prison. In these nightmares S.K. was usually being tortured or at least humiliated.

When S.K. was talking about his nightmares and the related memories, he became very tense and started breathing very quickly moving his shoulders but not using the diaphragm. Having observed this, the therapist taught S.K. some exercises to improve his respiration. In later interviews, the therapist sometimes interrupted the discussion of his nightmares in order to help S.K. to regain control over his respiration.

In the case of S.K., the treatment at first did not bring about much change with regard to the frequency or the content of the nightmares. Nevertheless, S.K. said that the interviews were useful, because this was the first time he could express his experiences without fear of burdening the listener too much.

In the fourth interview S.K. told the therapist that he was feeling worse than ever. At night, when he wanted to go to bed, he was overwhelmed by bad memories that were coming in a random order. He could not sleep more than three hours a night. He continued to have nightmares, but was not able to remember their content. He saw the deterioration in his condition as the result of watching the television news about the revolution in Rumania and the Dutch habit of letting off fireworks during the last days of December.

During this fourth interview the therapist even considered the possibility of changing to a different therapeutic approach: the testimony method. An advantage of this method is that it helps to invoke the bad memories in chronological order, and also facilitates the remembering of happier memories.

But the next week S.K. communicated the first signs of improvement. He had seen nightmares only during two nights. Their content had been slightly different: they were about situations in which S.K. was not the victim, but a bystander. The therapist asked him about the memories that were related to these nightmares, and specifically asked him whether the prisoners found ways to support each other after torture. This reminded him of some positive experiences.

After seven interviews, S.K. did not complain of nightmares any more. But he started to talk about another symptom that was bothering him. It happened about 20 times a day that S.K., unintentionally, suddenly cried out loud. He usually became aware of this by the startled reactions of his environment. It happened at home most of the time, but occasionally also in the library and in the subway.

The therapist gave S.K. the assignment of making notes about time and place of the occurrence of this symptom, and instructed him to reflect on his thoughts just before he caught himself shouting. During the next interview it became clear that the shouting was a reaction to intrusive memories, related to being tortured or watching others being tortured. That is to say, it was the side-effect of having a flashback. The symptom was already becoming less frequent, and occurred only at home.

During three interviews the therapist and G.F. discussed the notes S.K. had made about the flashbacks preceding the involuntary shouting. The therapist invited him to talk in detail about the worst memory that had come to his mind during these flashbacks. He also taught G.F. an exercise from the martial arts, in which he learned to coordinate his body in an aggressive movement, while shouting at the same time.

After 16 interviews, all symptoms had disappeared. Occasionally S.K. still became aware of the impulse to cry out, but he usually was able to control this impulse. From time to time, S.K. had some unpleasant memories of his years in prison, but he was able to cope with these memories. His achievements in his language course had become much better than before, and he looked quieter and happier. He said he did not need more therapy.

During a follow-up interview six months later, S.K. reported that he very seldom had a nightmare or a flashback, but that this did not bring him out of his equilibrium. He said he felt quite happy.

7 Therapeutic techniques aimed at less limited goals

The testimony method

Many of the authors who have written about the use of psychotherapeutic techniques with refugees or other victims of violence see the complaints which they first present to the therapist as stemming from unassimilated traumatic experiences that have interfered with personality development. In their work these authors emphasize the emotional integration of these experiences. They expect the assimilation of traumatic experiences and the insights obtained during the process to result in a reduction of the client's complaints in the long term. As Mollica (1987) has stated with regard to Indochinese refugees in the United States:

> Once the patient is ready to tell the trauma story, the narrative begins to give shape to many new possibilities. The patient's previous interpretation of his story as a hopeless loss of control is diminished. ... The story telling begins to give flexibility to what was rigid and fixed in time. ... The new story that emerges is no longer being a victim of one's own society—it becomes a story about human prejudices and the weaknesses of the so-called human civilizations in which we live. ... Our clinicians attempt to help our patients bridge this gap between the trauma story of helplessness and despair and the new story of survival and recovery.

Discussing traumatic events may be seen as a corrective emotional experience. De Wind (1970) uses this term to point out that it is a dramatic experience for the traumatized individual to realize that the therapist understands his fantasies and fears without rejecting him. Bleich, Garb & Kottler (1986) also speak of a corrective experience. They state that talking about traumatic experiences is so dramatic because it confronts the traumatized individual with frightening emotions. He is afraid of being overwhelmed by these emotions, but during the talk he realizes that he can undergo them and still hold out, and this is a corrective experience. In this connection, talking about traumatic experiences has been compared to the experience of bereavement (Spiegel, 1981), during which previously inaccessible emotions are experienced and expressed. This enables the individual to take leave, as it were, of the traumatic past and this opens the possibility of new experiences: a different, positive self-image, a new intimate relationship, involvement in a new ideology.

There is also a cognitive side to talking about traumatic experiences. For example, Piaget (1973) claims that the therapeutic effects of making memories conscious can be explained by the hypothesis, supported by experimental research, that remembering involves cognitive restructuring. Similar views can be found in Allodi (1982) and Spiegel (1981), who both emphasize that talking about traumatic experiences has a therapeutic effect, because it helps the client to realize what those experiences mean to him.

In the various publications on psychotherapy with refugees or other victims of political violence there are hardly any concrete descriptions of the therapeutic methods used.

The work of Cienfuegos & Monelli (1983) and Lira (1986) forms an exception. Their 'testimony method' was developed as a result of experience with the victims of the military dictatorship in Chile. It is so tied to the Chilean situation that it cannot simply be applied to the problems of refugees in other countries. But the line of thought behind the method is interesting and it will be discussed in detail below. The testimony method is a directive approach, but it can be used within the context of a therapeutic approach that is essentially non-directive, in the sense that the therapist tries to connect with what is bothering the refugee most.

Facts, emotions and their context

The point of departure of this method is to encourage the traumatized person to describe his traumatic experiences in as much detail as possible, as though he was giving evidence as a witness for the prosecution. He is not only encouraged to relate the facts, but also to express the emotions related to his experiences. The context of the traumatic experiences—the life history of the traumatized person and reasons for being politically active—are also discussed. Moreover, his capacities, coping skills and the way in which he copes with difficult situations become a topic of conversation.

The declaration is tape recorded and transcribed by the therapist, who then discusses the transcript fully with the client.

According to Cienfuegos & Monelli, the effect of this approach stems from the possibility of constructively channelling aggression in the form of a charge or indictment. In addition, the client gets a better idea of what has happened to him: fragmentary experiences become integrated in a life history. Because the experience of suffering has been symbolized in a different form (as a written statement) and its importance recognized by the therapist, the need to express it through somatization also disappears.

The effectiveness of the testimony method can be seen as the result of two forms of reconstruction. There is a cognitive reconstruction of the traumatic experiences in which things are ordered and the individual starts to understand his own strong and weak points. There is also an affective reconstruction of the traumatic experiences in which frightening, and therefore repressed, feelings are re-experienced and assimilated in an atmosphere of mutual understanding and emotional support. According to Agger & Jensen (1990), the result is that 'private pain is transformed in political dignity, (...) shame and guilt connected with the trauma can be confessed by the victim and reframed'. These authors see the testimony also as a cathartic, healing ritual.

Testimony as a therapeutic technique for refugees

The success of this method depends on the client's motivation. It is most successful in the case of those who know exactly what they want to talk about and who realize that it is important to talk about it. Success also depends on the coping skills the client has at his disposal. The testimony method is not applicable to all victims of organized violence. It is most successful when used for the victims of torture. The results are inadequate in the case of the relatives of missing persons: here special attention must be given to the process of bereavement (Cienfuegos & Monelli, 1983).

In Chile the method worked well in the case of peasants and miners; in other words, in the case of those who had little formal education and who were not used to talking about themselves or their emotions. The method is thought to be less successful with the well educated, who can write down their own story (Lira, 1986).

Although the testimony method was developed for people with modest verbal abilities, it can also be used with those who are used to talking about themselves and their emotions, but who have been in a situation in which they could not confide in anyone for a long time. The method seems to be particularly effective in the case of refugees who still experience repression as a reality in their everyday lives: for example, those who are still awaiting the outcome of a request for political asylum and have to live with the fear of being deported.

Moreover, having a written statement about their traumatic experiences, may be helpful in several ways. For instance, it can help the refugee to give information about his traumatic past in cases where this is necessary, without having to re-experience them again if he does not want to. For some refugees, after some time the written statement comes to function as a proof that they have not just had an unbelievable nightmare, but that their experience was true, because it is detailed and well documented.

The method also helps to make traumatic experiences which were severe, though not sensational or spectacular and therefore more difficult to describe, discussable. Finally, the method contributes to making accessible memories of pleasant moments experienced in the same period as traumatization.

During the first two interviews following the testimony method A.L., a young African, talked about his life in the period before he became politically involved. In the third, fourth and fifth interviews he talked about various experiences with violence and death, but also about the vegetation in his native country, and his interest in poetry.

The sixth interview formed a climax, and he told of the experience he found most terrible: he had not been able to associate with peers for two years.

With refugees, the testimony method can be applied in two different ways. First, the method can be used with refugees who are motivated to give evidence about the political repression and the violation of human rights in their country, either because they want to accuse the responsible authorities, or because they want to defend their request for political asylum. This way of applying the testimony method is characterized as a brief psychotherapy, with a duration of 12 to 20 sessions; although a case with a duration of 35 sessions has also been described (cf. Agger & Jensen, 1990).

Sometimes the therapeutic techniques of the testimony method cannot be applied exactly according to the aforementioned procedure. This happens, for instance, when a refugee does not only have to cope with traumatic experiences from the past, but is also facing problems in the present and/or has to cope with normal developmental tasks. The result is that the refugee will not be motivated all the time to give evidence about his traumatic experiences. In those cases the testimony method still can give a useful contribution to the psychotherapeutic process, but it has to be used in a different way: more flexible and supplemented with other approaches.

In the case of A.L. the interviews which followed the testimony method were interrupted by, and alternated with, talks about various topics. These were apparently introduced by A.L. because he was troubled or excited by them: political developments in his native country, news of friends and relatives, bad experiences with immigration officials, incidents which seemed to stem from misunderstanding of Western customs, somatic complaints and falling in love. In the therapeutic conversations about these topics, the therapist used supportive, symptom-orientated and occasionally uncovering psychotherapeutic techniques.

The testimony method seems less effective in the case of refugees who have had many traumatic experiences spread over an extended period of time (a number of years), and/or suffer from very incapacitating symptoms, and/or are convinced that they had psychological problems long before they were traumatized by organized violence.

Making traumatic experiences discussable

The main technical problem in applying the testimony method with refugees who don't have a very solid motivation to give evidence, is making traumatic experiences discussable. When a refugee shows signs—however ambivalent —that he wants to talk about his traumatic experiences then the therapist is confronted with the task of helping him. He can, of course, stimulate those who do not find it easy to talk about what is troubling them, by starting with one of the complaints for which the refugee requested help in the first place. For example, by asking about nightmares and discussing the thoughts, emotions and feelings which these evoke.

It is also possible to talk to the refugee about his normal everyday life and discuss events which have touched him emotionally: the emotional agitation caused by a current event may point to unassimilated emotional experiences from the past. In this connection it is useful for the therapist to be abreast of recent developments in the refugee's native country, and to be aware of other incidents which could stimulate the re-experiencing of traumatic experiences, such as the showing of films about the refugee's native country (cf. Genefke, 1984).

The therapist was trying to support B.L. in extending his social contacts and asked him how he had been getting on. B.L. replied that he had not done anything the last few days, just slept. The therapist knew that there had recently been a number of documentaries on television about the situation in B.L.'s native country, from which he had been forced to flee five years earlier. The therapist asked him if he had watched television during the last few days. This provoked a discussion of the many and complex emotions which the films had evoked in B.L. In that way, B.L. started to describe his traumatic experiences.

It sometimes happens that refugees who are known to have had very traumatic experiences would like to talk about them but that the conversation always breaks down. This is definitely not resistance to the therapeutic process, but the inability to express certain experiences. Explaining that some experiences are so terrible that words cannot describe them, and that the related feelings are inexpressible may have a supportive effect (cf. Puget, 1986).

The techniques of uncovering psychotherapy

Most writers on psychotherapy with refugees seem to proceed from the assumption that the most important thing is listening to what the refugee has to say, and relating this with what appears to be on his mind, but of which he is not completely aware. Some of them hesitate when it comes to asking intrusive questions, as happens in the testimony method or the methods described in the previous section. Like those who advocate the testimony method or symptom-orientated methods they stress the opinion that re-living traumatic experiences is painful and that it is only useful in the context of a relationship of mutual trust. However, they expect mutual trust to develop the quickest when the therapist assumes a non-directive attitude and tries to explore the feelings of the refugee, including the feelings he may foster regarding the therapist.

These therapists often use a psychodynamic framework. In their publications they are usually not very detailed in explaining their techniques, but in order to describe their work, they distinguish between different phases in the therapeutic process (see for example the case studies in Arcos & Araya, 1982; Cienfuegos, 1982; Monelli, 1982; Santini, 1986b; and the more general considerations by Groenenberg, 1984; Somnier & Genefke, 1986). Santini's division is the most elaborate. She distinguishes five phases:

Phase 1: distrust of the therapist Many refugees have had experiences that made them lose some of their confidence in other human beings. In some ways they tend to mistrust everybody, including the therapist. They test the therapists's reactions to find out whether he is really interested in their story, and whether he will patronize them. This means that their distrust leads them to hold back or to only talk at a superficial level about their traumatic experiences.

Phase 2: catharsis and reduction of symptoms In this phase the refugee talks about the terrible things he has experienced, expressing some of his emotions. This often brings some relief: the refugee becomes a bit less tense and his most disturbing symptoms (like headaches, nightmares and flashbacks) become less incapacitating.

Phase 3: working through In this phase the psychological meaning of the various traumatic experiences for the individual are analysed. To that end, the traumatic experiences are discussed in relation to one another, and against the background of his total life history and the attitude to life the refugee has developed throughout the years. Also the consequences of the traumatic experiences as reflected through present attitudes and behaviour (including attitudes and behaviour that are manifested within the relation to the therapist) are considered.

The techniques the therapist uses in this phase of uncovering psychotherapy, are described by such authors as Malan (1979) and Greenson (1967). To give a very brief summary: the interventions are directed at bringing to the surface feelings (often impulses) of which the refugee is not aware. These impulses are warded from awareness by feelings of anxiety and by defences. Generally speaking, the therapist tries to recognize the defence, the anxiety and the hidden impulse in that order.

The aforementioned impulses, anxiety and defences, can be recognized in relation to three categories: the parents, usually as they were experienced in the past; others, usually as they are currently experienced or as they were experienced in the recent past; and the therapist and/or the institution in which the therapist is working, as it is experienced here and now. The experience with traumatized refugees suggests that it can be useful to distinguish a fourth category: the people that were responsible for recent traumatic events (perpetrators and hangers-on).

According to Malan, the category in which the work of uncovering is done first, depends on what the client has on his mind. Once the hidden impulse has been interpreted with regard to one category, the therapist can try to switch to a different category in order to uncover the defence, anxiety and at last the hidden impulse. Until now it is the author's experience that talking about the refugee's feelings about early childhood experiences and about his parents is a more adequate start than talking about his recent traumatic experiences (cf. Santini, 1989).

Phase 4: behavioural changes   In this phase important topics of conversation are the social relationships of the refugee, for instance with his family, partner, friends (including political friends) from his native country and country of exile. His attitude and behaviour with regard to these persons are discussed, possibilities for behavioural change are considered, and eventually carried out step by step.

Phase 5: restoration   In this phase the refugee again looks back at his past. Here his feelings of guilt and bereavement are the main topic of conversation. They become assimilated and restoration can then occur: i.e. the individual gives up behaviour that was related to feelings of guilt and bereavement, which inhibited his welfare and adopts new behaviour which enhances his welfare. The latter may include behaviour which is rooted in the assimilated traumatic experiences, such as helping companions who are in a similar situation.

This division into five phases is useful because it provides a description of the many matters which are raised during the therapeutic process. The order of the phases is, however, not fixed: the first phase, that of distrust, may re-occur later in therapy, though in a different form, after there has been some catharsis and emotional assimilation.

While using psychotherapeutic techniques aimed at the emotional assimilation of traumatic experiences and personality change the therapist will be confronted by the following technical problems:

1. Recognizing and managing reluctance to discuss certain topics
2. Adjusting the extent of re-experiencing.
3. Understanding inner conflicts and defence mechanisms which are not generally known.

Recognizing and managing resistance

Resistance refers to the phenomenon that a refugee refuses to talk about certain events or aspects of events, which are relevant to the therapeutic process, even though he does remember them.

A.M. said that he saw mental images which reminded him of his experiences with the military regime in his native country. When the therapist asked him about them he changed the subject.

The Chilean psychologist Lira (1986) gives the following examples of resistance by torture victims. Some refugees minimize what they have undergone. They say that they were threatened and beaten but that 'nothing else' happened to them, and that others have had much worse experiences. Others can give detailed descriptions of the terrible things that have happened to them, but are unable to express the emotions which these experiences evoked.

The therapist can deal with resistance in various ways, depending on the capacities of the refugee. He can try to make him aware of the phenomenon and name it. He can explain that he understands and respects it but hopes that the refugee will be able to overcome it in the future.

When the refugee is motivated to overcome resistance the therapist can help him by getting him to narrate his experiences chronologically and in detail.

Adjusting the extent of re-experiencing

The re-experiencing of traumatic events during therapy can only have a liberating effect if it is adjusted so that the emotions which are evoked are not too strong for the client to cope with. It is impossibe to estimate beforehand the intensity of the emotions which discussion of a certain topic will evoke.

B.M. wanted to talk about her experiences before she was forced to go into exile. She brought along photos of friends and relatives. During the therapy session she spoke in an orderly but emotional manner about her memories. She seemed quite capable of distinguishing her past experiences and the emotions which these evoked in her from the reality of her present situation. At the end of the session she seemed calm and relieved.

But that evening, partly as a result of a news report from her native country, she had attacks of acute terror. It had apparently all been too much for her.

In this connection one must also be aware that when traumatic experiences are discussed it is not only familiar emotions which emerge but also various new emotions which the refugee did not register during his traumatic experiences (Galli, 1984).

Understanding inner conflicts and defence mechanisms which are not generally known

In psychotherapeutic contacts with refugees one may also encounter inner conflicts the content of which is less familiar to the average psychotherapist, as for example, in the following case.

C.M. said that she kept trying not to think about prison. But, she admitted somewhat embarrassed, she sometimes longed to be back in prison, though she did not know the reason why. That became clear later in the interview. She explained that she had been seriously maltreated a number of times during interrogation. Afterwards some of the other prisoners had taken care of her: they washed her, dressed her wounds, massaged her and comforted her.

In some cases, the inner conflicts of the refugee may be centred around feelings of guilt. As Kordon et al. (1986), pointed out, those who are tortured compare their reactions during torture to their ego-ideal and as a result may retain feelings of guilt or shame.

During his detention D.M. had been raped by three prison guards. During the rape he had an erection and because of that he felt very disgusted with himself.

A relatively well-known phenomenon is the inner conflict victims of organized violence may have about being alive. Having survived, while others died, may provoke thoughts as: 'Thank god it did not happen to me, but to my buddy.' Thoughts of this kind cause feelings of guilt and suicide ideation, and will be repressed from awareness (cf. Brainin, Ligeti & Teicher, 1990).

The inner conflicts of victims of organized violence about aggression may be very complicated, and what has been written about it may seem a bit confusing. For instance, Schwartz (1984b) claims that aggressive feelings in traumatized patients are sometimes a transformation of guilt feelings, which he describes—in psychodynamic terms—as aggression of the superego against the ego.

Somnier & Genefke (1986) give the example of a man who experienced as frightening the fact that he had not felt any aggression towards his torturers while he was being tortured.

Brainin, Ligeti & Teicher (1990) suggest that some victims of organized violence may repress any aggressive impulse, because they experience these impulses as a deformation, brought about by the perpetrators. For the author of this study, the last mentioned hypotheses is more recognizable than the other two, be it in a slightly different form.

E.M. had, during detention, been raped by a policeman. When he became aware of having sexual-aggressive fantasies, he was very disgusted with himself. He saw his fantasies as in inborn deformation, which made him as bad and disgusting as the policeman that raped him.

Because the therapist will, during interviews about traumatic experiences, be confronted with inner conflicts and defence mechanisms with which he is less familiar, he may also notice unusual reactions in himself (Krystal, 1984). These unusual reactions will be discussed in part III of this study.

The therapeutic relationship as an instrument

The relationship between therapist and refugee can function as an important therapeutic instrument for recognizing inner conflicts of the refugee. Once contact has been established the therapist can attempt to determine what kind of feelings the refugee has toward him. The answer to this can contribute to an understanding of the refugee's problems. Sometimes the nature of these feelings is very clear.

F.M., a 25-year-old ex-guerrilla was referred by his doctor because of depressions and insomnia. During the first interviews he evoked in the psychologist the association with a small boy who had fallen and grazed his knee. Moreover, he did not initiate conversation and only gave short answers to questions. He kept looking sadly at the ground.

The psychologist had the impression that F.M. initially distrusted him, to the extent that he was afraid of receiving humiliating responses if he spoke too frankly about his depressive feelings and their background.

The client usually has observable feelings towards the therapist from the first moment. Because he hardly knows the therapist these feelings are usually based more on a basic attitude or emotional barrier than on real experiences in his encounters with the therapist. Within the psychodynamic approach, the expression of a basic attitude during the therapeutic process is called transference. Feelings which are expressed as transference in the relationship with the therapist provide important information about the emotional aspects of the refugee's problems.

These emotional aspects may also become manifest in another way during the therapeutic interviews: in the feelings which the client evokes in the therapist. These feelings are partly determined by the way in which the client behaves: it could be said—in Runia's (1986) terms—that the feelings which the client evokes in the therapist cause emotional resonances which in turn partially influence the content of the latter's therapeutic reactions.

These reactions on the part of the therapist, based on emotional resonance, can become manifest in three forms (Abend, 1986):

1.   In the form of reactions for which the client unconsciously longs: sympathy, erotic attraction, condescension
2.   The client's behaviour toward the therapist may resemble the way in which people whom the client considers important behave toward him, so that the therapist then feels what the client has felt for years
3.   Empathy: 'normal' emotional reactions, given the refugee's descriptions of his experiences.

Moreover, the therapist's reactions are also partly conditioned by his own emotional needs or inner conflicts. His emotional reactions, whether or not they are expressed in behaviour or attitudes, are referred to as counter-transference. By reflecting on these reactions the therapist may gain a better understanding of the refugee.

The fact that F.M. reminded the therapist of a small boy who has fallen down, and the resulting inclination to take him on his knee and comfort him, says something about the therapist's own inner life. The therapist apparently found it pleasant to adopt a protective father or mother role. This is an inclination which he must keep under control in his contact with the client.

This association also says something about the non-verbal signals which the client transmits: looking sadly at the ground evoked, in this situation, the impression that he needed warmth, emotional support and reassurance that, in spite of the pain of the moment, everything would be alright.

Some refugees do not show any emotion, either in discussion with the therapist or in their behaviour. Their behaviour is correct and friendly and nothing else. But they do evoke feelings in the therapist (which he may experience during or after the encounter) and an analysis of these feelings (i.e. of the counter-transference) may give some insight into the refugee's own, initially hidden feelings.

G.M. was a friendly young man of 24, who had a rather vague problem, which he described as follows: 'I'm not enthusiastic about anything.' It appeared that long before he had been tortured, he had very traumatic experiences in the relationship with his father. In his contact with the therapist he was cooperative in the sense that he thought about the questions and gave thorough and balanced answers: in other words he did his best. His tone was serious, flat and slightly sad. During the first three sessions he did not laugh once.

The therapist had the uneasy feeling that he had to do something quickly, otherwise G.M. might sever contact and commit suicide. This led him to suspect that G.M. felt the need for someone who could give him advice and encourage him. To the therapist he seemed to be saying: Look, I'm doing my best, don't disappoint me, give me proof that you have something to offer that will give meaning to my life.

Transference and counter-transference in relation to refugees

As there is not much literature on transference and counter-transference in relation to refugees, the content of this section is also based on the literature on other victims of political traumatization: victims of the Second World War.

De Wind (1969; 1970) gives a number of examples of the intense transference of negative feelings, in which the client sees the therapist as the person who used violence against him. Refugees also sometimes transfer these negative feelings to the therapist: they may come to see the therapist who stimulates them to talk about their traumatic experiences as one of those who actually caused those experiences.

H.M. said that he wanted to talk about his experiences in prison, but had trouble in doing this. There were two reasons: the memories were painful and he did not expect the therapist to believe him. The latter reason led to a resentful attitude toward the therapist. This attitude could be interpreted as transference once the therapist found out that when H.M. was being questioned in connection with his request for political asylum the government official who interviewed him did not believe his story, and that his lawyer did not take what he said about his experiences seriously either.

Counter-transference phenomena in relation to war victims have been described by Danieli (1980). She describes feelings of guilt (I'm causing the client pain by reminding him of the past), repugnance (what other horrible things will I hear?), shame (how can people do things like that?) and shows how, in work with war victims, the therapist may come to feel superior or inferior in relation to the client.

In therapy with refugees similar forms of counter-transference may occur. In this context, powerlessness is not an uncommon emotion. Powerlessness can in turn cause antipathy toward the client (Lavelle, 1987; Truong, 1987).

I.M. described some of the details of the torture which he had undergone during his detention in a Latin American country. It was a horrible story, but the most frightening aspect was the way in which he tried to suppress his emotions. The therapist was unable to make I.M.'s fear of being overwhelmed by his own emotions discussable at that moment. His own feelings took him by surprise, particularly the feeling that he had nothing to offer in the face of so much suffering, that he had not experienced anything himself and therefore had no right to speak about such matters, and there was a feeling of aggression against the refugee who had put him into this uneasy situation.

Refugees who ask assistance while their request for political asylum is still pending, and whose problems are being aggravated by the uncertainty about their future and the fear of being sent back to their native country, often feel very powerless. During the registration interview, this feeling of powerlessness can be transferred to the helping professional, who may wrongly, and without making further inquiries, conclude that he cannot help the refugee at all or only by prescribing psychotropic medication.

Another form of counter-transference comes into existence when the therapist himself has been traumatized and experiences some similarity between his own experiences and those of the refugee. He may overrate these similarities and overlook essential differences. And even when he sees the factual similarities in experiences in their proper perspective, he may wrongly assume that the emotional meaning of these experiences for the refugee are more or less identical to his own emotional reactions. A related phenomenon can be described as follows: the therapist has strong emotional reactions to what the refugee tells him about his traumatic experiences, but he is not able to cope with these emotions and to contain them. He then transforms them to fantasies about the emotional reactions of the refugee, and uses them as interpretations during the therapeutic interview (cf. Bustos, 1990a).

The above example illustrates how counter-transference can impede the therapeutic process. Tiedemann (1987) describes how he attempted to avoid this in therapy with war victims by constantly reflecting on his own feelings. He kept asking himself whether he felt affection for the client and whether he felt at ease in his presence. If that is not the case then the therapeutic process is threatened; and Tiedemann suggests that this be discussed with the client.

Tiedemann uses the expression 'to feel affection' and 'to feel at ease'. Other therapists will become alert if they get the impression that they may not laugh, or that they are being hurried, or are becoming bored. Each therapist learns from experience which signals are important for him.

But in spite of this it is not always possible to prevent counter-transference from impeding the therapeutic process. By analysing his experiences with the assistance of experienced colleagues the therapist will be in a better position to realize what his own feelings are and to keep them under control. He will then be able to direct his attention back to his client's feelings and help him to express and assimilate them.

Crisis intervention

At the beginning, or in the course of the treatment of traumatized refugees, the therapist sometimes has to deal with an emergency situation in which the refugee is in a condition of psychological crisis. A psychological crisis is usually described as a condition of confusion, in which a person has to cope with very strong and uncontrollable emotions (cf. Butcher et al. 1988). It is the result of a problem situation which, if attempts to solve the problem fail, may result in extensive personality disorganization or emotional breakdown (Caplan, 1964).

Refugees are human beings, that can get into a condition of crises like any other human being, for the same variety of reasons and with the same variety of symptoms. In this section only those aspects of crisis intervention that are specific for the work with traumatized refugees will be discussed.

A traumatized refugee sometimes seeks the help of a mental health professional only because he is in a condition of psychological crisis. This may happen when the refugee has had severe mental problems for some time, but was reluctant to seek professional help.

In other cases, refugees enter a condition of psychological crisis because they have a problem that after some time, despite the efforts of the professional, does not become any lighter.

In both cases, the refugee usually suffers from severe post-traumatic symptoms like nightmares, flashbacks, sleep disturbances and concentration problems, as well as symptoms like delusions and loss of control over aggressive and self-destructive impulses. A crisis usually means a heightened risk of violent, suicidal or bizarre behaviour.

A therapist who works with traumatized refugees and looks for support in the professional literature, will find little. One can find the assertion that the concept of crisis is helpful in the treatment of refugees (Williams & Westermeyer, 1986), or the suggestion that crisis intervention services should be readily available to refugees in camps and during resettlement (Williams, 1987a). However, with the exception of a very short article on crisis intervention with Cambodian refugees (Bromley, 1987), studies on the techniques of crisis intervention with traumatized refugees are not available. This section will therefore principally be based on the author's own clinical experience.

A.N. was 30 years old, when he sought treatment because he was very nervous, had severe concentration problems, and was unable to sleep. He told the psychotherapist that he was haunted by intrusive memories, related to several periods of political detention during which he was sexually abused. He also complained of nightmares with a content related to the aforementioned memories. A.G. was a refugee from a Latin American country. His request for political asylum had been denied, and for two years he had been waiting for his case to be considered by a higher authority. A.N. was very worried about this.

A.N. obviously needed and liked to talk. The therapist devoted the first three interviews to listening to his complaints and the associations he spontaneously expressed in relation to his nightmares; simply in order to support his motivation for treatment while at the same time gathering some diagnostic information. The therapist also taught him a few exercises for quiet respiration and relaxation, which at least during the interviews had a positive effect. Moreover, he called in a psychiatrist who prescribed Temazepam in order to counter the insomnia.

After the third interview, a friend of A.N. was denied the status of refugee and expelled from the country. Three days later A.N. arrived for the fourth interview an hour early. He did not want to sit down in the waiting room, because he wanted to be ready to run in case the police came to kick him out of the country. He told the therapist that he had not been sleeping for three days and nights. Then he started to talk about the news he said he had heard the day before: that the country of exile was in armed conflict with his native country, which would be a reason for him to be sent back to his native country at once. It was, however, possible to convince him of the fact that there was no war going on, and that it was very unlikely for the police to grab a refugee from the waiting room. After—at least for that moment—contact with the reality had been restored, the therapist consulted a psychiatrist.

The psychiatrist on duty was wearing big leather boots that day. So A.N. stood up when he came in, hid behind his therapist and asked him if the psychiatrist wasn't a policeman. This fear being removed by some quiet talk, the psychiatrist prescribed anti-psychotic medication, which quickly had the desired effect. The therapist also informed the Ministry of Justice about the condition of A.N., which resulted in him receiving a residence permit. After this a therapy aimed at promoting emotional integration of traumatic experience was started.

Three components of the problem

The problem that causes the crises often has three components. The *first* component has to do with the past: the refugee has not been able to come to grips with some traumatic event or a lasting traumatic ordeal, or at least not completely. In this context one should think of physical and psychological torture, being subjected to political violence, combat experience, traumatic separation of family and friends and so on.

The *second* component belongs to present-day reality: the refugee is faced with some factual problem which blocks his plans for the future, or evokes a feeling of impotence. In this context I refer to occurrences like the confrontation with television news about war and political unrest, a racist incident in a public transport vehicle, seeing a film with a violent content, problems in finding a job or adequate housing, and incidents related to the request for political asylum.

The *third* component is what may develop from the interaction of the above components. Actual events may trigger unpleasant memories of a traumatic event, in a degree that the refugee is not able to handle.

B.N., a refugee from a Latin American country, had been trying to get a residence permit for three years. The uncertainty made him feel very helpless. This feeling became intolerable, so it seemed, because it triggered memories of the feeling of extreme helplessness he had felt when he was forced to see how his sister was raped by a policeman.

When a therapist is confronted with a refugee in a condition of crisis, his interventions may go in three different directions. The therapist may address himself to

- The individual refugee
- The social environment of the refugee, for example, his family, partner or close friends
- Institutions that have the authority to take decisions that may contribute to solving the practical problems of the refugee

Interventions aimed at the individual refugee

The first therapeutic reaction to a refugee in a crisis situation is to offer him the opportunity to tell him what is on his mind. The therapist starts with listening. While listening, he may sometimes observe (or suspect, if the refugee phones while being in a condition of crisis) that the refugee is walking around agitatedly. So he will advise the refugee to sit down. The therapist may also observe that the refugee is hyperventilating. In that case he may try to draw the attention of the refugee to this fact, explain to him what is happening, and convince him to join in an exercise that promotes adequate respiration (this can also be accomplished by phone).

While giving the refugee much opportunity to express himself spontaneously, the therapist can ask questions in order to identify the direct precipitator of the crisis (e.g. the refugee drank too much alcohol, received mail from his family, felt offended by the immigration police; cf. Butcher et al., 1988). In the meantime the therapist can observe the psychological state of the refugee and assess whether there are signs or symptoms that may indicate that the refugee is psychotic. These observations help him to decide whether it is necessary to consider admission of the refugee to a psychiatric hospital or the prescription of psychotropic medication.

After some listening, the therapist will try to make more active interventions. He will ask some questions, in order to get an orderly view of what is bothering the refugee. Doing this, the refugee may also succeed in looking at his problems from a certain distance. In combination with this, the therapist is sometimes able to provide factual information relevant to what the refugee perceives to be his problem, and to correct misunderstandings. If necessary, he can give explanations about post-traumatic symptoms.

After the problems have been clarified and brought back to realistic proportions, the refugee often can see some new perspective. That is the moment the therapist will try to mobilize the adaptive coping skills of the refugee in relation to his present-day problems. If necessary, he can give specific advice about coping with post-traumatic symptoms. He will also try to set realistic limits to self-destructive behaviour. At the end of a successful first interview in a crisis situation, the therapist has the feeling that he has a deeper rapport with the refugee than when the conversation started.

In later interviews, the therapist may opt for various interventions, depending upon the indications he perceives pro or con various types of psychotherapeutic techniques at the moment the interview takes place. For example, in the framework of a psychodynamic therapy aimed at promoting emotional integration of traumatic experience, he may try to clarify what transference processes were going on when the refugee entered a condition of crisis. Or he may, departing from a cognitive behavioural approach, focus on interventions aimed at the relief of incapacitating symptoms, like nightmares and intrusive memories.

Interventions aimed at the social environment

Sometimes a refugee in a condition of crisis is accompanied by a member of his family, a friend or a partner. In that case listening to them may serve to provide additional information. This information may include observations of possible stereotyped ways in which the concerned persons are relating to the refugee and, therefore, unknowingly, are contributing to the condition of crisis.

Interviews with persons that play an important role in the daily life of the refugee also present the opportunity to enlist their aid and cooperation in helping the refugee to cope with his problems. This may be accomplished by explaining to them the condition of the refugee and the therapeutic approach.

For instance, the therapist can discuss in which way the refugee's wife may help her husband to interrupt his brooding, or how she cautiously may assist him to return to the reality of the present when the refugee is caught in a flashback

When relational problems are contributing to the crisis, the therapist will have to resort to interventions derived from the various schools of family therapy.

Interventions aimed at institutions

Refugees often have to live in uncertainty about their future for a considerable time. As long as they do not have a secure legal status in the country of exile, they have justifiable reasons for fearing mandatory repatriation. This fear can frequently be seen as an important cause of the refugee entering into a condition of crisis. That means the therapist can decide to contact the authorities responsible for the continuation of this fear.

C.N., a refugee from an Asian country, was 19 when he was arrested for distributing pamphlets of an, at that time, legal opposition party. In prison he was severely tortured. During torture he was beaten unconscious several times. Eventually, he escaped from prison, went into hiding for some years, and at last fled to the Netherlands. There he requested political asylum.

His request was denied, but the government refrained from mandatory repatriation while his request was filed to be judged by a higher authority. C.N. asked for help because he was suffering from nightmares, insomnia, concentration problems, obsessive brooding, and because he sometimes lost control over his aggressive impulses. He had never had any of these complaints before he was imprisoned and tortured.

The therapist concluded that C.N. was suffering from a post-traumatic stress disorder, possibly in combination with some brain damage. In order to prevent a crisis, C.N.'s therapist contacted the Ministry of Justice and explained to the authorities concerned about C.N.'s condition, both in writing and by telephone.

Eight weeks later the therapist had still not received any answer from the Ministry, so he phoned the proper authority to remind him of the case. This person advised him to contact the head of the Medical Inspection of the Ministry. When the therapist got him on the phone, he was told that the Medical Inspection had decided against granting C.N. a residence permit. The Medical Inspection had the suspicion that C.N. was malingering, because his family doctor was not aware of him having mental problems. However, C.N.'s family doctor had referred C.N. to the therapist. There clearly was some misunderstanding. It turned out that C.N. had changed to a different family doctor two years before, and that the Ministry had contacted the previous doctor.

After 11 weeks, the Ministry informed the therapist that C.N. would be given a residence permit. However, this residence permit was restricted, meaning that it was given to make psychiatric treatment possible, and that C.N.'s psychological condition would be evaluated by the Medical Inspection of the Ministry after nine months.

When the therapist conveyed this news to C.N., it did not reassure him at all. For C.N. it meant that the risk of being expelled from the Netherlands at some date in the future continued. He felt that he had to live in uncertainty for nine months more. He was not able to listen to any reassuring information from the mouth of the therapist or people in his social environment. His symptoms became worse. C.N. expressed his lack of confidence in the therapist, and interrupted the therapy.

The therapist, who as a result of a similar experience one year before, had not been happy about the decision of the Ministry in the first place, again contacted the Ministry of Justice. In a protracted conversation with a member of the staff of the Ministry, who had no medical or psychiatric knowledge, he explained how the crisis was developing. The person concerned listened sympathetically and promised to convey the message to the proper authorities. After a few days the Ministry informed the therapist that a residence permit without restrictions would be granted. The interventions of the therapist consisted of making 10 phone calls and writing three letters, distributed over a period of 12 weeks.

In his contact with authorities, the therapist faces the task of persuading civil servants to assess an individual case, to do this as soon as possible, and to deviate from fixed rules and procedures. This job is complicated by the circumstance that he cannot restrict himself to addressing medical professionals, but has to communicate with people who can't be expected to possess special empathic capacities for understanding the reactions of someone who is suffering from a psychiatric disorder. If contact is made with a medical professional, one may of course not expect him to have much detailed expert knowledge on specific manifestations of psychiatric disorders in refugees from various cultural backgrounds. The contact with institutions usually requires a lot of patience, perseverance, tact, and also genuine interest in and understanding of the dynamics in which the civil servants concerned are functioning.

Some specific problems

In crisis situations, the therapist is faced with problems that require extra attention, not because they only present themselves when a client is in a condition of crisis, but because they manifest themselves more intensely and require extra vigilance or an instantaneous reaction from the therapist.

First, the therapist has to evaluate scrupulously whether reactions of the refugee that at first sight impress as overdone and theatrical, are to be considered as normal against the background of his cultural roots, can be waved as a passing form of overreaction, or should be considered as signs of a personality disorder (e.g. a histrionic personality disorder).

Second, when a refugee is in a condition of crisis, the therapist has to appraise the risk of suicidal behaviour (see Chapter 9 for a discussion of this topic).

While working with the refugee in a condition of crisis, the therapist should be aware of what is happening between him and his client in terms of transference and counter-transference. For example, when a crisis occurs the helping professional may be tempted to act as a saviour, give more help than is strictly necessary and in that way reinforce the helpless attitude of the refugee. Or, an insistent appeal for help of a refugee may provoke an aggressive counter-transference, which tempts the therapist to make a wrong diagnosis resulting in inadequate treatment.

In the aforementioned case of C.N., the aggressive and not very grateful attitude of the refugee made the therapist rather sulky. After C.N. left therapy, the therapist first contemplated the idea of dropping the case completely. A conversation with a colleague, in which the therapist ventilated his irritation, made him change his mind. After this he made the intervention to the Ministry of Justice which turned out to be successful. The therapeutic contact was restored.

The aggressive behaviour of a few traumatized refugees also constitutes a problem for the therapist. Sometimes, the aggression that the refugee ventilates is directly aimed at the therapist. But even when this is not the case, the aggressive outbursts are not pleasant to witness. They are, however, often unavoidable, either as aspects of the transference relationship, or as a rather desperate way of coping with feelings of fear and helplessness that in the condition of crisis have become unbearable.

When a refugee is in a crisis situation, the therapist will have to deal with the strong emotions of his client that inevitably will trigger strong emotions in himself. That can make crisis intervention a tough job. The therapist may try to comfort himself with the thought that many crises, although they bring a lot of emotional upheaval for both the refugee and the therapist, eventually prove to have been a decisive turning point, a fresh start for a positive development for all the involved parties (cf. Erikson, 1968, De Wit & Van der Veer, 1989).

Choosing therapeutic techniques

In the discussion of therapeutic techniques in this study, we have mentioned how they might be connected with the various theoretical approaches discussed in Chapter 2. It is obvious that the relations between psychological theories and psychotherapeutic techniques are not simple; often the effectiveness of a particular psychotherapeutic technique can be explained within more than one theoretical framework.

Therefore, diagnosing the problems of a refugee in terms of one or more theoretical approaches, does not automatically lead to the choice of a group of psychotherapeutic techniques. Moreover, a diagnostic appraisal is an ongoing process. Therefore choosing therapeutic techniques is often not an isolated event, but a series of experiments with various techniques, in which the therapist tries to find out what works and what does not.

In addition to this, the special problems of refugees often make it impossible for the therapist to stick virtuously to a fixed therapeutic procedure. The reason for this is the complexity in terms of the targets for psychotherapeutic techniques, as well as the influence day-to-day events have on the psychological functioning of refugees.

For instance, news about the political situation in the native country or the condition of relatives who are still living there, may bring back intrusive memories of traumatic experiences that were 'forgotten'. This can lead to a sudden increase in incapacitating symptoms or a revival of inner conflicts. Unexpected experiences with racism in the country of exile may bring adaptation problems to the foreground. Normal life events, like the birth of a child or the death of a parent, may trigger unexpected emotions, simply because they take place while in exile. Therefore, working with refugees forces the therapist to improvise. Helping refugees can be described as a process in which the therapist is constantly making decisions: about making certain interventions and refraining from other possible approaches; about digging deeper in some matter the refugee brings up, or ignoring it for the time being; about staying with or changing the subject, or purposely drifting away on what may be seen as a side track.

To become aware of his decisions during the therapeutic interviews, the therapist can monitor his own behaviour by using a tape or video recorder. When this is not possible, he can make notes of the conversation. Working with refugees this also may not be possible, especially when the therapist needs all his concentration for conducting the interview (e.g. if the refugee becomes very upset during the conversation, or when the therapist has to use a foreign language). In those cases the therapist can try to reconstruct what happened while he writes his report. The author usually uses the following checklist:

Name: Interview no: Date:
1. Intended beginning:
2. Other intended interventions:
3. Content of the interview: beginning (who started, and how. Was this conforming or deviant from what the therapist had in mind? This is usually easy to remember):
4. Content of the interview, middle:
5. Content of the interview, end: (Often it is easier to fill in item 5 before item 4. After writing down how the interview started and how it ended, one can try to reconstruct what happened in between):
6. Associations: (entries to be noted here are for example: 'Why do I keep forgetting the anamnestic data about this refugee?'; 'This man impresses me as being much younger than his chronological age'; and so on):
7. Feelings of the therapist about being with the refugee, and his speculations about the feelings of the client about being with the therapist: (for example, the therapist may have been bored for some time, he may have had the feeling that he had to say something really clever, he may have felt unfree to ask certain questions, he may have been moved to tears, or he may have felt impatience or aggressiveness. The therapist may speculate that the refugee likes him a lot but is afraid to become dependent on him, or that he at some moment experienced the therapist as an interrogator, or that he takes the therapist for the good guy while he is seeing the therapist's colleague, who prescribes him medication, as a powerful but inadequate woman):

8. New information with possible diagnostic value: (for example: a refugee tells the therapist casually that he used to be a member of a particular political group. From experience the therapist knows that this group has a very rigid ideology and seems to attract individuals who are in need of a group that can give them a kind of synthetic identity):

9. Signs of progression or drawback: (for example: a refugee told his therapist that he did miss his last interview because it was a warm day and he went to the beach with some friends. About this refugee the therapist concluded that: a. the refugee's superego had become less rigid; b. that he was becoming less dependent on the therapy; and c. that he was making progress in overcoming his inhibitions with regard to social contacts):

10. Did the therapist consider or effectuate a change in therapeutic strategy, or in any way deviate from the approach he had in mind? Did he think about any intervention that he decided to postpone?

11. Plan with regard to therapeutic strategy and intended interventions for coming interviews:

Sometimes, and with some clients very often, the therapist has to adapt to the actual developments in the life of the refugee. That means he has to change his strategy or at least to deviate for a minute or two. By making detailed reports, the therapist prevents these changes and deviations from being ignored. They will become conscious decisions which can be evaluated later.

Guidelines

Before offering a list of guidelines which can help the therapist to make his choice, the tentative character of this list must be stressed. The list is restricted to the therapeutic techniques that are discussed in this book, and other kinds of psychotherapeutic techniques that might be useful in working with refugees (like hypnosis) are omitted. Moreover, which therapeutic techniques are selected, is also a matter of personal preference and ability of the therapist.

Whenever a helping professional is considering the possibility of using psychotherapeutic techniques, he has to make an estimate of the motivation of the patient. Motivation for treatment is, in the case of traumatized refugees, almost always ambivalent. Thus estimating the motivation of the refugee, includes thinking of ways in which a very fragile motivation can be supported and stimulated.

Supportive psychotherapeutic techniques will have to be used in almost all cases. Supportive techniques can be employed as a sort of safe start, while the therapist is observing the problems and capacities of the refugee, and tries to get a view of the life-world of the refugee (cf. Vladár Rivero, 1989). They will also be first choice if there are not many people in the social environment of the refugee who can provide emotional support or if there is insufficient structure in his daily life (e.g. having a job, going to school or other routine activities).

Supportive techniques may help to reduce symptoms, to improve overall functioning, and to restart developmental processes. They can also be used within the context of therapy aimed at the reduction of incapacitating symptoms, or in combination with techniques of uncovering psychotherapy.

Therapeutic techniques for dealing with nightmares and flashbacks, will be used when these symptoms are very incapacitating, and the refugee is able to accept assignments. They are useful in working with refugees who have an immense history of traumatization.

The testimony method is useful when the refugee is strongly motivated to discuss his traumatic experiences, the traumatic experiences were not too much of a protracted ordeal, and the symptoms are not greatly incapacitating. The testimony method seems less effective in the case of refugees who have had many traumatic experiences spread over an extended period of time (a number of years), and/or suffer from very incapacitating symptoms, and/or are convinced that they had psychological problems long before they were traumatized by organized violence.

Use of the techniques of uncovering psychotherapy aimed at promoting long-term processes of emotional integration and personality change is indicated when the traumatic experiences deeply changed the refugee's attitude towards himself, other people and life in general, in an inadequate way. The use of uncovering techniques requires some psychological-mindedness of the refugee, a capacity to form and sustain relationships, and an ability to form an alliance with the therapist, which implies that the refugee is able to tolerate ambivalent feelings with regard to the therapist. Some refugees have these qualities, but do not appear to do so at the moment they request assistance. In such cases the therapist will start with a supportive approach, until it becomes apparent that the refugee needs and has the capacities to benefit from the techniques of uncovering psychotherapy (cf. Schwartz, 1990).

8 The use of psychotropic medication

Victor Vladár Rivero

The way in which psychotropic medication is used in therapy with refugees is not radically different from the way it is used to treat other victims of violence, like battered women, incest victims, war victims, veterans etc. However, in a number of aspects, working with refugees poses its own specific problems. These may manifest themselves in connection with diagnosis and the prescription of psychotropic medication. In addition, it is necessary to pay special attention to the way in which medication is attuned to other forms of treatment, particularly psychotherapy.

Diagnosis

An important problem in psychiatric work with refugees of different cultural backgrounds, is the validity of the diagnostic tools used. The diagnostic criteria of the DSM–III–R (APA, 1987) can only be strictly applied when both the patient and the therapist who makes the diagnosis come from the same Western background. When this condition has not been met, and that usually is the case in therapy with refugees, then the DSM–III–R has to be used with considerable caution. Various researchers (Bleich, Garb & Kottler, 1986; Solomon et al., 1987) have concluded that the complaints and symptoms related to post-traumatic stress disorders, and the way in which they are represented, may be influenced by the cultural background of the client.

For example, a refugee from South East Asia who says that he 'hears voices' cannot be compared to a refugee from Eastern Europe who says the same thing. The meaning of 'hearing voices' is completely different in the life-worlds of the two refugees. In the life-world of a refugee from South East Asia 'hearing voices' may be part of the normal process of mourning. This may also apply to the refugee from Eastern Europe, but in the latter case it is easier for the Western therapist to empathize with the content of the client's 'hallucination'. As a result, the therapist may be more likely to conclude wrongly that the refugee from South East Asia is suffering from psychosis. In order to make a decision on treatment it is important to determine whether 'hearing voices' stems from a schizophrenia, a major depression with psychotic features, or is an aspect of the re-experiencing which is related to post-traumatic stress disorders.

Therefore, the complaints and symptoms of the refugee have to be evaluated against the background of the client's life-world. The term 'life-world' (Schutz, 1975) here refers to the cultural, political and socio-economic background of the refugee, as well as the way in which he experiences this. In order to cope with these diagnostic problems, cooperation with therapists from other cultures is necessary. It is also preferable to make the diagnosis in consultation with representatives from other disciplines—social workers, social-psychiatric nurses, psychologists and psychotherapists with different specializations—who, because they may have longer or more intensive contact with the client and/or because they come from a different cultural background, are more aware of the refugee's life-world. The same applies to the process of deciding which treatment is most appropriate.

A psychiatrist working with refugees has to deal with a heterogeneous population. Not all refugees are victims of extreme violence. Not all of them suffer from trauma-related psychiatric disorders. Although we focus in this chapter on trauma-related disorders, we should not forget that among refugees any psychiatric disorder may be found and should be treated in the usual way.

About the prevalence of psychiatric disorders among refugees, only few studies are available that use DSM-III-R categories. On the basis of clinical experience (see chapter 2 of this study: cf. Mollica, 1987; Hauff, 1990; Kinzie et al., 1990) it can be stated that a relatively large number of them have complaints which point to an anxiety disorder, and post-traumatic stress disorder, in particular. There are often complaints which suggest mood disorders—including major depression and dysthymia. Also some refugees show symptoms of somato-form disorders. Besides this, many trauma victims manifest symptoms of dissociative disorders (Van der Kolk & Van der Hart, 1989), especially when they were traumatized at an early age (Terr, 1991). That also holds for refugees. Occasionally we use the diagnosis reactive psychosis, or, preferably, post-traumatic disintegration psychosis (cf. Rümke, 1960). A co-morbidity up to 80% has been reported of post-traumatic stress disorder and mood disorder, the mood disorder being a major depression in half of the cases. The co-morbidity found between post-traumatic stress disorder and other anxiety disorders (especially panic disorder and generalized anxiety disorder) is about 50%. However, these data are based on research with various instruments and divergent populations and should, therefore, be used with caution.

The most important step in treatment of refugees with a post-traumatic stress disorder is careful assessment and diagnosis of co-morbid conditions in terms of the DSM-III-R. To facilitate diagnostic assessment, it may help to visualize the co-morbidity of the various DSM–III–R categories. Therefore we developed the following figures.

Figure 8.1 illustrates the two most important diagnostic categories found in trauma victims; it shows that there is not a clear boundary between anxiety disorders and mood disorders. Figure 8.2 suggests that in the marginal area of these disorders, we find symptoms indicating aggression and somatoform disorders. In Figure 8.3 post-traumatic stress disorder is shown as a square, that overlaps with all the aforementioned categories. In Figure 8.4 the dissociative disorders and reactive psychosis were added, leaving only a small area for patients with post-traumatic stress disorder in a narrower sense.

In refugees, either anxiety symptoms or depressive symptoms may be prominent, or they may both be present. Other possible combinations seen in refugees are, for instance: panic disorder in combination with post-traumatic stress disorder and disregulation of aggression, or post-traumatic stress disorder in combination with major depression with symptoms of a somatoform disorder, or panic disorder in combination with dissociative symptoms.

Personality disorders are not easy to diagnose in refugees coming from all parts of the world. Correct diagnosis of these disorders is very important in order to estimate the possibilities for psychotherapeutic treatment. The literature about pharmacotherapy of these disorders warns against high expectations

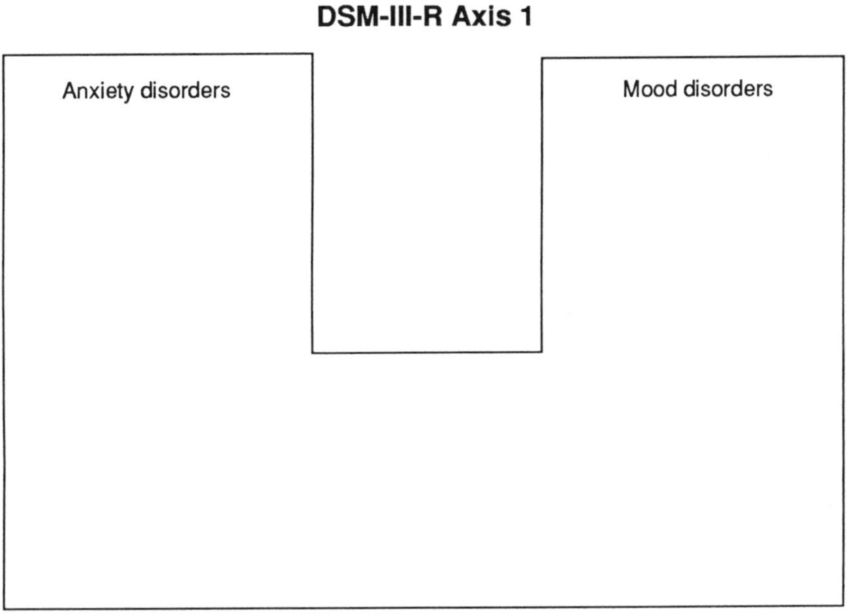

DSM-III-R Axis 1

Figure 8.1: Anxiety disorders and mood disorders are two important diagnostic categories of trauma victims. (Reproduced by permission of V. Vladár Rivero.)

DSM-III-R Axis 1

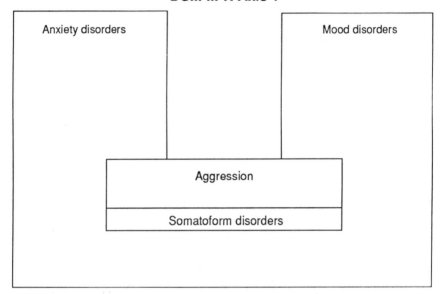

Figure 8.2: **Aggressive and somatoform disorders are found in the marginal area. (Reproduced by permission of V. Vladár Rivero.)**

DSM-III-R Axis 1

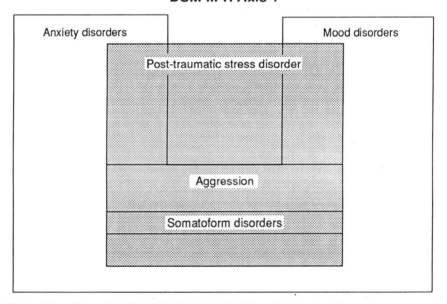

Figure 8.3: **The projection of post-traumatic stress disorder on Figure 8.2 shows the possibilities of co-morbidity. (Reproduced by permission of V. Vladár Rivero.)**

DSM-III-R Axis 1
Clinical manifestations in traumatized patients

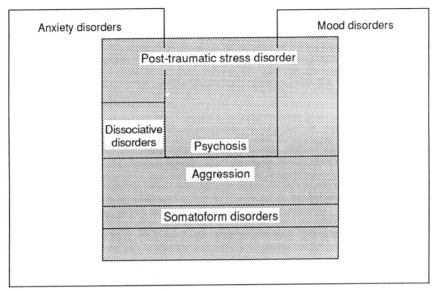

Figure 8.4: Including dissociative disorders and reactive psychosis leaves only a small area for patients with the narrower post-traumatic stress disorder. (Reproduced by permission of V. Vladár Rivero.)

about the results (Gunderson, 1986). Therefore, they are omitted in this chapter. However, it should be stressed that refugees with a supposed personality disorder may also suffer from symptoms of one of the aforementioned disorders and should then be given adequate treatment.

The prescription of psychotropic medication

In this paragraph discussion will be limited to the prescription of psychotropic medication for refugees who have been diagnosed as having an anxiety disorder, and, in particular, a post-traumatic stress disorder, in combination with symptoms of other disorders. The literature on this subject does not provide an unambiguous picture. But researchers are agreed that, generally speaking, psychotropic medication can help in relieving symptoms, and that it can also be used to support psychotherapy, particularly behaviour therapy (Friedman, 1988). Reference will be made to studies on the use of medication in populations of people traumatized in a similar way to refugees, for the greater part Vietnam veterans, for only little research on this topic was directed at a refugee population.

Criteria of choice   It is well known that a number of medicines can lead to a reduction in the complaints and symptoms which are related to post-traumatic stress disorders. These include benzodiazepines, lithium carbonate, beta blockers, alpha-adrenergic agents, anti-psychotic drugs, tricyclic anti-depressant agents, serotonine re-uptake inhibitors and MAO inhibitors.

Positive effects have been reported of tricyclic anti-depressants like imipramine and amitriptyline, MAO inhibitors and serotonine re-uptake inhibitors (fluoxetine). In patients with mixed symptoms from various disorders, anti-depressants seem to counter the depressive symptoms, while they have less effect on the intrusive and avoidance symptoms of post-traumatic stress disorder. There are however indications that amitriptyline and fluoxetine reduce avoidance symptoms, while imipramine reduces intrusive symptoms and MAO inhibitors alleviate sleep disturbances and block nightmares (Bleich, Garb & Kottler, 1986; Burstein, 1984; Davidson et al., 1990; Ettedgui & Bridges, 1985; Falcon et al., 1985; Frank et al., 1988; Friedman, 1988; Jaranson, 1988; Klein, 1987; Lerer et al., 1987; McDaniel, 1986; Mellman & Davis 1985; Shen, 1983).

Of the benzodiazepines Alprazolam, in particular, has given good results (Feldman, 1987). Small doses of lithium carbonate seem to work well with patients for whom symptoms of extreme aggression, irritability, anxiety and insomnia are central (Kitchner & Greenstein, 1985).

Proceeding from a neuro-physiological hypothesis Kolb (1984; 1987) claims that the use of propranolol (a beta-adrenergic blocker) or clonidine (a centrally active alpha-adrenergic agonist) may also produce positive results.

It may be concluded from various publications (e.g. Lin, 1982) that people from different ethnic origins may react in different ways to psycho-pharmaca. Although some of these studies lack methodological consistency, it seems justified to conclude that many Asian people may react to lower doses of anti-psychotic and anti-depressive medication than Caucasians. Other studies (cf. Yang, 1985) indicate that, in Asian patients, lower blood levels of lithium are effective than in Caucasians.

Although attempts have been made to develop treatment protocols for patients with post-traumatic stress disorder (Silver, Sandberg & Hales, 1990), more research is needed before the treatment of these patients can become a rational stepped care approach in the style of the treatment plan for depression described by Guscott & Groff (1991).

Experience with psychotropic medication   The author's experience with the prescription of psychotropic medication has been obtained mainly in an out-patient clinic. The contact between psychiatrist and refugee was usually the result of an explicit request by the latter, or a request from, and/or in consultation with another therapist who has discussed the possibility of medication with the refugee.

When psychotropic medication is prescribed for refugees it is necessary to devote extra time to explanation. The printed instructions are usually in a language which the refugee has not yet fully mastered and are incomprehensible to him. It is important that the person who is to take the medicine should be fully aware of why it has been prescribed, how it works and what effect it will have on his condition. He should also know the correct dosage, how long it may be used for and what possible side-effects there will be.

Side-effects, together with the failure to achieve rapid relief from symptoms, are often responsible for the early termination of medication (Mavissakalian & Perel, 1985; Yost, 1987) or high rates of non-compliance with prescribed medication.

In patients that have been physically abused or tortured, side-effects like palpitation of the heart, can trigger series of associations or cognitive representations. For these patients, it is a small step from a slight palpitation that is inexplicable, to the palpitations he experienced during torture or while waiting for what turned out to be a mock execution.

Moreover, abnormal physical reactions caused by medication may strengthen a refugee's doubt about his physical functioning. This may, for example, bring him to present many vague somatic complaints. As a result, the clinician could incorrectly conclude that the refugee is suffering from a somatoform disorder. Some more examples: a refugee who, after suffering genital torture, suffered from erectile disorder and was very worried about the quality of his sexual fantasies, panicked when, after a prescription of trazadone, he developed priapism. In female refugees, side-effects such as a diminishing of vaginal secretion during sexual stimulation or urine incontinence may trigger the fear of being damaged and not being able any more to have children (Vladár Rivero, 1991). Obstipation or hard stools may trigger similar strong feelings of fear in refugees that have undergone anal torture. Refugees using benzodiazepines sometimes report, during the first days or when medication is withdrawn, symptoms of derealization and depersonalization, which may provoke fear of losing control. This may eventually result in a crisis situation.

However, when refugees are well informed about the consequences of using medication and their possible side-effects, they are often able to deal with the aforementioned reactions. They should, of course, be allowed plenty of time to discuss the side-effects from which they are suffering. The clinician should actively ask about side-effects, both when medication is attuned and during long-term treatment.

Mrs. A.P., who came from one of the Latin American dictatorships, was referred to us for psychotherapy by a psychiatrist. She had come to him with the symptoms of an anxiety disorder and the psychiatrist had prescribed amitriptyline. This treatment reduced the symptoms considerably.

The question of whether there had been a major depression remained.

A.P. explained that in the country she had left she had been given dosulepine and that this had made her feel better. It had been particularly good in helping her to sleep. She asked us to prescribe the same drug. She let it be known that she did not want to discuss her traumatic experiences with us, though she was pleased to know that she could do so if she wanted, because she knew that 'you know a lot about that kind of thing'.

The therapist told her that he hoped that she may want to discuss her past with us at a later date. He then informed her about the advantages and disadvantages of switching to a different medicine before prescribing the drug which she had requested.

This led to a reduction in the side-effects, such as a dry mouth and constipation, and A.P. slept better and dreamt less, as she had predicted.

In addition to appointments to check her medication, we also offered to bring her into contact with a female psychotherapist.

Medication has now been completed and A.P. accepted the offer to visit the psychotherapist regularly. The therapy sessions with her have a supportive and cautiously explorative character.

Some refugees report that, when they start using the prescribed anxiolytic or anti-depressant medication, there is an increase in flashbacks, nightmares or sleep disturbances. For example, when they first use fluoxetine, some refugees experience an increase of anxiety symptoms, depressive symptoms or eventually panic attacks. In those cases, it is important that therapist and refugee have come to an agreement about what will be done if this happens: continuing the use of the medication, interrupting it, or phoning the therapist. It goes without saying that, in a case when a co-therapist is involved, he should be informed about all the possible effects and side-effects of the medication, the kind of information that has been given about this to the refugee, and which procedure has been settled on in case the refugee feels he cannot handle the side-effects.

Apart from these side-effects, some refugees have an aversion to the use of psychotropic medication and the doctors who prescribe them. This aversion can often be interpreted as a healthy distrust which may be based on experience with doctors who 'treated' them so as to enable the torturers to continue their work, or doctors who administered psychotropic medication and/or other drugs such as pentotal, scopolamine, curare derivatives and LSD, by force (Vladár Rivero, 1986).

B.P., a refugee from the Middle East who had been receiving treatment for a relatively long time, reported that he was once again suffering from fear and auditory hallucinations. The psychiatrist diagnosed 'psychotraumatic disintegration psychosis' and wanted to prescribe haloperidol as an anti-psychotic medication. B.P. became very suspicious and tense when the name of the drug was mentioned. From inquiries it became clear that B.P. had been given haloperidol by force by a doctor who had also been present while he was tortured. When this had been discussed B.P. accepted the medication. His symptoms reduced and medication could be terminated after five weeks.

Aversion to use psychotropic medication may also result from different, unexpected causes.

C.P., a refugee who was suffering from a mixture of depressive and obsessive compulsive symptoms, refused to take medication. During later interviews, it became apparent that he associated the prescribed drug with the cyanide capsule he had carried with him for years during the time he was a member of an opposition group. He was supposed to take the capsule in the event of being arrested. When this happened, he did not swallow the capsule. Seeing the capsule in the pharmacy triggered all the feelings of fear, shame and guilt connected with the cyanide capsule.

The therapist should also be aware of the possibility of self-medication. Sometimes the refugee may use alcohol or cannabis products to reduce anxiety, or chew leaves of the Khat plant, which has a mild stimulating effect (Kalix, 1988). Refugees may continue, without informing the therapist, a course of medicinal treatment which had been started in another country. They may even import medicaments.

In general, the prescription of psychotropic medication only is indicated when the symptoms of the anxiety disorder are so serious that they impede normal functioning. For example: when insomnia or disturbed concentration make it difficult to continue with a language course, or when the re-experiencing of traumatic events, panic attacks or nightmares become unbearable. When a refugee is suffering from a major depression, adequate medication should be prescribed. Suicidal thoughts and suicidal behaviour should also be evaluated carefully (Hendin & Pollinger Haas, 1991).

Medication can be prescribed in four situations: in a crisis situation, as part of long-term psychiatric treatment, as treatment in combination with psychotherapy, in support of ongoing psychotherapy.

Medication in crisis situations

In a crisis situation, medication is prescribed for a short period. In the meantime other forms of assistance are offered. In this way an attempt is made to reduce anxiety and contribute to the establishment of a new equilibrium.

D.P. was referred to us by his family doctor, who urged immediate assistance. D.P. had complained of insomnia, attacks of anxiety and nightmares. During the first meeting it was not clear how this crisis situation had developed. The psychiatrist gave D.P. medication for a week in the hope that this would help him sleep and reduce his anxiety. He thought that this would facilitate an examination of the causes of the client's complaints during the next session. It was agreed that the medication could be terminated or changed after a week.

When a refugee has had complaints for a long time and consults a therapist because he finds himself in a crisis situation, insomnia usually plays an important role. Then the prescription of benzodiazepines is indicated. In such cases the author usually prescribes these for one week: temazepam (10 to 40 mg before going to bed) or flunitrazepam (1 to 4 mg before going to bed). When the refugee is so tense or frightened that anxiolytic medication is considered to be necessary, oxazepam (10 to 150 mg per day) or clorazepate (10 to 150 mg per day) may be prescribed. In the latter no extra sedative is prescribed to counter the insomnia, but the refugee is advised to take an extra dose of the same drug before going to bed. The prescription of benzodiazepines is terminated as soon as possible, and after three weeks at most.

When there are signs of a psychosis, anti-psychotic medication can be prescribed.

E.P., a male victim of sexual violence, told his therapist that he had not taken a shower for a week because the last time he did this, he had seen the shower head slowly change into an enormous penis. The psychiatrist that was called concluded that E.P. was having hallucinations and delusions and prescribed anti-psychotic medication. After a few days, E.P. again was able to enter the shower cubicle.

The question can be brought forward whether, in case of a post-traumatic disintegrative psychosis, one should prescribe anti-psychotic medication, or first prescribe anxiolytic medication and only switch to anti-psychotic medication if the effect has been insufficient. This procedure has been proposed for the reason that it can be very difficult to differentiate between psychotic symptoms and the symptoms of a dissociative disorder, especially if the refugee and his therapist come from different cultures. In some cases diagnostic instruments for dissociative disorders can be valuable (Steinberg, Rounsaville & Cicchetti, 1990; Boon & Draijer, 1991).

In the case of E.P., it became clear during later sessions that showers and rooms with tiles induced in him a condition of dissociation that had come into existence during sexual torture. A few months later his symptoms came back. Then anxiolytic medication (chlorazepate) was sufficient.

Medication as part of longer-term psychiatric treatment

It is preferable not to prescribe any of the benzodiazepines mentioned above for long-term psychiatric treatment. The possibility of dependence has been described extensively in the literature. After protracted use (longer than four months) withdrawal symptoms (e.g. depersonalization) may appear which can be more serious than the complaints for which the drug was prescribed in the first place (Schoepf, 1981).

If the refugee continues to have serious depressive complaints then an antidepressant should be prescribed in a dosage which suits him. We refer in this connection to the extensive literature on the use of these drugs (e.g. Guscott & Groff, 1991).

If complaints which point to a post-traumatic stress disorder and/or a panic disorder persist, in other words, if the crisis situation in which the client finds himself has not diminished to such an extent that the symptoms have reduced then we consider the following rules to be applicable:

1. The diagnosis must be evaluated
2. Depending on the individual characteristics of the client a suitable dosage of an anti-depressant should be sought
3. If after six to eight weeks, when maximum dosage as used with depressions have been prescribed, there is no positive effect, medication is stopped. If necessary, an anti-depressant from a different group can be tried (Davidson, 1990)
4. The prescription of benzodiazepines should be stopped after three weeks, or earlier if possible.

In order to find a suitable dosage of an anti-depressant, the prescription starts with small doses and gradually increases the dosage until the symptoms abate. A reduction in the client's insomnia, nightmares, panic attacks, flashbacks, listlessness, avoidance reactions and alcohol use, and an increase in his appetite, can serve as indications.

The author has experience with amitryptiline, imipramine, fluoxetine (20 mg a day), maprotiline (between 10 mg and maximum 150 mg per day). There is no agreement in the literature on post-traumatic stress disorder with regard to the best initial dosage and the rate at which this can be increased. In the case of some clients it helps to prescribe neuroleptic (perfenazine) in combination with anti-depressants rather than simply increasing the dosage of the anti-depressant. There is also no agreement in the literature on the value of determining the blood levels. There are some indications that anti-depressive medication must be continued at least eight weeks for adequate evaluation (Davidson et al., 1990).

The termination and/or reduction of medication should be gradual, and should depend on the course of the therapy, and whether or not there has been a recurrence of symptoms. There are hardly any publications on this aspect of therapy, and no follow-up studies. We advise the use of experience in the treatment of patients with mood disorders; depressive and panic disorders as an example.

Medication as treatment in combination with psychotherapy

In most forms of psychiatric treatment, three phases can be distinguished. The first phase is the phase in which the therapist wins the trust of the refugee and a working alliance develops. Often crisis intervention is needed in this phase. When the crisis is solved and a treatment plan can be made, a second phase is entered. In this phase the therapist will bring the symptoms of which the refugee was or still is suffering, into connection with his traumatic experiences.

After F.P's panic attacks and depressive symptoms had been treated successfully with medication (fluoxetine), it became clear that these symptoms could be understood as a result of trans-generational traumatization. This could be elaborated during therapy. In this case the first stage had lasted eight weeks, the second stage 18 months. After an evaluation of both the medicinal as well as the psychotherapeutic part of the treatment, it was decided to stop the medication.

Termination is the third phase. After a successful medicinal treatment, medication can be stopped. It has to be decided whether the psychotherapeutic treatment can also be terminated, or has to be continued. When medication is stopped, it is important to instruct the refugee about what he has to do if the symptoms return. How this is done, depends upon the treatment setting.

Medication as support in ongoing psychotherapy

When a refugee has complaints which make medication necessary this does not mean that other possibilities, such as psychotherapy, are excluded. We have already stated that medication is sometimes only used during a short period and serves to assist the refugee in establishing a new balance in his life in a crisis situation. If medication has to be continued and there is reason to refer the refugee for other forms of therapy, then it is necessary to consider the way in which they interact and the possibilities for attuning them.

Van Bork (1986) claims that various drugs influence the incidence and content of dreams in different ways. Dreams and nightmares are often an important starting point in the provision of psychotherapy for refugees. Prescription of medication in such a way that nightmares disappear completely could therefore interfere with the psychotherapeutic process. However, sometimes this is necessary for a while, especially when the nightmares interfere too much with daily functioning and cannot be adequately dealt with during psychotherapy (this may happen for example when a refugee lives in fear of mandatory repatriation). Continual consultation with the psychotherapist concerning the effect of medication is therefore desirable. On the other hand, the course of a therapeutic encounter can sometimes lead to consultation with the psychiatrist for considering the prescription of psychotropic medication. This may happen, for example, when a refugee becomes depressive, psychotic, or frightened as a result of bad news about his family or the political situation in his native country, and this cannot be dealt with immediately during the psychotherapeutic sessions.

During the process of diagnosis and deciding which treatment is most adequate, the pros and cons should be discussed with the psychotherapist and the prescriber of medication whether they are the same person or not.

In conclusion, although there is a growing amount of literature on pharmacotherapy of patients with trauma-related disorders, relevant information for clinical practice has to be sought in the literature on the treatment of patients with mood disorders and panic disorders. Careful assessment and diagnosis of co-morbid conditions lays the foundation for a rational approach to the use of psychotropic medication in the treatment of victims of war, torture and repression.

Part III

SPECIAL GROUPS AND SPECIAL PROBLEMS

Introduction

Refugees form a very heterogeneous group which, on the basis of their own special characteristics, backgrounds or present situations, can be subdivided into countless subgroups. All these groups have to deal with special problems, and when they seek assistance they confront the helping professional or volunteer with special tasks.

Part III of this study begins with a description of the special problems of refugees who have requested political asylum, but have not yet been admitted as residents in the country of exile and therefore live with the fear that they may be expelled. The chapter (9) about this group will focus on the increased risk of suicide among refugees seeking asylum. It is based on experience of the Dutch political situation, but most of the content is relevant to other countries that have a restrictive policy regarding the admission of refugees.

The remaining chapters are devoted to the children of refugees (chapter 10), adolescents and young adults (chapter 11) and victims of sexual violence (chapter 12). The book will conclude with a chapter on the consequences of working with refugees for the helping professional (chapter 13).

9 The risk of suicide among refugees seeking asylum

Waiting and feelings of insecurity

With regard to the legal status of refugees in the country of exile four groups can be distinguished:

1. Refugees who were invited by the government
2. Refugees who arrived through their own initiative, requested political asylum, and received it
3. Refugees who requested political asylum, were denied it and are therefore considered to be illegal immigrants
4. Refugees whose request for asylum is still pending.

A large number of the refugees to which the author and his colleagues have attended (more than 60%) belonged to the last-mentioned category. They requested assistance while they were waiting for an answer from a committee of the Ministry of Justice, or a decision in their case in court. Some of them had already been waiting for more than five years.

For refugees who have undergone some traumatic experience in their native country, the prolonged uncertainty about their acceptance as a refugee has negative consequences for their psychological well-being. Having to wait for years for a decision by others, which carries with it enormous consequences for their own future, puts the refugee in a very dependent position. For the refugee it combines with the continuation of the fear of being sent back to the country where he underwent traumatic experiences. When the refugee is not able or does not have the means to move on to a country that is less restrictive and slow in admitting refugees, waiting for a decision about political asylum produces the combination of dependency, fear and feelings of insecurity based on very real experiences, and no possible alternative action. In other words, helplessness.

In spite of all the support that psychiatric and psychological assistance may provide, in the cases of refugees who must endure a very long wait for a decision concerning asylum, one often sees such a progressive deterioration in their psychological condition that the refugee may enter into a psychotic state or become suicidal.

Of those refugees seeking asylum to whom the author attended, 80% were traumatized refugees whose psychological condition seemed to be deteriorating as a result of the prolonged uncertainty about the possibility of mandatory repatriation and return to the source of trauma.

A.Q. was 26 years old and came from a dictatorship in the Middle East. He applied for political asylum in the Netherlands after spending a few months in prison in his native country for political reasons. During detention he was tortured. One and a half years after filing his request for political asylum, he requested assistance. The most important reason for his request for help was his fear of going mad. While he was waiting for a decision on his application for political asylum a friend with whom he had been detained and who was also waiting for the decision of the Dutch authorities, had gone to seed. Another friend, in the same predicament, had committed suicide.

A.Q. complained about insomnia, nightmares, concentration problems, loneliness and frequent episodes of crying. He was no longer able to continue his language lessons and felt guilty about this.

All these complaints started about six months before A.Q. requested assistance. During his first years in the Netherlands, A.Q. had functioned rather well. He had learned to speak Dutch on a basic level and had made a few Dutch friends. But lately he had started to avoid his friends, and said that he was forgetting what he had learned of the language.

After further exploration of A.Q.'s complaints and life history, the following diagnosis was reached: post-traumatic stress disorder, signs of a major depression, exacerbated by continuing uncertainty about obtaining a residence permit, the very real fear of being sent back to his native country and problems related to his forced separation from his parents. The proposed treatment was supportive psychotherapy and medication. A.Q. was very enthusiastic about the treatment and, even though he had difficulties with the language, he made good use of the therapy which was offered. But in spite of this his condition deteriorated and his therapist concluded that there was a real danger of suicide. The deterioration of A.Q.'s condition could be related to reports of misuse of power by the government in his native country and what he considered to be impolite treatment by immigration officials, to whom he had to report every week. The suicide of his compatriot, after he had been refused asylum, and an interview with an official from the Ministry of Justice, in which the latter made it known that he did not believe a word of A.Q.'s story, all led to an increase in his symptoms.

Factors associated with suicide

Statistical data on the number of suicides or attempted suicides among refugees requesting asylum are not yet available. There are also no studies of the background of suicidal behaviour among these people. A study of the literature to find factors which may be relevant in understanding suicide among refugees or traumatized individuals generally only produced one article (Curtis Alley, 1982), which will be discussed below. What follows is based on the general literature on suicide and clinical experience with refugees.

Expulsion   In 1897 the sociologist Durkheim published a study of suicide in which he introduced the concept of *anomie* to explain suicidal behaviour. Since then *anomie* has been associated with the absence of integration in social structures and the occurrence of a process of expulsion or exclusion (Goddijn, 1969).

A characteristic of the social situation in which refugees seeking asylum in Western countries find themselves is the existence of forces which do not work towards their integration in this society but towards their exclusion. Refugees have been expelled from their native countries because dictatorial governments made life impossible for them. The policy of Western governments seems to be aimed at restricting the number of people seeking asylum, and as a result many refugees are not recognized as such and deported. The individual asylum seeker experiences this process of exclusion in his contacts with government officials. Sometimes their behaviour or the procedures they have to conform to are such that, even though they may be intended as humane, the refugee experiences them as humiliating and offensive.

Social isolation and loneliness   Since Durkheim, a lack of social cohesion in a community has been considered to be a factor which is related to the incidence of suicide. This social phenomenon manifests itself on the individual level as social isolation and loneliness.

In the case of refugees with psychological problems, the flight has often separated them from their relatives and friends. Moreover, they are relatively isolated from the indigenous population. This is partially a result of language problems, xenophobia, government policy and the previously mentioned process of exclusion which makes integration into indigenous society almost impossible. Political differences or fear of the secret police of their native country may contribute to social isolation from compatriots. Also, the fact that some refugees suffer from post-traumatic stress disorder may contribute to social isolation. In the latter case one may think of refugees who avoid compatriots because they remind them of traumatic experiences, such as torture or murders organized by the government. Refugees who request help often mention feelings of loneliness.

Unemployment   Another factor which is often related to the risk of suicide is unemployment (Matthijs, 1982). In some countries asylum seekers are excluded from the labour market, they are not allowed to work. They therefore do not have much money for recreational activities. Those with a post-traumatic stress disorder or a depressive disorder usually have difficulty concentrating and this makes it difficult for them to follow courses or read. One needs to be very inventive to find something useful to do with one's time under such circumstances.

The breaking off of relationships   Instability in relationships or the breaking off of relationships with those who are important to the individual or the loss of a significant loved one through death is generally considered to be related to an increased risk of suicide (Curtis Alley, 1982). This is often the case with refugees, who have been forcefully separated from their parents, family, friends, partner or children.

Extreme dependency and powerlessness   The last social factor which is related to an increased risk of suicide can be referred to as extreme dependency and powerlessness. One may think of conditions in which the individual is totally dependent on powerful persons or institutions for his welfare, while these persons or institutions cannot be brought to act in a way which alleviates his distress, and all attempts to free himself from this dependency fail. The individual then comes to see suicide as the only possible way of exerting some influence on his own life, and it becomes a reaction to a long-lasting feeling of powerlessness (see Diekstra, 1983).

Powerlessness is often the dominant affect in the lives of refugees at the moment they come into contact with a therapist. During their traumatic experiences (during torture, for example) they felt utterly powerless. The fact that they are unable to help friends and relatives who have remained behind exacerbates this feeling. Dependence on a government, which, for reasons which are not always easy to understand (and not only for asylum seekers), sends large numbers of refugees back shortly after arrival while letting many others remain in uncertainty for years, also evokes strong feelings of powerlessness.

Powerlessness is an emotion which is difficult to cope with, even in situations in which the individual feels relatively safe. In situations which are experienced as extremely dangerous—being sent back to a country in which one has been exposed to state terror—it becomes amplified by hopelessness about building a new future in exile. Some individuals cannot cope with these emotions and may commit suicide. The suicides of a number of Iranian refugees at Zavethem airport in Brussels on 6 March 1987 can be understood in this light: they committed suicide at the point at which they were to be deported back to Iran. Cases like this, however, are seldom reported by the media.

Guilt   Especially people who were traumatized by combat experience may feel extensive guilt in relation to surviving their missing, wounded or dead buddies. They may also feel guilty about what they did to their adversaries on the battlefield. This guilt may be extra strong if the veteran in some way enjoyed committing violence. This guilt feeling may, in combination with the wish to recreate the excitement that was experienced during combat, result in extremely risk-taking behaviour (Solursh, 1989).

B.Q., a 25-year-old refugee from an Asian country, was referred for therapy after he had tried to commit suicide by cutting his radial artery. During the first interview, he told the therapist how he, as a guerrilla, had been involved in sniper attacks on military patrols. After this interview, he crossed a motorway on his bicycle, and almost caused a concertina crash. When the therapist asked him why he had done this, he said: 'I don't know, it was just an impulse.'

Depression and other psychiatric disturbances   That depression and other psychiatric problems increase the risk of suicide is not a matter of discussion. In addition, individuals who have been admitted to a psychiatric hospital earlier in their life, who attempted to kill or kill themselves before, or who have a relative who committed suicide, are more likely to commit a suicide attempt than individuals without these characteristics (cf. Kerkhof, Van der Wal & Hengeveld, 1988).

A developmental perspective

Research has shown that most attempted suicides occur in the under-40 age group (Diekstra, 1983). The statistics also show sex- and nationality-related variations. Most suicide curves show a peak in the period of adolescence and young adulthood. So age seems to be a risk factor in itself. This fact constitutes a challenge to developmental psychology.

On the basis of empirical research Diekstra has concluded that adolescents and young adults do not think about suicide in the same way as older people do. Young people are more likely to view negative social conditions, such as the loss of a job or the breaking off of a relationship, as a reason for suicide. Diekstra concludes that when an adolescent is confronted with problems which block his future perspective he will be more likely to develop a hostile attitude to life and the desire to escape from it.

The style or structure of young people's thinking about suicide can also show specific characteristics. They tend to think in terms of polarized extremes and radical solutions, rather than in terms of nuances and compromises (cf. Chandler, Ball & Boyles, 1988; Diekstra, 1984). This can be explained in terms of the temporary negative by-products of cognitive development during adolescence (De Wit & Van der Veer, 1989).

Refugees who were treated by the author and were thought to have a dangerously high suicide risk were mostly young adults who had been seriously traumatized during adolescence and had been in situations of real mortal danger for themselves and their family or friends. During the course of therapeutic interviews it became clear that they tried to repress memories of their experience of the nearness of death and their behaviour in the situations of mortal danger. As a result, their cognitive development, including the development of moral reasoning, seemed to have stagnated since adolescence: that is to say, as long as it was concerned with matters of life and death. Their rigid way of thinking results in a selective attention to radical solutions in a situation in which there is no clear perspective for the future, and a tendency to assume a self-punitive position. A similar observation was made with regard to Vietnam veterans (Williams, 1987b).

If one wants to view the psychological development processes of adolescents more generally then the concept of identity may be helpful. The point of departure is that adolescents are confronted with the task of becoming individuals, but individuals who have good relations with their social environment. These two factors are related and constitute the main developmental task during adolescence: the development of an individual identity.

Four components are important for experiencing this identity: a feeling of inner sameness and continuity; a feeling of personal freedom (in the face of all the unavoidable limitations placed on every individual in any society); having a goal or an ideal or a plan for which one can work; and the feeling that, with regard to the essential aspects of one's personality, one is accepted and recognized by one's social environment (Erikson, 1982).

In the case of young refugees the process of identity development has often not been completed. Their feeling of inner sameness and continuity is threatened by a radical discontinuity in their environment: going into exile means leaving behind familiar surroundings and coming into contact with a different culture. Their feeling of personal freedom is threatened by the many restrictions which accompany their refugee status. Many refugees may have had an ideal or goal in their life before they were forced to flee, which they will have to adjust to the new circumstances in which they find themselves. But, most importantly, they do not feel accepted and recognized as refugees and victims of violence. In Western societies refugees are not necessarily accepted as victims of political oppression, even when it is obvious that they have been the victims of violence. They are involved in a struggle for recognition with the authorities, which may be protracted and for which the rules are far from clear.

The feeling of not being recognized or accepted results in a sense of loneliness which cannot easily be abated. Loneliness, as has been mentioned above, is one of the factors related to suicidal behaviour.

Protective factors

The presence of the above mentioned factors in refugees points to an increased risk of suicide, but by itself cannot be taken to mean that there is a real danger of suicide. The majority of the refugees seeking asylum who requested assistance from the author had been able to control their self-destructive impulses for a long time. Although they had been traumatized and uprooted, they functioned adequately until the moment they finally lost their optimism about getting political asylum. How can their initial strength be understood?

The concept of protective factors (see, for instance, Kazdin, 1987), which was initially developed to explain individual differences post factum, might be helpful.

This author's experience with Kurdish and Iranian refugees seeking political asylum shows that in the case of every individual at least some protective factors could be assumed. Most of them used to have a broad repertoire of behaviours which they can call on to cope with difficult situations. From their life histories it could be concluded that, before they were traumatized by political violence, they were flexible, energetic and self-assured, and could always cope reasonably well with difficult situations. Apart from a few exceptions these refugees said that they came from close families in which they had a good relationship with their parents. Most of them had completed secondary school and seemed intelligent and articulate.

The fact that these refugees requested assistance (most of them did this in an adequate manner, without manifesting suicidal behaviour or threatening suicide) can in itself be seen as a result of such protective factors.

In the discussion about protective factors it has been pointed out that they should not be seen as impenetrable. Even the most resilient individuals can be broken. Or, to use metaphors which are often heard in this connection: even the strongest and most flexible materials can, through exposure to extreme and repeated stress, crack as a result of fatigue (Graafsma, 1987).

Given this, the therapist should take into account the possibility that refugees may have waited a long time before seeking assistance, and that when they do they may already have reached the point of exhaustion. Some of the refugees with whom the author worked seemed to be on the point of losing control over their self-destructive impulses, as well as over the capacity to distinguish between fantasy, flashback, nightmare and reality.

Signs of suicide risk

Refugees with psychological problems usually initially consult social workers or doctors who are not specialists in psychiatry and therefore do not have the knowledge necessary to make a psychiatric diagnosis. Indeed, because of language problems it is often difficult for experienced therapists to make a diagnosis. Translations of diagnostic questionnaires which relate to symptoms of fear and depression (cf. Mollica et al., 1987) may be useful here.

In this connection the above-mentioned publication on suicide among refugees (Curtis Alley, 1982) also offers useful suggestions. Based on research among Indochinese refugees who have made one or more attempts at suicide, its author lists the following factors which correlate with the risk of suicide:

1. The presence of a reactive depression, related to the loss of a familiar environment, alienation from the native country, changes in socio-economic status and forced settlement in a different culture.
2. The loss of someone who was important, through death, divorce or abandonment. In the case of children and adolescents this includes forced separation from parents and the fear of never seeing them again.
3. The feeling of not having a goal in life, that everything is meaningless.
4. Feelings of anger or rage. In addition to this, the general literature on suicide (Diekstra, 1983) points to two factors which are related to increased suicide risk:
5. Earlier attempts at suicide in a person's life history. Refugees can be asked about this, though caution is advisable. It is the author's experience that these earlier suicide attempts were mostly very serious ones, that occurred as the result of extremely traumatic experiences, which the individual had tried to repress. In such cases questions about previous attempts to commit suicide can evoke strong emotions, related to these traumatic experiences. In addition, some refugees come from cultures in which suicide is taboo and therefore not easily discussable.
6. Thoughts and images of suicide. It is the author's experience that in the case of refugees suicidal images occur mainly in nightmares, for instance nightmares in which they are invited to commit suicide by friends or relatives who had been killed.

There was some doubt whether the term reactive depression accurately characterized the condition of the above mentioned A.Q. His complaints definitely suggested its applicability, but during the therapeutic interviews there were too many modulations in his mood to justify the use of the diagnostic label depressive disorder. During the first contacts A.Q. flourished, probably because he could at last tell his story. During the course of treatment, however, his nightmares became more depressive: he dreamed that he had been deported back to his native country, where friends were killed or committed suicide, and woke up crying. After the suicide of a compatriot and an interview with a government official, who made it clear that he did not believe A.Q.'s story, the modulations in his mood reduced and he became clearly depressive.

Dilemmas

The therapist working with suicidal refugees finds himself in a remarkable situation. There is not a very firm basis for effective therapy because the refugee may be deported at any moment, but the therapist *has* to make some attempt to alleviate the refugee's suffering. This is the first dilemma.

The therapist who wants to help the refugee will want to avoid suicide and decompensation, but he will feel helpless because he cannot influence the social factors which led to an increased suicide risk. If the therapist decides that psychotherapy is desirable then he encounters the fact that the minimal necessary condition for effective treatment is absent: as long as the refugee has the realistic fear of being deported he will need to use all his defence mechanisms. Also, the therapist cannot avoid contributing to the refugee's stigmatized status by making him into a patient: in many of the cultures from which refugees come it is considered scandalous to consult a psychiatrist.

The therapist may decide on one or another form of psychosocial and psychotherapeutic counselling, perhaps supplemented by medication, and he may present himself as a neutral sounding-board. He may assume that it is the refugee's own responsibility if he decides to commit suicide.

In the case of a serious risk of suicide or decompensation the therapist may consider the possibility of admittance to a psychiatric institution. But he should then realize that this admittance will not alter the factors which led to the increased suicide risk in the first place, and it can lead to increased stigmatization as well as increasing the fear of 'going mad'.

After they have made a diagnosis, recognized that there is a risk of suicide or decompensation and carefully weighed both suicidal and protective factors, some therapists may decide to abandon the neutral sounding-board role. If the client agrees, they may then contact the relevant government organizations and try to influence them by informing them of the refugee's psychological problems. In the Netherlands this usually means that the therapist, after consulting colleagues, will pass his diagnosis on to the Medical Inspectorate of the Ministry of Justice, with the request that the refugee in question receives a decision about his request for asylum as quickly as possible. Experience has shown that the said Inspectorate then acts adequately by advising the ministerial department involved to admit the refugee for humanitarian reasons. In most cases the result of this has been that the therapist then had more scope for therapeutic intervention, which in turn had a favourable effect on the client. However, in a few cases the therapist's intervention was not successful and the uncertainty continued.

When the therapist decides to contact government institutions in relation to a specific case he is dealing with he should, however, first carefully consider the possible disadvantages.

The first of these is that by making his diagnosis known to others the therapist may contribute to the stigmatization of his client, who may already be ashamed of the fact that he requires psychiatric help.

If the above-mentioned intervention is successful it may have consequences for the process of transference within the therapeutic relationship which could not have been anticipated beforehand. The client may come to see the therapist as extremely powerful, and this may serve to exacerbate his own feeling of powerlessness. He may come to resent the fact that the therapist did not intervene sooner. He may be so thankful that he feels very much indebted. In a few cases such feelings of gratitude led to the client offering the therapist a present. This was of course turned down, but it had to be done in such a way that the client did not feel offended. This may go wrong if cultural differences cause misunderstandings and the refugee may end up feeling powerless and resentful. Feelings of powerlessness, resentment or extreme gratitude toward the therapist, either separately or in combination, do not constitute an optimal basis for psychosocial assistance or psychotherapy.

Finally, other refugees may consult the therapist in the hope that he will use his influence with the authorities to help them in the same way, and when he does not they may feel aggrieved.

No simple rules can be laid down as to how to avoid the aforementioned dilemmas. Consultation with colleagues about each new case is both useful and necessary. Such consultation can help the therapist guard against becoming too protective or too involved. But in the last instance it is the therapist who is directly confronted with a suicidal refugee who must make the decisions. If he strictly adheres to his therapeutic role he will have to be content to wait and hope. In a number of cases in which the author decided to wait, the refugee himself came up with a solution: he quit therapy and left the country.

10 The children of refugees

Special problems of refugee children

The children of refugees are at risk of acquiring special psychological problems. These may relate to traumatic experiences related to the political situation in their native country, to the loss of a familiar environment, and/or to difficulties in adapting to life in exile.

Traumatic experiences   Sometimes the children of refugees have themselves been victims of violent experiences which could be called traumatic.

A.R., the 11-year-old son of a refugee from Africa, had been hit by two dumdum bullets during a shoot-out. His brother, who is two years older, was burned seriously when their house caught fire after it had been bombed. A.R. had nightmares.

Other children have witnessed violence in which their parents were involved. For example, they may have been present when soldiers raided their house, took away their father and maltreated their mother (see Santini & Escardo, 1981; Viñar, 1985 for a detailed description of similar cases).

B.R., an eight-year-old boy, was referred because of bed-wetting. He cried a lot, had temper tantrums and did not play with other children. The problems began after he had seen his father mishandled and arrested. Since this experience he had been very dependent.

Some children are primarily the victim of problems which stem from their parents' experiences with violence and persecution. When their father or mother are imprisoned, children may suffer emotional distress due to the sudden, involuntary separation. Parents' traumatic experience then have an indirect effect on their children.

C.R., a girl of 10, had been in exile with her parents for two years. Her mother claimed that she had changed a lot recently: she spent a lot of time in her room, was rude to her mother and did poorly at school. Inquiries revealed that she had good contact with her classmates at school and the teachers had no complaints about her behaviour. But serious problems had arisen between her parents: her mother had difficulty adapting to life in exile and she reproached her husband, who had been seriously maltreated during his detention, for getting involved in politics.

The loss of a familiar environment   For almost all children of refugees, moving to another country means that they have to leave behind relatives, friends, pets and other belongings to which they are emotionally attached. Moreover, they usually do not have the opportunity to say goodbye.

D.R., who was 10 years old, had lived with his grandparents for five years. When his parents began to have political problems they picked him up from school and fled to a neighbouring country, without telling the grandparents. D.R. had not had the opportunity to say goodbye, and the only belongings he had taken along were the clothes he was wearing.

Adaptation problems   In exile, the children of refugees almost always have problems adapting and learning the language. They have to get used to a different school system. Sometimes they experience racism. In their relations with peers they become acquainted with different norms and values relating to children's behaviour from those of their parents. If they conform to the new norms this is not always well received by their parents.

Because children learn foreign languages faster than their parents, they often have to play the role of interpreter between their parents and various institutions, which burdens them with various problems. All this taxes the problem-solving capacities of these children.

The literature which is relevant for the provision of assistance to the children of refugees is heterogeneous. A distinction can be made between that which is based on the experiences of therapists and social workers and that which is based on scientific research.

Children and political violence

The literature based on scientific research which is relevant for the psychological problems of, and therapy for, the children of refugees relates mainly to traumatization. In this research the psychological consequences of traumatic experiences are studied. In addition, many researchers devote their attention to coping mechanisms, which are important for the child's assimilation of traumatic experiences. The research relates to children of different ages who have undergone a variety of traumatic experiences (see Handford et al., 1986 for an overview).

Part of this research is directly concerned with the reactions of children to political violence. For example, in Denmark research was carried out into the psychological functioning of 85 Chilean children, whose parents had been arrested and tortured before going into exile (Cohn et al., 1980; Cohn, 1982).

This study revealed that most of the children had psychological problems, mainly relating to fear. They reacted with fear to intruding noises, such as the screeching of tyres, sirens or loud voices. Some were afraid of people in uniform. Many had insomnia, and when they did sleep they were disturbed by nightmares, which were usually about death, murder and abduction, with their parents as victims and soldiers or policemen as the perpetrators.

Some children started to wet their beds, or became more depressive and introverted. Others lost their appetite and had stomach aches or headaches. Concentration problems, poor memory and aggression are also common problems.

Research on the psychological problems of Chilean children whose parents had been the victims of political violence but who had not gone into exile, Argentinian children in Mexico and Chilean children in Canada produced similar results (see Allodi, 1980).

These studies also showed that the children in question were, given their age, very dependent on their mother. The seriousness of the symptoms seemed to correlate with the age of the child, the duration of the traumatic situation and the extent to which the family received support from the social environment. Extreme dependence in relation to the parents was stronger in children who had themselves been directly confronted with violence or who had been born in exile. In most of the families one of the parents had been absent, as a result of imprisonment or abduction, for a period of time. Children in these families had more serious complaints if they had not been told the real reasons for the absence of the parent.

According to Allodi, the absence or, in some cases, death of the father and/or mother as a result of political violence causes the child to lose his feeling of safety: the protection which (one of) his parents provided has disappeared. If one parent remains he cannot completely take over the role of the other. He will have his own emotional problems, fears and grief which he has to assimilate, and as a result will be less able to support the children. As a result the children will feel helpless and vulnerable; fear becomes the dominant emotion for them and it determines their relationship to other people.

In providing therapy for these children play seemed to be a good approach, particularly if the mothers played with their children. The result of play therapy was that the children were less sad, had more social contact and their self-image became more positive.

On the basis of later research (Allodi & Rojas, 1983a; 1983b; cited in Protacio-Marcelino, 1984) on the functioning of Chilean and Argentinian children in Canada it can be concluded that the psychological problems resulting from political traumatization hardly manifest themselves in children who feel protected by their parents or parent substitutes.

Chilean psychologists have attempted to establish whether there is a connection between persecution by the police or the army and the mental problems of children (Alamos, 1986). For this purpose they developed a projection test called DITT. It contains scenes or images which are familiar to children but which are open to different interpretations, so that they can project the thoughts that are occupying them.

The nine children who took part in the research had all been exposed to police or military violence, and they interpreted the scenes represented in the test as portraying situations involving repression.

For example, when shown a picture of a helicopter all the children said that it belonged to the police and that they were coming to raid their neighbourhood. Not one said that the helicopter was just flying over. When confronted with a picture of a street scene all said that it was a demonstration or protest action. The thought that it might be a neighbourhood celebration or a procession did not arise. In another picture there were people sitting round a table and one chair was empty. Here the children said that a brother or grandfather was missing. In reaction to this many children expressed fear and the feeling of being treated unjustly (Perez, 1986, personal communication).

The coping behaviour of children of political prisoners was the subject of research by Protacio-Marcelino (1984, 1989). The children in her study manifested the following forms of coping: asking parents and other adults for explanations, aggressive behaviour toward those they considered responsible for their parents' arrest and playing games based on the theme of arrest and imprisonment.

Protacio-Marcelino found that some factors improve children's adequate coping behaviour: knowledge of their parents' political ideas; previous experience of arrest, detention and separation from their parents; an open and democratic way of family life; organized and supportive contact with those who have similar political views; participation in collective protest actions; and the support of human rights groups, both inside the country and in other countries. There are also factors which can have a negative effect on children's coping behaviour: financial problems in the family; poor health; an authoritarian educational style in which the father is dominant; conflict between parents; difference of opinion between the parents and other relatives; conflicts with neighbours.

Lastly, the nature of coping behaviour changes during the course of time. Immediately after the arrest of their father the children's coping repertoire was very limited. All their attention was directed to the mother and they demanded attention and explanations from her. The mothers found it difficult to fulfil these demands. During this phase many children manifested mental and physical symptoms. Later they incorporated their wider social environment in their coping behaviour and the symptoms abated.

Children and other traumatic experiences

This section is based on research on various forms of traumatization: natural disasters, nuclear accidents, war and the murder of one or both parents. Children may, as a result of experiences with extreme violence, manifest the symptoms of post-traumatic stress disorder. This was shown in research on children's reactions to a sniper attack on their primary school, in which one pupil was killed and 13 wounded (Pynoos et al., 1987a). A considerable number of the children involved had nightmares, intrusive thoughts and concentration problems; they were easily frightened, repressed their feelings and tried to avoid situations which reminded them of the traumatic event. It was also found that a number of the children manifested bereavement reactions: they dreamed about the girl who had been killed in the shooting, or they thought they had seen her after her funeral. The children hardly spoke about these experiences with adults. Although their sadness lingered for a long time, it was hardly manifested in their behaviour so that their parents did not notice and they had to cope without the support of their social environment (Pynoos et al., 1987b).

Two types of trauma

The empirical evidence about post-traumatic reactions in children has been reviewed by Terr (1991). This author divides traumatic conditions in children in the following rough categories: traumatic experiences that came as a single, sudden and unexpected blow (type I); traumatic experiences consisting of long-standing, repeated and therefore anticipated ordeals (type II); and traumas that appear to settle between the aforementioned major types, e.g. one blow creates a long-standing series of childhood adversities.

Regardless of the age at which they become a victim, traumatized children have the following characteristics: strongly visualized or otherwise repeatedly perceived memories, repetitive behaviours, trauma-specific fears, and changed attitudes about people, aspects of life and future. Repetitive dreams are not included in this list, because they are not often seen in children under the age of five. Infants physically demonstrate that they are dreaming by making mouthing movements or little sounds in their sleep, and toddlers may scream from sleep without awakening, but this kind of dreaming is often too primitive and inexpressive to establish that traumatic dreams are actually taking place.

Trauma-related memories seem to come to the mind of a child at leisure: during times they are bored with classes, at night before falling asleep, and when they are at rest, e.g. watching television. As opposed to adults, they rarely have sudden flashbacks while they are busy. Even very young children who are not able to talk about their experiences, may later play out or draw elements from their traumatic experiences.

Repetitive behaviour can be observed in play, even by children who have no verbal memory whatsoever about their traumatic experiences. The repetitive behaviour is a re-enactment of the traumatic event, and it may be continued, in a somewhat disguised way, into adulthood. Acting out experiences is usually an adequate coping mechanism for children, but in the case of extreme traumatic experiences it is not effective. Acting out (without therapeutic help) does not reduce the fear. In play, children never manage to give the story a happier ending than the one they experienced in reality. And they are not aware of the relationship between their play and the real traumatic events.

Trauma-related fears are limited to specific things. They are easy to spot, once one knows what the trauma might have been. These fears also may last many years.

Changes in attitudes after trauma manifest themselves in a limitation of the future perspective, as manifested in statements such as 'I live one day at a time', and lack of confidence in other people.

Children who suffered from unanticipated single traumatic events (type I) have symptoms that differ from the children who suffered from more enduring traumatization. The characteristics related to single shocking events are: full, detailed memories, misperceptions, hallucinations and mistiming (Terr, 1985) and belief in 'omens': the children believe that they can predict accidents and disasters because they are paranormally gifted. Terr (1983) did a follow-up study, five years after the event, of 26 children who had been involved in a school bus hijacking. At the time of the research some of the children were already adolescent. Nineteen of them believed that before the hijacking there had been a number of signs which pointed to what was about to happen. Five of them reproached their parents for not having taken notice of these signs. Ten of the children thought that they were capable of predicting events in the future and eight thought that their dreams had predictive value.

This belief can also be found in adolescent refugees who have been severely tortured or were forced to witness executions.

Terr explains this belief in prediction as follows: children who have been rendered totally helpless and placed in a frightening situation later try to make these experiences controllable. The child prefers to attach feelings of responsibility or guilt to the events than to accept helplessness and coincidence as reality (Terr, 1989).

Long-standing or repeated exposure to traumatic events may result in various emotional reactions: an absence of feeling, a sense of rage, or unremitting sadness, and, of course, fear. The absence of emotional reactions is the result of denial (the child tries to look normal, whatever has happened and avoids talking about himself), psychic numbing, self-hypnosis and dissociation. Rage may be acted out in self-mutilations, physically damaging suicide attempts, or antisocial behaviour. It may be covered by extreme passivity.

In addition to Terr's observations, it should be mentioned that the emotional reactions to traumatic experiences that are verbalized by children, are often contradictory. This is the conclusion drawn by Handford et al. (1986) on the basis of research into children's reactions to a nuclear accident. One of the children said: 'I think I will get sick and will have to go to hospital and die. But I don't really think about it.'

The emotional reactions of children to a single traumatic event may continue for considerable time. The parents in Handford et al.'s study had lost their fright reaction after six months, but it was still measurable in the children after a year and a half, even though the parents did not notice it. According to a study about the reactions of victims of the *Herald of Free Enterprise* ferry disaster (Yule & Williams, 1989), the majority of the children involved in this accident still showed considerable signs of psychological morbidity after more than a year.

After a single traumatic event, children report more distress when their parents are not present, especially when their parents also were involved in the traumatic event. The children seem to be aware of their parents' distress and try not to burden them (Yule & Williams, 1989).

The way in which these children react to a traumatic event is, when one takes a closer look, in some ways related to their level of mental development. In this connection, we refer to the aforementioned conclusions of Terr (1991) about post-traumatic dreams. Another example can be found in the study by Handford et al. (1986) about an accident in a nuclear plant. They observed that children who were older than 13 rationalized and intellectualized the disaster, and only those older than nine years had dreams about it.

Trauma often means loss. Eth & Pynoos (1984) investigated the reactions of children to significant loss, for instance the death of a parent. They conclude that children are capable of a wide range of grief responses, whose expression is influenced by the child's level of development, personality and cultural milieu. The tasks of mourning in childhood are similar to those for adults. The child must first accept the loss through reality testing and then tolerate the experience of pain and grief. The child may feel sad, angry, guilty, lonely, tired, confused, preoccupied and perhaps even ill. Because young children have a short attention span, their sadness or pain may go unnoticed by their adult caretakers. In addition to this they are sometimes excluded from the adult bereavement rituals.

When the loss is discussed with them in a proper way many children will express grief and seek comfort and support.

Children's reaction to single traumatic experiences differ in some respects from those of adults: amnesia relating to the traumatic events does not occur in children, they do not manifest psychic numbing, though they do try to avoid feelings related to the traumatic events (Eth & Pynoos, 1984); they do not experience sudden, unexpected visual flashbacks of the traumatic event that interrupt their behaviour or disrupt their concentration, and their work performance rarely suffers for more than a few months after the trauma (Pynoos et al., 1987b).

Post-traumatic reactions in children and the responses of their parents

Children's emotional reactions to traumatic experiences are often more intense than their parents realize (Handford et al., 1986). Rigamer (1986) found that parents' reactions to their children's stories frequently entailed denying the seriousness of the situation. They tried to comfort the children in spite of the dangers which the latter had perceived correctly. They often did not let the children finish their story. Rigamer thinks that the parents thereby unconsciously undermined their children's normal coping behaviour. Their comforting words only caused the children to become more distressed.

Children's emotional reactions to traumatic experiences are less intense if their parents show the same feeling and reactions with regard to the events. This can be concluded from the research on the effects of the nuclear accident already mentioned above (Handford et al., 1986). Children whose parents react differently are more distressed than those whose parents agree.

Research on Australian families who had been involved in a fearful forest fire has shown that if the parents cannot cope adequately with the traumatic experiences this will be reflected in the reactions of their children (Cowell McFarlane, 1987). The extent to which children exhibited post-traumatic behaviour was determined more by the over-protective, fear-inducing behaviour of the mother than by the real effects of the fire. Galante & Foa (1986) studied the effects of an earthquake in Italy. They concluded that children were in a better position to cope with the effects of the disaster if relatives were present to give them emotional support. Reverting to a normal daily routine and having the opportunity to talk about their experiences and feelings also contributed to their ability to cope with the events.

Post-traumatic reactions and other factors

Some children do not, at least in the short term, seem to be affected by an experience which could be considered traumatic in the extreme: the murder of one of the parents, whereas others show the symptoms of post-traumatic stress disorder. Malmquist (1986) studied 16 children who had lost a parent in this way and concluded that those who had a well developed sense of self-respect and self-confidence before the event found it easier to cope with the resulting fear and grief. He assumes that self-respect and self-confidence develop as a result of painful experiences which are less serious and in which a parent or parent figure gave emotional support.

The child's mental health prior to traumatic experience also influences his post-traumatic reactions. Handford et al. (1986) found that the children who had a psychiatric disturbance before the nuclear accident were the ones who showed the strongest shock reactions afterwards.

Delayed or disturbed development

Research on the functioning of 120 Israeli boys who were between one and three years old during the six-day war in 1967 has shown that traumatic experiences can also affect development (Meier, 1985). These boys had experienced a period of intense stress, during which their fathers had been absent for military service. When compared with a control group of boys who had been born later they were found to be slow in toilet-training and learning to talk. They also had more eating disorders, more family conflicts and later more problems at school.

Newman (1976) studied the effects of a serious flood in which many people were killed. He concluded that children born after the disaster, of parents who had experienced it, also showed signs of delays in their development.

Summary

Research on the victims of political violence and disasters has shown that the negative effects of traumatic experiences are not always demonstrable. When they are they may take various forms in children, and some of the symptoms point to delayed development or regression. The symptoms in children only partially overlap those in adults. They may develop in the short term or the long term, and can even appear in children who were born after the traumatic events. Fear is the most important underlying emotion, together with grief, aggression and, in the case of political violence, the feeling of having been treated unjustly. The way in which the child copes with these emotions depends on the stage of development he has reached. The intensity of the child's feelings are sometimes underestimated by the parents.

The seriousness of the child's complaints depends on his mental health prior to the traumatic experience, and on personality variables such as self-respect and self-confidence. Emotional support from his social environment is also important.

In relation to all these factors the family in which the child grows up plays a decisive role: a traumatized child places greater demands on the family. In the words of Anthony (1986): 'In situations of intense fear there are no children; only children in their family.'

The experiences of therapists and social workers

The practical experiences which are relevant for providing assistance to the children of refugees, and which are available in written form, can be divided into three categories: experiences with Latin American children, experiences with the children of Second World War victims, and experiences with children who have been involved in extremely violent or otherwise traumatic incidents.

Latin American children

Relatively little has been published on therapists' experiences with children who are victims of political violence. The material which is available is, with a few exceptions, from Latin America or concerns the children of Latin American refugees. The articles in question are mainly concerned with the children's problems, the relation to their family, the goals of therapy and the methods used.

The children's problems   The Chilean institute Fundación para la Protección de la Infancia dañada por los Estados de Emergencia (PIDEE) [Foundation for the Protection of Children Damaged by the State of Emergency] (see for example Alamos, 1986; Herrera Rivera, 1986; Van der Veer, 1987d) is specialized in treating children (and families) who have fallen victim to political violence and repression. These children often have a negative self-image: since their traumatic experiences they feel inferior and dumb and do not think it is worthwhile for anyone to like them. They place high demands on themselves and feel guilty because they cannot fulfil these demands. Although, their social behaviour, both inside and outside the family, seems to have changed. The children isolate themselves, are aggressive and intolerant or extremely dependent and uncertain. Their achievements at school have also deteriorated. Moreover, the children's picture of the future, if they dare to think about the future, is coloured by fear and desperation, or by the resolve to see justice victorious.

Children from Latin American refugees in Denmark have the same kind of problems (Lukmann & Mortensen, 1988). Many of these children also suffer from anxiety symptoms and somatic complaints such as stomach ache. In such cases it is difficult to determine the source of the symptoms: the confrontation with political violence, trans-generational traumatization or the stresses of life in exile.

Eth & Pynoos (1984) sum up the problems of refugee children from El Salvador. Most importantly, they noted long-term impairment in remote memory: the children were often not even able to relate their traumatic experiences in the proper chronological sequence. Their results at school were poor, which points to a disturbance of other cognitive functions. Some children come from rural areas where youngsters below the age of 14 were being trained and armed for combat. Many of them exhibited several incapacitating avoidance behaviours after arriving in the United States. The continual witnessing of violence is, according to Eth & Pynoos, not an adequate basis on which to gain control over one's own drives and impulses. They noted that these children often behaved anti-socially.

Children's problems in relation to the family   In addition to the contribution of Becker & Weinstein (1986) that was discussed in chapter 2, interesting observations can be found in the work of Reinoso (1985) about families that have been traumatized by political violence. It is mainly concerned with families in which the father is missing or has been murdered. The children in these families manifest the expected nightly fears, that can be partially interpreted as the fear of growing up and meeting the same fate as their father. In addition, the mother is often ambivalent towards the death or disappearance of her husband—particularly if she did not feel involved in his political activities—but the negative side of this ambivalence is not expressed, though it is felt by the children. At the same time, the children tend to idealize their missing or dead father. This all results in an ambivalent relationship between mother and children.

The goals and method of therapy   Some of the articles from Latin American or on the children of Latin American refugees can be characterized as case studies, and as such they are difficult to compare. They are also not very explicit about the therapeutic methods used. They are interesting for us because of their different therapeutic goals.

In some cases the therapist directs his attention to the child as an individual. This may be to help the child cope with a distrust of adults, resulting from a series of traumatic experiences which led to the breakup of the family (Luna, 1982), or with the memories of parents being tortured while the child watched and identified with them (Viñar, 1985). In other cases the therapist directs his attention to the whole family. He may explain that the problems of the child who is considered to be 'abnormal' are related to the experiences of the whole family, and the effects of these experiences on their situation (Schwartz, 1982).

Group-play therapy (Viñar, 1985) constitutes another approach, aimed at promoting the assimilation of current fear-inducing experiences.

Experiences with the children of war victims

The experiences of therapists and social workers in helping children to cope with war traumas are also relevant for providing assistance to the children of refugees. According to various authors (e.g. Levine, 1982), traumatization negatively effects the parents' capacity to bring up their children. Traumatization in parents may also be manifested in their mood and behaviour; they may become chronically dejected or be unable to keep aggressive impulses under control. Such moods or behaviour patterns may evoke similar moods and behaviour patterns in the children, or other patterns of more or less adequate coping behaviour.

When parents are secretive about traumatic events they can still have an effect on the emotional climate in the family, but in a way that the child does not understand and can therefore interpret wrongly.

E.R.'s father had spent some time in prison, where the sanitary conditions were so bad that they formed a serious threat to health. He hardly discussed his experiences with his wife. E.R. was born after his father had been released, and in the following years his father became very concerned about E.R.'s bodily hygiene. The problems for which E.R. sought help as an adolescent were coloured by the need for physical affection and he experienced his own body as 'dirty'.

In connection with the transfer of the effects of traumatic experiences from parents to children Van Blaaderen-Stok (1986) claims that children perceive —unconsciously—the feelings which their parents have as a result of traumatization but which they never express. The children experience these feelings as their own. Family therapy can serve to make this unconscious transfer of parents' feeling to their children and the internalization of these feelings by the children explicit, thus making prevention possible.

Children and extreme violence

From the publications about the treatment of children who witnessed extreme violence two very different examples will be reviewed. The first is a study of the application of behaviour therapy to a child who, at the age of four, witnessed a bombing in which many people were wounded (Saigh, 1986). It is a description of the treatment of a six-year-old boy from Lebanon who suffered from memory impairment, frequent outbursts of anger, depressive symptoms, attacks of fear and nightmares. The method used was *in vitro flooding*. The treatment, which lasted for 10 sessions, led to the disappearance of the symptoms. Unfortunately, it is not clear from Saigh's article whether the bombing was a relatively isolated traumatic experience or whether it was part of a larger process of traumatization. He also does not mention whether and how the boy's parents were involved in the traumatic experience. As a result it is not clear what possibilities Saig's method offers for the treatment of the children of refugees.

Children who have been the victims of direct or indirect traumatization are generally treated with the usual methods of child psychotherapy and family therapy. In the treatment of these children play therapy has an important place next to family therapy. Death, soldiers, prison and torture are the most important elements in these children's play.

It is not often that the specific content of traumatized children's problems has led to a description of specific methods. The work of Pynoos & Eth (1986) forms an interesting exception. These authors describe a method which can be used to talk to children about traumatic or violent experiences, such as the murder of one of their parents, in which they were involved.

In their approach it is important that the therapist speaks to the child as soon as possible after the traumatic events. However, in practice, with refugee children, the traumatic events in question usually took place a long time ago and are therefore more difficult to discuss (cf. Bleich, Garb & Kottler, 1986). For this reason Pynoos & Eth's method cannot be adopted without modifications. But it does give a good overview of matters that can be covered once the discussion of traumatic experiences is under way.

Pynoos & Eth consider their method suitable for children from three to 15 years old. They speak to the children individually, i.e. in the absence of relatives or caretakers. The sessions generally last for about an hour and a half.

They describe their method as a sequence of three phases. In the first phase of the interview the therapist gives the child the task of making a drawing. Their instructions are: 'Draw whatever you like, but something you can tell a story about.' Their experience is that the traumatic experiences are so dominant that they will be represented in one way or another in the drawing or accompanying story.

On the basis of the child's drawing and story the therapist attempts to get a picture of the emotional meaning that the traumatic experience has for the child, and of the coping and defence mechanisms the child utilizes in order to keep going and not be overcome by fear. In this connection children in this phase of therapy can be divided into four groups.

The first group of children fantasizes about a happier end to their story. A second group ignores things which remind them of the traumatic events, for example by not mentioning part of the drawing in their story. In the third group the children relate what they have experienced immediately, without showing any emotions. In their stories various details are excluded. In the fourth group the children avoid talking about what has happened by worrying about possible dangers in the future.

In the second phase of the interview the therapist discusses the child's traumatic experiences directly. He does this by taking one aspect of the drawing, relating it to the traumatic event and attempting to articulate the *wishes* or *desires* which are expressed in it. For example: 'I'll bet you wish that your father could have been saved at the end', in the case of a child who fantasized about a happy ending; or: 'I'll bet you wish that by saying what happened over and over again, you would get used to it', in the case of a child who told his story without any apparent emotion; or: 'I'll bet you wish that your father were still here to protect you'. in the case of a child who did not say anything about his traumatic experiences but only mentioned possible future dangers.

Such interventions often lead to strong emotional reactions on the part of the child. In an atmosphere of emotional support the therapist can then ask the child to tell him about his experiences. Toys (dolls, weapons) may also be of some help. The child is encouraged to focus attention on what happened when physical injury was caused: the punch, the stab, the moment of rape. The therapist asks about various perceptions, including sounds and other physical sensations. It is important to be aware of details to which the child attaches special meaning. The therapist can then ask the child what he considered to be *the worst moment.*

The next topic concerns the *explanations* which the child gives for his experiences. This entails such questions as: 'Why would somebody do something like that?' In the case of older children their behaviour during the traumatic events, and possible alternatives, given the situation, can become a topic of conversation. Then the feelings of the child towards those responsible can be discussed.

This second phase of the interview is concerned with emotional assimilation, getting an integrated picture of what has happened and differentiating between the perpetrator, the victim and the child as witness. The discussion of a traumatic experience can then lead on to the revelation of other traumatic experiences or nightmares which are related to these events.

Finally, the therapist can discuss the child's *fears and worries about the future.*

According to Pynoos & Eth, the third phase in the interview with traumatized children begins when therapist and child can look back on what has preceded. The therapist can then emphasize how understandable and realistic the child's reactions were. The original drawing and accompanying story is then related to subsequent discussions.

The therapist also emphasizes that feelings of fear, grief, anger and helplessness were justified. He explained that memories of traumatic experiences, and related emotions, will occasionally return, and he points to the possibilities for the child to obtain emotional support in his immediate social environment. The therapist may praise the child for his courage in discussing his experiences. He may also ask the child which aspects of therapy have helped him and which have not. Pynoos & Eth state: 'As we end the interview we give expression of our respect for the child and the privilege of having shared the interview experience with him.'

Conclusion

The following goals determine the therapeutic process:

1. Promoting coping behaviour, in the child and, where possible, in other members of the family
2. Offering a protective situation to the child, to one or more members of his family or to the family as a whole, in which feelings related to traumatic experiences can be assimilated and, partly as a result of the therapist's explanations, cognitive restructuring can take place
3. Promoting self-confidence and self-esteem in the child and other members of the family
4. Promoting communication and mutual understanding in the family
5. The prevention of transference of traumatization from parents to children.

These goals stem from the development-psychological assumption that child therapy is not only concerned with solving a current problem, but also with restarting a development process which has, in some respects, been arrested. This assumption also forms the basis for therapy for adolescents and young adults, which will be discussed in the next chapter.

11　Adolescents and young adults

Exile and/or trauma

The adolescents and young adults with whom the therapist working with refugees comes into contact can be divided into two groups. The first group contains those who have been the direct victims of traumatization during or before adolescence. Their traumatic experiences interfere or interfered with their psychological development during adolescence. Their problems may be characterized as the 'normal' problems of refugees, but can be understood better by viewing them against the background of the phase of life in which these refugees found themselves at the time of traumatization, and the developmental task they are facing at the moment they are requesting assistance.

The second group consists of adolescents and young adults whose parents are refugees. Many of them have not undergone traumatic experiences directly, although they may have suffered indirectly in cases where their parents were traumatized. However that may be, in their case the developmental tasks of adolescence are complicated by their position as a member of a family of exiles.

Adolescents and trauma

There is not much literature on adolescents and young adults who have been directly traumatized, based on scientific research. So the work of Kinzie et al. (1986) and Sack et al. (1986) can be seen as pioneering. Both publications are concerned with research on the functioning, in the United States, of 40 Cambodian youths of between 14 and 20 years who had spent some time in concentration camps during the Pol Pot regime. They were compared to six Cambodian youths in the same age group who had also fled to the United States but who had not been in concentration camps.

The youths had about two years of primary education when they were imprisoned in the camp, where they spend about four years. They escaped and fled to Thailand, where they spent two years before being granted asylum in the United States, where they went back to school. The research was carried out two years after their arrival in the United States. In the concentration camp most of the youths had been subjected to forced labour: 15 hours a day, 7 days a week. They were separated from their parents, witnessed maltreatment and death and suffered hunger. Two-thirds of them had lost at least one member of the family (a mother, father, brother or sister).

From interviews it was clear that in 27 of the 40 adolescents with concentration camp experience a psychiatric disorder could be diagnosed: depressive disorder, anxiety disorder, post-traumatic stress disorder or a combination of these. Those who lived with other members of their family had less problems than those who lived alone or with Cambodian or American foster parents.

The symptoms hardly resulted in anti-social behaviour and were experienced inwardly. The youths tried their best not to think about the past and to deny its meaning for them. At school they were hard working and attentive students and their teachers did not suspect that they had such serious problems. Those whom psychiatrists had diagnosed as having psychiatric disorders did not cause disruption in class. They were often described as dreamy and introverted by their teachers.

Clinical experience

Therapists have also not published very much on seriously traumatized adolescents or young adults. What follows is based on the author's own experiences with youths aged between 14 and 25, mainly male and coming from Asian, Middle Eastern and African dictatorships who live as refugees in the Netherlands. All of them had undergone extreme traumatic events, most of them between the ages of 14 and 20. The mental problems of these youths were expressed in the form of insomnia, frequent nightmares, fear, depression, somatic complaints, fits of anger, sexual problems, concentration problems and study problems. These complaints can be understood as the result of the interaction of problems stemming from four sources.

1. The normal problems of adolescence and post-adolescence, particularly relating to becoming emotionally independent from parents, the development of a separate identity and an independent existence
2. Problems caused by re-activation, during adolescence, of the unsolved problems from previous development phases
3. Problems which stem from traumatization during adolescence
4. Adjustment problems related to life in exile, which may complicate the normal developmental tasks of adolescence.

A few examples will illustrate these problems. In each example one of the four sources will be central. The individuals in these cases have in common that they were detained for political reasons and seriously maltreated during adolescence.

A.S., a refugee from the Middle East, was offered exile in a European country. After spending a few months in a reception centre he was provided with a house in a new suburb. He was 19 at the time. He consulted his doctor about vague somatic complaints, and it soon became clear that he had various psychosocial problems: he felt alone, could not handle money and was unable to decide whether to look for a job or to study.

This refugee had the normal problems of someone of 19 who moves out of his parental home and becomes independent, but he got into difficulty because he did not have any contact with peers with whom he could identify, and he lacked the support of familiar adults. This was related to his status as a refugee.

B.S., a 22-year-old African student, could not sleep well and felt depressive after he had failed an exam. He asked the therapist for advice in a rather forceful manner.

It appeared that during the last year he had spent almost all his time studying. It was important for him to get his diploma, but language problems made this difficult. When it came to his study he imposed high standards on himself. This can be explained by his background: conflicts with his authoritarian father, who did not want him to study further, had an important effect on B.S.'s present state of mind. It seemed as though he was devoting his life to proving himself to his father.

In this case one can assume a neurotic development. The sharpening of inner conflict between increased impulses and the superego which is normal during adolescence has, in B.L.'s case, not led to a weakening of his superego, which is derived from identification with the father and is therefore rather harsh. B.L. has deflected the conflict between his impulses and his superego by choosing a rather ascetic way of life. This form of defence has been applied so rigidly and for so long that, following Anna Freud's (1958) criteria, one may speak of a neurosis.

In the meantime, B.S. was having difficulties with the language and, consequently, his study results suffered.

C.S., a 24-year-old man from South East Asia, requested help because he felt very shy when associating with peers. He wanted a girlfriend, but his relationships with girls in the country of exile always ended in a disappointment.

C.S. had undergone traumatic experiences when he was 18. He had experienced bloody battlefield events and his girlfriend had been executed for political reasons. His shyness can be understood because he was afraid that peers may ask him why he had left his native country. He was afraid that he would start to cry and that people would pity him.

His relationships with girls never worked out because, as the relationships became more intimate, he was reminded more and more of his girlfriend who had been executed.

In this example it is clear how unassimilated traumatic experiences impeded C.S. in carrying out one of the development tasks of the phase of life which he was in: the establishment of intimate relationships.

D.S., a 23-year-old African refugee, felt lonely. He had difficulty establishing contact with peers, particularly girls. Before he left his native country he had lived by himself for a while, and during this period he had friends and girlfriends. But he did not understand the way in which young people in his country of exile associated with one another.

For this refugee, a normal developmental task of adolescence in which he had been successful in his native country, became problematic in the cultural environment of the country of exile.

Three developmental themes

The problems of young refugees can, generally speaking, be grouped around three developmental themes: integration of aggressive and sexual impulses, separation from the parents and building an independent future.

Integration of aggressive and sexual impulses　According to Blos (1962) adolescence begins with an increase in the strength of both aggressive and sexual impulses. The first developmental task of adolescence is the integration of these increased impulses, that is to say, finding ways of dealing with them in an adequate, socially acceptable way. This developmental task becomes more complicated when the adolescent has undergone traumatic experiences, either directly or more indirectly.

E.S. was 14 when he was sent by his school counsellor. He had fallen asleep at school several times in the past two weeks. He said this was the consequence of his sleeping problems. He never slept more than three hours each night. He was afraid to go to sleep, because he often had horrible nightmares. The nightmares were about soldiers burning down the village where he used to live, killing the men, raping the women. The nightmares always ended with a soldier threatening to kill him with a knife.

E.S. had undergone some traumatic experiences, but nothing like what happened in his nightmares. However, these kind of things had happened in his country, and as a child he probably had heard many stories about rape and killing of innocent civilians.

The therapist started therapy, departing from the hypothesis that E.S. was entering adolescence, and was experiencing an increasing amount of aggressive and sexual impulses which would produce aggressive and sexual fantasies, which could easily become mixed with memories of the stories E.S. had heard about rape and violence during his childhood. He assumed that E.S. would probably have difficulty in accepting these fantasies, because they were associated for him with violent crimes against humanity.

After E.S.'s father had agreed that therapy was indicated because of the deterioration of E.S.'s achievements at school (E.S. did not want him to know that he was suffering from nightmares), therapy started. The therapist used techniques aimed at dealing with nightmares and controlling aggressive impulses, in combination with giving E.S. information about psychosexual development. The nightmares lost their sexual component immediately, and soon became less frequent.

Separation from the parents Adolescents are confronted with the task of becoming less dependent on their parents. This also applies to adolescents in exile, but from them the task is made more difficult by the fact that they are forced to leave their parents.

Young adult and adolescent refugees have often not seen their parents for years. Contact with them has been severed at a moment when the psychological process of separation and individuation, which occurs during adolescence, had not yet been completed.

These young refugees sometimes badly need their parents' emotional support. They are often very worried about their parents and feel they have failed in their responsibility towards them. Sometimes they have made promises before leaving —that they will finish their studies, for example—which they now cannot keep.

For them, contact with their parents is important, but difficult to maintain by post. In their native country letters may be opened by the authorities and the postal services are unreliable. Many of the letters never arrive. When they invite their parents to come and visit them in exile all sorts of problems relating to the application for a tourist visa develop. Sometimes these difficulties lead to an alienation between parents and children, which is incompatible with emotional independence.

F.S. was 21. His parents had to make great financial sacrifices to pay for his trip to Europe. He later tried everything to get them to come and visit him for two months. Their application for a visa had been made a year and a half previously and they still did not know whether it would be granted. F.S. worried a lot about this delay and could no longer concentrate on his studies. His parents wrote to him regularly and asked him how he was getting on with his studies. He increasingly isolated himself in his room and avoided his friends. He stopped opening his parents' letters.

If these young people do maintain contact with their parents they are afraid to be too open about their daily life because their parents might, as a result of their traditional attitudes, disapprove.

G.S., a young man of 24, who came from an Asian country, had a relationship with a woman who was a few years older and he wanted to marry her. He was afraid to write and tell his parents about her because he knew that, because of their traditional attitudes, they would want him to marry a younger woman. He felt unable to explain everything in a letter and was afraid that they would be hurt and have a bad image of him.

The feelings which young refugees have towards their parents are usually very complex. They miss their parents' emotional support but feel hindered by the expectations and norms which they assume their parents have. They feel guilty about not living up to these expectations or violating these norms. Some of them had to go into exile because of political activities of which their parents did not approve. They reproached themselves and thought: I should have listened to my parents. For some, political activities were the result of a first attempt to make an independent choice, but if the first step has such disastrous consequences the person is not likely to take a second flippantly. And if they have experienced that those for whom their parents have political sympathies did not shrink from the use of torture, then this will also influence their attitude to their parents.

Other refugees carried out their political activities with the approval of, or more or less under orders from, their parents, and reproach them for not having provided protection (though they are initially not aware of such negative feelings).

A visit by the parents can sometimes contribute to the assimilation of these conflicting feelings.

Building an independent future   Adolescents generally develop plans for their future. This is not easy for young refugees: they are usually very uncertain about their future. The future perspective which they had before going into exile has been destroyed and their world view and self-image have been shaken by their traumatic experiences. As long as their request for asylum has not been granted they are not sure whether they will be able to build a new future in exile. They fantasize about returning to their native country, but do not know when this will be possible.

H.S. was 25. He had been waiting for a decision on his request for asylum for four years. He had been having a relationship with a girl for three years and they were planning to get married. But he only wanted to marry her once he had been given refugee status because he did not want people to think that he was only marrying her to get a residence permit. In the meantime he often thought about returning to his country and so ending the long wait for a decision. This caused him a lot of worry, as a result of which he became more and more dejected.

The building of a new future perspective is more than just a development task for these refugees, it is also an aspect of dealing with the trauma. The refugee has to learn to live with the fact that some of the possibilities he dreamed about are, temporarily or permanently, closed to him because the situation in exile is not suitable for their realization and that the alternatives are not clear.

Studying or learning a trade can be important in helping these youngsters to build a future perspective. The parents of young refugees have usually had to make great financial sacrifices for their flight into exile. They have often given their children instructions to 'achieve something' (see also Bruers, 1985). These youths feel obliged to become very successful for their parents' sake. But the language barrier, the different education system and disturbed concentration as a result of psychological problems all impede this. They experience failure in their studies as a failure to live up to parents' expectations, and the parents—at least if the refugee can keep in contact with them—are often unable to understand the reasons. This makes the process of emotional separation from the parents and the building of a future perspective, which is better attuned to the new situation, more complicated.

Talking constructively about the future within the context of therapy is only possible once the refugee feels some degree of safety and certainty, for example, when he has been granted a residence permit and at least some of the traumatic experiences and related emotions have been discussed during therapeutic sessions.

Counselling and therapy

In providing assistance to young refugees the therapist is confronted with problems similar to those encountered in therapy with other adolescents. The most important problem is their fluctuating motivation: asking for and receiving assistance conflicts with the adolescent need to feel independent (De Wit & Van der Veer, 1989). Fluctuating motivation requires a flexible and accommodating attitude from the therapist.

I.S., a 20-year-old refugee, telephoned for an appointment: he wanted to come and have a talk the same day. The therapist agreed to see him but he arrived half an hour late. The therapist adjusted his schedule, so that they would still have an hour in which to talk. At the end they made another appointment, but when the time arrived I.S. did not show up. The therapist sent a letter inviting I.S. to come and see him, but I.S. did not show up. He telephoned an hour later, apologized and asked for a new appointment, for which he was on time.

I.S. who had undergone extremely traumatic experiences and was occasionally very depressed, did not keep two-thirds of the appointments the therapist made with him. Sometimes he took the initiative to make a new appointment and sometimes he left this up to the therapist.

In this way a faltering therapeutic relationship developed in which I.S.'s feelings towards his parents were discussed and, occasionally, aspects of his traumatic experiences.

Adolescents and young adults who came with their parents

In the chapter on the children of refugees it was shown that life in a military dictatorship can bring children into dangerous and threatening situations which may negatively influence their psychological development. These negative effects may only become visible years later during adolescence. Moreover, adolescents that belong to a family of exiles, have to face special adjustment problems and intercultural conflicts. The remarks about these points will be based on the descriptions of the problems and psychotherapeutic treatment of Latin American adolescents (Santini, 1986c; Bustos & Ruggiero, 1985; Castillo, 1984) in exile, a study of cultural factors in the treatment of South East Asian adolescents (Lee, 1988), and the author's experiences with adolescents and young adults from Latin America and the Middle East.

In developmental terms the problems of these young people can be summarized as follows. They have to carry out the normal development tasks of adolescence in an environment they experience as strange and sometimes hostile. In such an environment, a lot of courage is needed to experiment with independent behaviour and new social roles.

The processes of separation from the parents and identity development are complicated by conflicting feelings such as resentment and contempt on the one hand and solidarity on the other hand. These feelings may have reference to both their parents, the community of exiles and their native country. Some of these adolescents were not consulted about the decision to go into exile. They felt helpless, like packages being sent from one country to another. In some cases this helpless feeling has become part of their self-image and their attitude to life: they think that they have no influence at all on what happens to them. Because of this they sometimes have feelings of resentment towards their parents and they reproach them.

But these adolescents also feel solidarity with their parents, because they have the same cultural background, belong to the same minority group and experience the same problems in adapting.

Conflicts related to differences between the values of their parents and members of the extended family or the community of exiles at one side, and peers and educators that don't belong to the community of exiles at the other side, also complicate aforementioned processes. Because of their contacts with peers, teachers and other adults in the country of exile, these young people experience more liberal attitudes than those of their parents, for example relating the role of women, sex and the independence of the youth from their parents' authority. These adolescents often want their parents (or their extended family) to adopt the same life attitudes as those of their classmates and the same lifestyle as the parents of these classmates. But their parents tend rather to emphasize familiar attitudes and customs and expect their children to behave accordingly. This can lead to conflicts and tensions. In discussions with these adolescents one can often hear that they do not want to hurt their parents, but that they think they look ridiculous if they conform to their parents' expectations. They say that they feel caught between two cultures. To that extent their situation is comparable to that of the adolescents described in Mussen & Bouterline Young's (1964) classic study of second-generation migrants.

J.S., a 19-year-old boy from a Middle East country, complained that his parents scolded him for being too Western. His peers however considered him to be a cissy, because he did not like to participate in their rather sexist behaviour towards the girls in their school.

The psychosocial development of these adolescents can run along different trajectories. The following division (cf. Brassé, 1987; Santini 1986c) is just one example.

1. 'Modern' adolescents: they adapt very much to the dominant lifestyle in the country of exile. They speak the language and have good contacts with age-

mates outside their ethnic or national group. They reject most of the values of the culture of their native country.

2. 'Traditional' adolescents: they only socialize with peers from the same cultural background, reject many of the norms and values of the country of exile, and criticize peers from the same background who have adapted more to life in the country of exile.

    Some of these adolescents join political committees. If they do that, they may experience that their contribution to such groups is not taken very seriously by adults, so that they withdraw in disappointment. They sometimes notice doubts in their parents about the political ideals for which they had fought and for which they had ended in exile. At times they wonder whether they would feel at home in their native country. This all contributes to inner confusion and disorientation.

3. 'Converted' adolescents, who for some time adapted very much to life in the country of exile, but after some time returned to traditional values.

4. Adolescents that live 'between' two cultures: in external matters they follow the trends in the country of exile, but apart from that they conform very much to what is expected from them by their traditional parents. They tend to spend most of their leisure time with peers that have the same background. They often have little education, cannot find a job, and feel discriminated against. They seem to balance between the demands of two cultures and try to please both sides.

5. 'Marginal' adolescents. It seems that for these adolescents, the normal skirmishes with their parents have become exacerbated because of their living in exile. They resulted in the adolescent running away from home. Most of these 'marginals' are boys who have developed an antisocial behaviour pattern, which may include alcohol or drug abuse.

6. Adolescents that retreat in social isolation from their peers. This usually results in psychological problems.

For these adolescents, the self-confidence necessary for identity development is undermined by study problems and youth unemployment among ethnic minorities. These adolescents have to study in a different language than the language spoken at home. They also have to adapt to different teaching methods. Because of language problems studying requires a lot of effort and as a result they often end up not achieving what they are capable of, given their intelligence. This diminishes their motivation to continue studying and as a result their achievements suffer further. The result is reduced self-confidence and an undervaluation of their capabilities. Sometimes they even drop out of school.

Not speaking the language fluently and without qualifications, foreign youths find it more difficult to get jobs than their indigenous peers. The possibilities available are heavy, dirty jobs, or illegal jobs which are underpaid and uninsured. Most of these youths are not keen on this and just hang around getting bored and thinking up fantastic plans instead of building a realistic future perspective. Their parents are not capable of really helping them in this.

Role reversal in their families may result in these adolescents adopting a pseudo-adult attitude that makes relations with peers difficult, so that they lack their support in the process of identity formation. Some of these young people have in some way taken over the role of (one of) their parents, either because their parents were suffering from the psychological consequences of traumatic experiences, or because they were slower in adapting to life in exile than their children. Moreover, these adolescents often feel that they cannot share the most important and drastic experiences in their lives with their new friends. This impedes the development of the kind of relationships with peers, based on mutual trust, which are so important in adolescence.

As a result, some of these young people continue to cling to their role as pseudo-adult and confine themselves to the family environment. They do not identify with peers and do not experiment in the way which is normal for adolescents. Consequently their personality development stagnates.

On the other hand, some of these young refugees adopt an exaggerated childish attitude, given their age, at least in some situations. They are afraid to make choices and decisions.

In summary, adolescents and young adults who have gone into exile with their parents and those who have themselves been directly traumatized and gone into exile alone, have extra problems in developing an independent adult lifestyle. Moreover, for some of them their future perspective is very limited.

However, many of these adolescents succeed, by themselves or with help from those in their social environment, in solving their problems. Sometimes psychotherapy—individual or in a group with other adolescents who have similar problems—can help them to overcome their difficulties. The therapy can be aimed at overcoming traumatic experiences, but should also have the objective of reactivating the normal processes of psychological development, by supporting the adolescent or young adult when he tries to regain control over his daily life.

12 Victims of sexual violence

MALE VICTIMS

According to what male refugees tell us, or to what is written in reports of human rights organizations (e.g. Comision de derechos humanos de El Salvador, 1986), sexual violence is part of the regular repertoire of crimes against humanity that are committed by the prison guards, soldiers and policemen in countries where refugees come from. According to a Danish study (Agger, 1989) 52% of the male refugees seeking treatment at a specialized centre for torture victims, had experienced sexual torture. Even in a European country like Turkey, sexual torture of men is anything but a rare incident. In a study by Yüksel (1991), of the 16 males who applied for help to the Psychiatric Department of the University of Istanbul after having experienced torture since 1988, all had experienced sexual torture, including application of electricity to the genital organs, threats that the victim will become homosexual and application of some instrument to the anus. In his study of 35 ex-political prisoners in Turkey, Kaptanoglu (1991) found a rate of 35%.

Sexual violence is one form of political violence that may have traumatized a refugee. Its special quality exists in the fact that this form of violence lays hold upon a person in matters which in most cultures are not easily open for discussion and surrounded by shame and irrational beliefs. For male victims, undergoing sexual violence may, apart from the effects that are to be expected as a result of any form of traumatic violence, contribute to serious doubts regarding their sexual identity, relational problems and disturbances in sexual functioning. The special impact of sexual violence, is thought to be a result of the intense feelings (including guilt, shame and self-blame, cf. Roth & Newman, 1990) and the moral conflicts in the victim that are provoked by sexual violence.

With regard to the quality of sexual violence, a distinction can be made between two forms: forcing the victim to take part in sexual activity, and genital torture (cf. Lira and Weinstein, 1986). One form of involuntary sexual activity, is anal rape. This inflicts physical pain on the victim, as well as a wide variety of confusing and conflicting sensations and emotions, like rage, disgust, and powerlessness. Although there is a popular belief that men with homosexual preferences will enjoy being raped, these victims also suffer when they are submitted to forced anal intercourse or any other form of involuntary sexual activity. In some countries (e.g. Eastern European countries during communist rule) it is more or less a rule that when a prisoner is known to have a homosexual preference, he will be raped by the guards.

During rape, the victim, whatever his affective preference may be, may have an erection or an ejaculation (Sarrel & Masters, 1982). This can be a very confusing experience, because many men believe that having an erection or ejaculation means that they have enjoyed the experience, which belief leads to feelings of guilt. It may be possible that some victims also have some feeling of pleasure while they are being raped, but having an erection, an orgasm or an ejaculation during anal rape in general can be seen as a pure physiological reaction that comes without the consent of the victim.

Other forms of involuntary sexual activity, like forced masturbation or fellatio, are not necessarily painful in a physical sense. But they also provoke a broad spectre of conflicting emotions.

Genital torture can be defined as the infliction of physical pain to the genitals which brings the victim to associate pain or panic with sexuality. Examples are: blows or kicks at the genitals, wringing of the testicles, and electric torture of the testicles. Both forms of sexual torture are often accompanied by suggestions of the perpetrator that they will have a detrimental effect on the masculinity of the victim, on his reproductive capacities and on his sexual functioning.

The consequences of sexual violence

If one looks at sexual violence *from the psychiatric approach* it may lead to various symptoms, including a reduction of sexual interest or pleasure, failure to attain or maintain an erection during sexual activity, premature ejaculation, delay or absence of an orgasm, and disturbing thoughts or feelings during sexual activity (e.g., fear of hurting or injuring the partner, flashbacks of the traumatic incident).

From a psychodynamic point of view the following can be formulated. Sexual violence is an interaction in which the parties involved experience conflicting feelings, including lust and aggression. Moreover, in male victims 'the incidents can provoke active sexuality, thereby activating castration anxiety, and/or provoke passive, receptive sexuality, thereby activating homosexual anxiety and identity feeling' (Agger, 1989, p. 309).

It must be added here that, from a psychodynamic point of view, the individual meaning of the traumatic sexual experience will be related to the individual's personal history, especially his experiences in relation to sexuality and the quality of his sexual identity before he was traumatized. Therefore, there will be important inter-individual variation with regard to such matters as castration anxiety or homosexual anxiety.

After being raped at the age of 16, A.U., who considered himself to be heterosexual before he was imprisoned, was afraid that he would not be able to have sexual contact with a woman and that trying it would probably result in a fearful, humiliating experience. But he never had fear of being or having become a homosexual. He said that he heard about boys at his school having a love affair, including a sexual relationship, a few months after he had been raped. He explained to the therapist how amazed he had been at that time, because he could not understand that a sexual relation between men could be anything else than disgusting violence.

B.U. was raped at the same age, but he was afraid that the experience might have made him a homosexual, although he frequently had heterosexual contacts after he escaped from prison. He said he had become aware of this fear for the first time after seeing a documentary on television, in which an expert said that some male victims of sexual violence become themselves sexual offenders.

C.U. was raped at the age of 22. He had considered himself to be homosexual since he was 18. The most disturbing effect of the rape for him was that memories of what happened sometimes provoked aggressive sexual fantasies.

From the point of view of family therapy, the hypothesis can be made that many men will be reluctant to discuss their experience of sexual violence with their partner. They are burdened with a secret, which will hinder the communication and contribute to relational problems. If the male victim has problems in sexual functioning, and his partner is not aware of the background of these problems, she (or he) may easily misinterpret them (for instance, the partner may become suspicious and think that the victim is having an affair with another sexual partner).

From a *cognitive-behavioural point of view,* the following hypotheses can be proposed. Sexual violence triggers intense aversive emotions such as panic and disgust, and disturbing thoughts. For many people, these thoughts and emotions are incompatible with sexual pleasure. These emotions and thoughts can become conditioned to certain stimuli that occurred during the traumatic situation. Occurrence of similar stimuli later in life, for example during sexual contact but also in completely different situations, may provoke flashbacks of the traumatic sexual experience which disturb normal functioning.

D.U. was raped in a police office at the age of 16 after being detained for political reasons. Fourteen years later, he was having a romp with the 10-year-old daughter of a friend. The girl accidentally hit his bottom. D.U. shouted: 'don't do that', and was startled by the rage he heard in his own voice. While telling this to the therapist, he recognized he had felt as if he was about to be raped.

Treatment: basic principles

Various forms of traumatization may eventually result in sexual dysfunction; so the symptom of sexual dysfunction does not always mean that the refugee has suffered from sexual violence.

When E.U. requested assistance, he said that his most important problem was that he sometimes failed to attain an erection when he was making love to his girlfriend. Although he had spent some years in prison during adolescence, he denied that he had suffered from sexual violence. In the course of therapy, E.U. talked spontaneously about many traumatic experiences and present-day problems. Impotence did not seem to be a very urgent matter, the most important disturbing symptoms seemed to be nightmares and flashbacks. After 10 interviews, the therapist reminded him of his problems in sexual functioning. E.U. then said that the problem had disappeared. He thought it had been the result of drinking alcohol before going to sleep, which he had been doing because he had difficulties falling asleep. As soon as his nightmares had become less, he had stopped drinking.

On the other hand, the therapist should be aware of the fact that sexual violence in prisons and police offices is not exceptional, and that when the refugee does not mention it after a first question, this doesn't mean it has not happened to him.

F.U. had been in prison for three years during adolescence. He said that he had been tortured, but gave a negative response to a routine question of the therapist about sexual violence. During the therapeutic sessions, F.U. told many stories about his amorous adventures with women. Only after a year he was able to tell the therapist that he sometimes failed to maintain an erection during sexual intercourse. He associated this with experiences he had when he was about five years old. After exploring his memories about the experiences, the therapist asked for a second time about sexual violence in prison. This time, F.U. described a severe form of genital torture that had resulted in internal bleeding.

Sexual violence is a traumatic experience, and treatment of the victims of sexual violence may proceed along the same variety of trajectories as the treatment of other traumatized refugees. So the techniques of supportive therapy may be useful, along with techniques aimed at such symptoms as nightmares and flashbacks, the testimony method (cf. Agger, 1989) or the techniques of uncovering psychotherapy.

The traumatic sexual experience is often an incident during a long process of traumatization. Moreover, the treatment takes place at a moment when the refugee has to deal with current acculturation problems and present-day difficulties. Therefore, the therapist should take care not to be too selective in his attention to this particular matter.

G.U., a refugee from a Latin American country, had been raped many times during detention. He sometimes had flashbacks, triggered by movies on television that showed love scenes. After a first discussion about his prison experiences, 10 of the weekly interviews were spent discussing a variety of present-day problems. After this, G.U. started to discuss his flashbacks, mentioning only the physical sensations. The therapist taught him some methods of gaining control over these bio-physiological reactions. After another 10 sessions, G.U. started to talk about his fears in relation to sexuality and his experience of sexual violence became the focus of attention in therapy.

Special supportive techniques

In the treatment of male victims of sexual violence, a complicating factor is the reserve against discussing sex-related matters in many cultures. For some male refugees, it is an extra threshold to discuss sexuality with a woman therapist; while others feel more awkward when the therapist is a man. Making a conversation about sex possible can be rather difficult, and requires a lot of tact.

Talking about sexuality can sometimes start during the first interview. This happens when the refugee himself stresses the importance of the subject. happens when the refugee himself stresses the importance of the subject.

H.U. obviously wanted to come to the point immediately, and get it over with. He had been referred to the therapist by a student counsellor. He had met this counsellor six times. In the last interview he had told him that he suffered from nightmares about his experiences with sexual violence in a police station. The counsellor then advised him to seek assistance from a psychotherapist.

H.U. told the complete story in 30 minutes to a therapist who was a complete stranger. Later he said: 'I had no choice, I needed help urgently.'

In other cases, especially when the refugee has other troubles on his mind, the therapist may prefer to wait until a therapeutic relationship has developed before he starts to discuss sexual violence.

In the case of I.U., the therapist suspected that sexual traumatization had taken place because, by coincidence, he was well informed about the situation in the prison where I.U. had been detained. However, he decided not to bring up the subject, because I.U. seemed to be very vulnerable. After a year, in which I.U.'s functioning improved, he cautiously started to explore I.U.'s experiences in prison. I.U. then confirmed that he had been raped.

In order to make a conversation about sexual violence possible, the therapist often has to take a directive stance 'in which he combines distance with empathy, friendliness with straight professionalism' (Tsui, 1985). This attitude can, to give just one example, be actualized by explaining to the refugee that in order to help him adequately, diagnostic information about very private matters is needed. The therapist may add that he is aware of the sexual violence that takes place in the police stations and prisons of the refugee's native country, and mention some examples. He also can express his understanding for the fact that many people are not very eager to talk about these matters. Then he can ask the refugee if he himself was a victim of any kind of sexual violence, or witnessed other prisoners becoming a victim of sexual violence.

It is important for the therapist to have some information about the nature of the sexual violence the refugee experienced. For this reason, some discussion of the exact nature of the violence is often indicated. If the refugee is not able to talk about (parts of) the traumatic experience, it can be helpful to instruct him to tell the story in the third person, as if he were talking about someone else (cf. Perren-Klinger, 1991).

As soon as it is clear which kinds of sexual violence the refugee has experienced, the therapist can examine whether the refugee is misinformed about certain things, or has questions he never dared to ask.

J.U. had been raped several times by a prison guard. After this, he had to be hospitalized because he suffered from prostatitis. One of the doctors in the hospital had advised him to avoid sexual contact for some time. Since then, J.U. believed that any form of sexuality, including masturbation and spontaneous ejaculations during the night, could be dangerous.

In this context the therapist can also examine the possible realistic components of the fears the refugee entertains about the consequence of sexual violence.

K.U., 21, had been sexually abused during his detention. He was aware of the fact that this experience had a negative effect on his sexual relationship with his girlfriend. He had even been able to overcome his shame and talked to her about it. Nevertheless, his behaviour towards her continued to be influenced by unpredictable spells of fear and disgust.

During therapy K.U. said that he had not discussed everything with his girlfriend. He had not told her that he was sometimes afraid of being impure and unclean and of passing this on to her through sexual contact. He considered this fear to be irrational, and a sign that he was going mad. Later it became apparent that it was related to the fear of being infected by the Aids virus. After he had undergone an Aids test (with favourable results) his fear disappeared and the relationship with his girlfriend improved.

Another important topic is the refugee's norms and moral values with regard to sexuality. It is necessary to explore this topic, because moral condemnation of certain forms of sexuality may complicate the exploration of the consequences of sexual traumatization, and because advice the therapist might consider giving in order to improve sexual functioning, should not be irreconcilable with the refugee's moral values.

In the case of L.U., who had been raped during detention, the therapist was hesitant to ask questions about his present-day sexual functioning, because L.U. seemed to avoid the subject. He said to L.U. that he wanted to ask him questions about this, but that, in order to come up with the right questions, he first needed to know something about L.U.'s opinions with regard to various types of sexual behaviour. Then he brought up the topic of masturbation, and gave a brief summary of the differences in opinion in the country of exile about this form of sexual behaviour. Then he asked L.U. about his thoughts about these different opinions. L.U. responded to the question, saying that he always had seen masturbation as a sign of moral weakness, but that he now thought that it was a normal thing. At the end, L.U. was ready to discuss his masturbation fantasies in relation to his prior sexual experiences, including the rape.

Discussion of the moral values about sexuality may lead to a discussion about sexual fantasies. A refugee may have fantasies that are coloured by his traumatic experiences. These fantasies often are not compatible with his moral standards, and may provoke an intense fear of being abnormal.

L.U. admitted that he had sexual fantasies about his girlfriend in which he actively approached her. This made him afraid because he associated his fantasies with becoming a rapist himself. The therapist then said that, as a psychologist, he considered sexual fantasies to be a normal and adaptive mental activity. He also said that fantasies can be coloured by memories, for instance the memory of being angry at the man who raped him. He added that fantasies are different from actions and that not every fantasy can or should be put into practice. He then said to L.U. that he had no reason to fear that L.U. would be unable to control his sexual behaviour, and asked if L.U. himself was afraid of losing control. L.U. said he wasn't, since he understood now what was happening.

For refugees who were traumatized during childhood, the sudden upheaval of sexual and aggressive impulses during early adolescence (cf. Blos. 1962; De Wit & Van der Veer, 1989) may even provoke panic.

M.U., a refugee from an African country, was 16 when his foster parents consulted the therapist. They said that for six weeks M.U. had been unable to sleep for more than one or two hours. He also suffered from nightmares and flashbacks. Psychotropic medication had been prescribed, but without much effect.

M.U. had been raised in a detention camp for political prisoners, in which he had seen many atrocities, including the rape of his sister and the killing of his father.

In two individual sessions, the therapist taught M.U. various exercises for quiet respiration and relaxation. In a session with M.U. and both foster parents, the therapist explained that all boys of 16 are bound to be very hot-tempered at times, and that they may be startled by their own aggressive impulses. Then the therapist said he wanted to say something about sex. He explained that all teenagers have sexual fantasies. He added that he had not yet had the opportunity to talk about these matters with M.U. but that he knew from other boys that these fantasies can become very confusing, especially if they become mixed with memories like the memory of seeing someone being raped.

Then the therapist added that he was ready to talk about matters like this with M.U. if necessary. The session was concluded with some pedagogical advice for the parents.

Three days later M.U. reported to the therapist that he had slept rather well the last three nights. Then he told that he had fallen in love with a girl he had met a few days ago.

After three months, he was still free of symptoms and functioning as a normal adolescent.

FEMALE VICTIMS
Mia Groenenberg

Political violence against women is often aimed at women who, either directly or indirectly, resist being in the harness. They may do this by actively participating in political resistance organizations or by expressing an attitude to the role of women which is not in keeping with the dominant norms. In other cases, violence against women may be aimed at obtaining information about the political activities of the woman's spouse or acquaintances.

Political violence which is used against women usually has sexual aspects. These may be expressed in the form of threats of rape, forced undressing or the performance of sexual acts. Rape is usually involved.

An indication of the incidence of sexual torture is difficult to get because the victims tend to hide this to avoid stigmatization. Of 20 female refugees from various cultures seen by the author during the last three years at least 60% had undergone sexual violence in one way or another. A Danish study has shown that of the women who were reported to a centre for the treatment of the victims of violence, 80% had been sexually tortured (Lunde and Ortmann, 1990; cf. Mollica & Son, 1988; Agger, 1989).

The consequences of sexual violence

The physical consequences of sexual violence for women include injury or mutilation, infections or venereal diseases, deflowering, and pregnancy, sometimes followed by abortion. Irrespective of the culture from which the woman comes, this is associated with great humiliation and the fear of permanent damage.

Looking from the various theoretical approaches mentioned in the paragraphs on male victims, the psychological consequences of sexual violence for women are basically the same. But on a lower level of abstraction, some special observations can be made.

The precise nature of the psychological consequences of sexual violence is related to the image a particular culture or sub-culture has of women and their social role, and of the relationship between the sexes. In some cultures, deflowering may result in the woman no longer being considered acceptable as a marriage candidate. In other cultures, rape may lead to a woman becoming stigmatized as a 'whore' and to her being ostracized by her husband and family.

From a psychodynamic perspective on sexual violence, Agger (1989) places the emphasis on the ambiguity of the interaction between victim and perpetrator, in which both aggression and lust can play a role on both sides. The connection which is made between sex and aggression during sexual abuse makes rape a complex experience which evokes strong feelings of guilt and shame. The ultimate goal of rape is to break the image which the woman has of herself as a person who can love and experience sexual intimacy (cf. Lira and Weinstein 1986).

Research has shown that women who have been tortured often have complaints, such as nervousness, insomnia, headache, depression, reduced self-esteem, guilt feelings, etc. Moreover, in cases in which sexual abuse was part of torture, more mental problems were found which interfered with cognitive function, such as lack of concentration, memory disorder, nightmares, intrusive thoughts, suspicion, delusions, etc. Such women also have more sexual dysfunction, namely sexual anxiety and avoidance. Three years after sexual abuse a considerable disruption of sexual functioning was still found (Allodi & Stiasny, 1990; cf. Lunde and Ortmann, 1989; Yüksel, 1991). How the process of overcoming the consequences of violence, including sexual violence proceeds, is dependent on a combination of factors. Firstly, the woman's own personal history, her experience in life and her ways of coping.

A.T., 23-year-old woman from an African country, had frequently enormous outbursts of anger, especially when she was treated in an authoritarian way. She attributed this to the humiliating manner she was treated by the soldiers in prison, who had forced her to dance naked and raped her. During the therapy she remembered how angry she felt as a child when she witnessed how her mother was beaten up by her authoritarian father.

A second important factor is whether the woman considered herself to be politically active and was aware of the risks of her activities or not.

B.T., an 18-year-old refugee from a Middle East country, was arrested by secret police because they wanted information about her brother. During the interrogations she was violated. She had never been politically active, nor was she aware of the activities of her brother. As a consequence of this violence her family advised her to leave the country. In the country of exile she got very depressed and asked herself why this had to happen to her.

C.T., a 25-year-old women from the same region, was an active member of an illegal political organization. She was indignant at measures the government took towards women and tried to make other women conscious about what happened. She was arrested, tortured and spent four years in prison. After her release she suffered from nightmares and attacks of anxiety. In spite of her symptoms she tried to continue her political work together with other women in the country of exile.

The way in which the woman has been socialized as a woman and the way in which she experiences her own sexuality, is also an important factor. All this is influenced by the values and norms of the family or clan in which she grew up. In this connection, the following distinction (Murdock, 1965; cf. Mernissi, 1985) can be used:

1. Societies in which there is a strong internalization of sexual prohibitions during socialization, such as in Western societies.
2. Societies in which the sexual urge is contained by the imposition of external precautionary measures, such as societies in which women are supposed to use a veil.

Mernissi (1985) adds that this distinction reflects a difference in view on female sexuality in such a way that, in the first case, women are considered as sexually passive beings, and, in the second case, as sexually active beings. If this hypothesis is correct, we may expect that in societies of the first kind, a woman that suffered sexual violence will be considered as a victim. In societies of the second kind, the woman can be blamed for the sexual violence she suffered. This may lead to a conflict with her social environment.

Women from Latin America   In Latin American cultures, in which the influence of Christianity is great, the male-female relationship is characterized by 'machismo', in which the emphasis is on the virile man, manly honour and sexual achievement. There is a double standard as far as women are concerned: on the one hand they should be decent, obedient and self-sacrificing, while motherhood is highly valued. On the other hand women are supposed to please men and function as a sexual object for them. Here the emphasis is on being competitive with other women with regard to physical attraction.

Sexual violence towards a woman means loss of dignity for her and her husband can experience it as an attack to his honour.

D.T. 25 years old, from Latin America, was picked up by the secret police and raped because she could not reveal her husband's hiding place. Her husband experiences her rape as a personal humiliation. She refuses sexual contact because it reminds her of the violence she has undergone; then he becomes aggressive and abuses her and the children.

Women from Islamic cultures   According to Islam, women are considered to be strong, threatening, sexually active individuals who should be kept under control in order to prevent them from tempting the men to forsake their social and religious duties (Mernissi, 1985). From this perspective rape is blamed on the woman herself and may result in social rejection (cf. Amnesty International, 1991). To avoid ostracism many women keep silent about rape.

E.T. was 17 when she was arrested by the secret police in her native Middle East country, because they were suspecting her brother of illegal political activities. During interrogation E.T. was tortured, and this included rape. After five days she was released.

After this experience she broke off the three-year relationship with her fiancé, whom she was shortly due to marry. She told him that she did not love him any more, but the real reason was that she was no longer a virgin. She did not think that she could tell him this because he would then either reject her as his wife, or he would marry her, but then she would never know whether he had done so from the bottom of his heart.

All this also applies to women who come from traditional African cultures with an Islamic patina, such as Somalian culture. In addition, women from Somalia and neighbouring countries have often also undergone a genital operation. Various forms of this operation can be distinguished (Thompson, 1989):

- *Incision*: making an incision in the clitoral prepuce
- *Sunna* or *circumcision*: removing the clitoral prepuce
- *Excision* or *clitoridectomy*: excision of the prepuce, removal of the clitoris and all or part of the labia minora
- *Infibulation* or *pharaonic circumcision*: excision of the clitoris, labia minora and labia majora. The two sides of the vulva are then stitched together with thread, or pinned with thorns, leaving a match-stick sized hole for the passage of urine and menstrual blood

Infibulation is widely practised in Somalia, Djibouti, Sudan and parts of Ethiopia and Mali, particularly by nomadic peoples. It is assumed that the practice of infibulation started in the Egyptian empire, long before the origin of Islam. In Somalia infibulation is carried out when girls are about seven years old. In the countryside the operation usually is performed by a traditional midwife. During the operation the girl is restrained by a number of older women. With a razor-blade, a piece of glass or a sharp stone the clitoris, labia minora and part of the labia majora are removed. The labia majora are pierced with thorns and then tied together with a cord. The wound is covered with a special oil and herbs to stem the bleeding. The girl's legs are entwined from the waist down to the toes, and she cannot get up for three or four days. She only receives a little fluid and soft food in order to keep the production of urine and faeces to a minimum. After this the thorns are removed and the legs tied more loosely. If the operation was not successful, i.e. if the opening is still too large, then it will be repeated. The mother and female relatives are usually present during the operation. In the city the operation is usually carried out illegally by health workers. They use a local anaesthetic, surgical instruments and anti-biotics. In Somalia it often occurs that women get the infibulation done after divorce or the death of their husband in order to have a chance of re-marrying (cf. Bartels & Haaijer, 1990).

Little is known about psychological consequences of circumcision. Some claim that girls look forward to it with feelings of pride and excitement, which give way to fear on the day of the operation. It may be assumed that these operations often constitute traumatic experiences.

Political violence in the form of rape is a traumatic experience in itself, which moreover leads to a reliving of the trauma of the infibulation or related operations. In some cases rape means that the effects of the operation must be violently undone.

F.T., 20 years old, from an African country, fled from her home city when it was bombed. She was picked up, together with other women, by soldiers and interned in a camp. During the day the women had to cook for the soldiers and at night they were taken naked to the soldiers' tents. She was raped repeatedly every night. 'The first time I tried to resist because I was a virgin and my vagina was still sewn up, but they violently opened it up. Afterwards I bled profusely, but it did stop', F.T. said. She also explained that she continued to resist and that the soldiers had shaved her head, stabbed her in the leg with a bayonet, put out cigarettes on her body and knocked her unconscious. F.T. was liberated from the camp after three months. She was referred to the therapist in connection with nightmares and problems in the sexual relation-ship with her husband.

Women from cultures influenced by Confucianism Although the author has some experience with women from cultures influenced by Confucianism, e.g. Vietnamese women, she never had the opportunity to discuss the consequences of rape with them. In the literature about this topic the following conclusions can be found.

In South East Asia the consequences of rape for the woman concerned are influenced by an image of women as the essence of purity, the pure source of all life (Mollica and Son, 1988). In these cultures Confucian philosophy strongly influences the relationship between men and women. The man has a central role in the family and the woman is subordinate. The woman is supposed to depend fully on her husband and her pleasure should consist of pleasing him. Innocence and naivete are highly valued characteristics in women. A woman should be a virgin at marriage. Reproduction is considered as the only purpose of sex (after Truong, 1989; cf. Ashman & Ngo, 1981).

Vietnamese women who fled without a partner were often raped during their flight. In refugee camps they often had to make themselves sexually available in order to obtain the necessary assistance and support from male compatriots (Truong, 1989; Van Willigen 1988). These women saw their traumatic experience as the hand of fate and as a punishment for mistakes in a previous life. Their compatriots considered them to be dishonoured and therefore not entitled to claim respect (Truong, 1989).

Rape and the relation with the immediate social environment   One consequence of rape could be that the woman becomes pregnant. Some women consequently have an abortion. In many cultures unmarried motherhood and abortion are not accepted and this may lead to ostracism and great shame for the woman concerned. In some cases the abortion itself is a new traumatic experience. When a rape leads to the birth of a child it can be expected that the mother and those in her primary social environment will have ambivalent feelings towards the child.

G.T., a 21-year-old refugee from an African country, had been arrested during a police raid. She was raped in prison and was pregnant when she was released. The baby was born in the Netherlands.

From the start, the relationship with the baby, a boy, was extremely ambivalent. When he cried she felt aggression surging up inside her. She doubted whether she was capable of bringing her son up properly and considered placing him in a foster home. When it appeared that this would be realized she refused to cooperate.

Many women who are raped during a raid on their house or in prison were not themselves politically active. They became victims because their husband, father or other male relative was involved in political activities. For these women rape means that they lose the illusion that they will be protected by the men in their social environment. Often very mixed feelings can arise. The rage that is evoked by the violence can, often indirectly, be expressed towards the husband.

H.T., 36 years old, from Latin America, was raped in her house by two men from the secret police in the presence of her husband and daughters, 12 and 14 years old, because they could not find certain documents which her husband was supposed to have hidden in the house.

She was referred to the therapist in connection with various tension complaints, nightmares and problems in the relationship with her husband. When he approached her sexually she saw in her imagination how he watched her being raped and she then saw herself through his eyes in that humiliating situation.

Often women have an aversion to sexual intercourse after they have been raped, even if, before the violence took place, they had a good sexual relationship with their husband. One of the reasons could be that during the husband's sexual advances the woman experiences flashbacks which are related to the rape situation. Another reason could be concealed anger towards the husband because the woman sees him as implicated in what has happened to her. All this may contribute to relational problems.

The problems which the female victims of rape have with their husbands sometimes have repercussions for the relationships in the family as a whole. A consequence might be that the woman clings more to her children or becomes overprotective of them.

H.T. did not discuss the violence with her daughters, but she behaves in an overprotective manner towards them. She must be continually reassured by her eldest daughter, as it were.

I.T. tried to avoid the aggressive explosions of her husband when she denied him sexual contact by sleeping with her son of 3 years old. Even in therapy she avoided the confrontation with the true nature of her problems by taking her son along with her.

It may be assumed that the feelings of anger which are related to the rape are transformed into an aversion to men in general. It is probably for that reason that many of these women initially want absolutely no contact with male therapists.

Consequences for counselling and therapy

Unlike male refugees, female refugees hardly ever mention sexual dysfunction as their main problem. More often they express their problems as problems with the children or with their husband. Therefore, their individual problems due to sexual violence could easily be overlooked. For example, it often occurs that a woman comes forward with the question of how to cope with her husband, who is suffering from post-traumatic symptoms but does not seek help because he is afraid of being found weak, or that she only mentions problems with the children that tempt the therapist to restrict herself to pedagogic advice.

Whatever problem a female refugee presents first, it is necessary to take into account that the woman may have undergone violence in various ways and that this is often not easily discussable.

In the first place, in some cultures people do not speak about individual problems since the collective experience is primary. For example, in Vietnam the word 'I' does not have just one single equivalent. The way a person refers to himself depends upon the relationship he has to the person he addresses himself to (Phan, n.d.). A woman may therefore tend not to express verbally her individual complaints, but accentuate her worries about the welfare of her husband and children.

Besides this, talking about sex is taboo in many cultures. For example in traditional Vietnamese society women are not supposed to discuss issues relating to sex, and metaphors and poetry are used to communicate such matters.

Moreover, women who have become the victim of sexual violence choose to keep this a secret because of the possible social consequences.

It sometimes happens that rape is only mentioned in a late stage of treatment. Sometimes the therapist suspects that rape has occurred but the client avoids talking about it. It is important to devote a lot of attention to the development of a good working relationship with the client and to emphasize that anything discussed will be in the strictest confidence. This is to give the client a feeling of security which makes talking about even the most painful, intimate experiences possible. A confrontational approach can exacerbate fear to such an extent that the client drops out of therapy.

In the first phase of treatment the emphasis will be on the situation here and now, including complaints and symptoms. If there are material problems then the woman will be shown how she can help herself and in this way become less dependent on others. Cultural differences can be discussed, as well as her youth, upbringing, etc. Gradually, emotional problems can be touched on, in relation to her symptoms, for example. In this connection, and also because her contact with her own body can be disturbed as a result of the violence, body-orientated interventions may be indicated.

These interventions include exercises aimed at relaxation, concentration, feeling one's own strength and limitations, and the channelling of aggression. Passive relaxation methods, such as the progressive relaxation method of Jacobson (1938), are less suitable because the fear of losing control may arise and anxiety might be induced. Exercises in which the client reaches relaxation through active, dynamic strategies are preferable (Yüksel, 1991). Physical exercises can be very supportive and can readily be done in groups (Santini, 1990).

Post-traumatic symptoms can be treated through such methods as described in Chapter 6.

If the client can share her traumatic experiences with the therapist then this may provide relief, but just talking about these experiences is insufficient to achieve a permanent improvement in the client's condition (cf. Agger, 1989). The theme of sexual violence can evoke a reliving of traumatic experiences which leads to increased fear. In order to overcome this fear it is important that the client learns to integrate these experiences in a vision of herself and the world in which she lives.

Agger uses the concept of 'reframing' to point to the fact that the traumatic experiences of victims of political violence need to be placed in a political context in order for them to be integrated. This reframing can occur through the testimony method (see Chapter 7). Because violence against women is closely related to the image of women in a particular culture, and assimilation of violence is related to the internalization of that image by the individual woman, it is necessary to devote attention to the way in which she has been socialized with regard to the female role. During this process other experiences of sexual abuse sometimes surface.

M.T., a 30-year-old woman from a Latin American country, had sexual problems as a result of being raped by a number of men from the secret police. During intercourse she re-experienced this and had complaints which suggested vaginismus, as a result of which she suffered pain. With mixed feelings she sometimes accepted the sexual advances of her husband. In the discussion of her sexual development during therapy it surfaced that she felt guilty towards her husband because of a sexual relationship which she had for a few years during her youth with two of her brothers.

It also occurs that the woman in question has never received any sex education and does not know exactly what has happened to her. Explanation is called for in such cases. An examination by a gynaecologist may be useful in order to check suspected physical damage. This should be thoroughly prepared in consultation with both the woman herself and the gynaecologist in order to prevent further traumatization.

If women have sexual problems with their partner the therapist may consider discussing the connection between the woman's symptoms and her experience of violence in his presence. This is, of course, only possible if the woman agrees. Many women prefer to keep the sexual violence a secret because of feelings of shame or fear of punishment, or because they do not want to burden their husband. Very often the woman first needs to restore her self-image before she is ready to discuss her problems with her partner.

With regard to counter-transference, it can be said that working with women from cultures with views on femininity that differ completely from our Western views, may raise ambiguous feelings in the therapist. This may happen, for example, when a female refugee tells the therapist that she wants her daughter to undergo clitoridectomy, or when a victim of rape asks to be referred to a doctor to have infibulation redone. The strong feelings connected with sexual violence also may cause the therapist to over-identify with the women as a victim, while failing to be an identification model who can assert herself and is able to discuss aggressive feelings and sexual desires. Lastly, the therapist may not be able to contain the feelings of helplessness that is demonstrated by the female refugee and wrongly or prematurely turns to a confrontational approach.

N.T., a woman from a Middle East country, had been tortured and sexually abused during a period of four years. She suffered from many post-traumatic symptoms, including panic attacks. She came to therapy regularly for a year, but was reluctant to discuss her experiences during detention. One day, N.T. told the therapist she had failed an important test at school. During the test an ambulance had passed, and the sound of the siren had triggered a flashback that destroyed her concentration. This story gave the therapist the feeling that she herself had failed. She decided to change her approach, from cautiously uncovering psychotherapy to a behaviour therapy (systematic desensitization), and proposed this to N.T. The next two appointments were cancelled by N.T. with the excuse that she was ill. In the next session it turned out that nightmares and flashbacks had increased after the last interview. This had kept N.T. from travelling to the therapist's office.

The therapist interpreted N.T.'s behaviour as a sign that she had been experienced as a person who causes trauma. As a consequence, she put considerable effort into restoring the relationship with N.T. She gave up the desensitization plan, and decided that the most important contribution she could give to N.T.'s well-being at that moment was offering her a space where, for one hour a week, she could feel safe.

13 The consequences of working with refugees for the helping professional

Burnout, counter-transference and vicarious traumatization

Every mental health professional hears sad and unpleasant stories whatever the background of his clients. That is part of his job. Depending on the nature of the institution for which the clinician works, the type of assistance he provides and the background of his clients, he will hear more unpleasant stories or need to go into them more deeply. In the work with refugees, the helping professional will certainly get his piece of the cake, and should be prepared for the psychological consequences of eating it.

In the international literature (Van der Ploeg & Vis, 1989; Van der Ploeg, Van Leeuwen & Kwee, 1990; McCann & Pearlman, 1990) the psychological consequences of working with 'difficult populations' are often discussed under the heading *burnout*. This concept refers to the phenomenon that after a while some therapists become depressed, bored and discouraged. They show all kinds of somatic symptoms, and sympathy is replaced by a cynical and indolent attitude towards their clients.

On the one hand, this may partly be based on certain personality characteristics of the therapist, such as a tendency to perfectionism, a dedicated, idealistic attitude, the need to prove himself, difficulty in saying 'no', difficulty in delegating tasks and the tendency to have expectations about the results of care provision which are too high. On the other hand, burnout may be related to factors which do not have anything to do with the personality of the therapist and on which he cannot exercise much influence, such as problems in the organization for which he works, professional isolation and lack of professional success because the clients cannot really get better.

Because of the related descriptions, the concept of burnout offers a number of interesting points of recognition. For the enthusiast there is even a burnout questionnaire (Maslach & Jackson, 1986). But the burnout concept offers few theoretical points of departure, and only describes the most extreme and unfavourable consequences of working with difficult populations in very general terms.

Counter-transference   Another group of publications which can be considered relevant have counter-transference as key word. Counter-transference can be defined as the therapist's total emotional reaction vis-à-vis the client in the therapeutic situation (Kernberg, 1975; see Shapiro, 1984).

Working with refugees who have been seriously traumatized in the relatively recent past, but who did not previously have very serious mental problems, is somewhat different to working with people whose personal functioning has been coloured by traumatization from early childhood. As a result, certain forms of counter-transference which are encountered in the literature on incest victims, such as doubt on the part of the therapist about whether what the client describes really happened (Goodwin, 1985), are not relevant, or not relevant in the same way, in the case of refugees.

For those who work with refugees, the publications written from a psycho-dynamic perspective and relating to working with Vietnam veterans offer many points of recognition. For example, Haley (1974, 1978; see Schwartz, 1984a) writes that listening to stories of war crimes made her 'numbed and frightened', but that it also evoked all kinds of aggressive impulses.

In the literature on counter-transference in the provision of care to people who have been traumatized a narrower definition of counter-transference is sometimes used. The concept of counter-transference is then reserved for the therapist's emotional reactions which can be seen as the result of an interaction between the stories which the client tells him and his own unsolved inner conflicts. The client's horrible stories evoke impulses in the therapist which cannot be easily integrated, and against which all kinds of defence mechanisms, such as repression, splitting, projection and denial are brought to bear. This defence can result in various forms of dysfunction during the therapeutic interviews and in the interaction with colleagues (Benedek, 1984; Blank, 1987; Bustos, 1988, 1990a, 1990b; Chu, 1988; Danieli, 1980; Lindy, 1988; Shapiro, 1984; Schwartz, 1984a).

The counter-transference concept is part of a complex theoretical framework. In particular, it directs attention to the inner life of the therapist as an individual, but thus limits itself to the drives and impulses within the therapeutic interview. It thereby offers few points of departure for explaining changes in the therapist's behaviour and attitudes outside the therapeutic situation. The attempts by Bustos (1988, 1990a) to explain conflicts in a care-providing institution in terms of counter-transference and the defence forms which it evokes provide an interesting exception.

Vicarious traumatization The psychological effects of working with traumatized clients have been discussed under the title 'vicarious traumatization'
(McCann & Pearlman, 1990). The contribution of this approach consists mainly
of descriptions of specific symptoms which the therapist may manifest (such as
nightmares, intrusive memories and avoidance behaviour), the changes in
thinking which can be the long-term consequence of listening to horrible stories,
and the existential questions which they can place before the therapist.

The psychological consequences of working with refugees can, according to
the author's clinical experience, be elucidated by dividing them into three main
categories. These are: consequences for functioning during the therapeutic
contact, temporary consequences shortly after the therapeutic contact, and
long-term consequences.

During the therapeutic contact

Listening to a refugee who is trying to make clear how political repression and
the violation of human rights have dislocated his life, can at first lead to unusual
empathic reactions on the part of the therapist. These are reactions which are
based on normal sympathy, but somewhat unusual within a therapeutic
situation. For example: the client tells a moving story so vividly that the
therapist gets cold shivers, or feels tears welling up in his eyes.

According to Kernberg's (1975) definition of counter-transference, these
unusual empathic reactions could also be considered as counter-transference. In
any case, the line between an unusual empathic reaction and emotional reaction
which is strongly dependent on the personal idiosyncrasies of the therapist
cannot always be clearly drawn.

A.V. told the therapist a very moving story, while he cried. As the therapist listened
tears welled up in his eyes. The therapist empathized with his client's sadness, but
also experienced a kind of euphoria because he had been able to feel so close to this
client.

In addition, being confronted with all kinds of atrocities and injustices can lead
to the kind of inadequate reaction which can, in psychodynamic terms, be
referred to as counter-transference in a narrower sense, and which can be partly
understood against the background of the therapist's own inner conflicts. A few
examples: the therapist experiences an impulse to embrace the weeping client,
although he considers this to be an inadequate reaction from a professional
point of view. After a while the therapist may realize that he has avoided certain
questions, questions which were obvious given the objective of the therapeutic
contact. It is possible that he does not notice certain of the client's statements,
for example, statements which express aggression towards himself, or which
evoke aggression in him. It may also occur that the therapist ignores remarks

which, for him, refer to an emotionally loaded topic and adroitly (but not wholly consciously) changes the subject (cf. Benedek, 1984).

Something similar occurred in the contact with B.V., a refugee whom the therapist liked from the first moment he met him. In the course of 10 interviews, during which B.V. talked about what had happened to him in prison, the therapist came to consider B.V. to be a very good-natured, sensitive person. During the 11th interview B.V. told the therapist about his involvement in a horrible war crime. He described the event, but the therapist did not understand exactly what had happened. The therapist did not ask any questions which would have given him a clearer picture.

It may also occur that the therapist asks various explorative questions, but with a slightly reproachful, accusing, condemning or disapproving undertone, or that he is tempted to express an explicit moral judgement with regard to the client's behaviour.

The stories of traumatized clients can, as was mentioned, evoke strong emotions in those who listen to them. The therapist will generally attempt to keep his emotions under control to such an extent that he can keep his concentration on his client, or at least not burden the client with his own emotions. The behaviour which is aimed at keeping one's own emotions under control could be characterized as coping behaviour. For example, the therapist feels horror as a result of what the client has said, but puts this aside by consciously taking a few deep breaths. He then attempts to empathize with the client, and considers an intervention. Or, if he cannot manage that, he explains to the client that it has become too much for him for the moment and that he would prefer to break for a cup of coffee, or continue on another occasion.

Shortly after the therapeutic contact

During the discussion of traumatic experiences the therapist will sometimes succeed in setting aside the emotional meaning which the client's stories have for him; by simply concentrating on the client's feelings (cf. Draijer, 1987). Shortly after the therapeutic contact the therapist will have to assimilate the story he has just heard. As a result, he may find it difficult to set it aside. He will not be able to concentrate on other matters for some time. Or he may feel temporarily incapable of social interaction, because he cannot open himself up to others, particularly when they make a demand on his capacity to empathize.

C.V. had told the therapist a series of extraordinarily lugubrious stories about his experiences on the front in the war between Iran and Iraq. The interview lasted a quarter of an hour longer than expected. The next client, D.V., was in the waiting-room. He looked very unhappy. With the door handle still in his hand he told the therapist that his cat had died. Although the therapist knew from experience what it can mean to lose a pet, he nonetheless had difficulty suppressing a giggle.

It is also possible that the therapist feels a strong desire to share the story he has just heard with someone else. This may lead to an inner conflict: for example, if he does not want to burden his colleagues, house-mates or friends, while at the same time realizing that as long as it keeps bugging him he will not be very pleasant company. In the interaction with colleagues a sick joke sometimes has a liberating effect.

Furthermore, it is also possible that the therapist has difficulty recognizing certain feelings which he experienced during the therapeutic interview, such as powerlessness, melancholic pessimism, blood-lust and sexual aggression, and as a result cannot dismiss them from his mind. He becomes tired, feels tense and cannot concentrate (cf. Mollica et al., 1990). This may also be expressed in other ways, for example in reluctance to write a report after an interview, or great relief when a certain client cancels an appointment.

When the therapist recognizes such confusing impulses, emotions and alarming thoughts, this does not automatically mean that he can directly relate to them his contacts with clients. As a result he is not sure what to do about them.

Another source of confusing feelings is that the therapist is confronted with the client's feelings of powerlessness. These feelings are based on facts for which the therapist is himself responsible to a certain extent. For example: a seriously traumatized client on whom therapy has a positive effect leading to a reduction of symptoms, regresses when his request for recognition of his refugee status is rejected. The therapist not only feels hindered in carrying out his work; being a voter he may also feel partly responsible for the government policy which led to the rejection of his client's request for asylum (Van der Veer, 1989b).

Therapists sometimes have intrusive memories, graphic impressions and/or disconcerting fantasies of the traumatic events described by the client.

The last client of the day, E.V., looked miserable and agitated. The therapist poured a cup of tea for him and said: 'You look as though you haven't slept well'. 'I haven't', E.V. answered. 'I've had some more terrible nightmares.'
'Do you want to say something about them?'
'I can't remember very much about them. Except that I was back on the front. We drove into a village that had been attacked by enemy soldiers the previous day. It was a terrible sight. The main street was full of bodies. The enemy had apparently rounded up all the villagers and killed them. It looked as though they had been slaughtered with bayonets. There were the bodies of old women, babies, mothers with a child in their arms. They were cleared away with bulldozers. The gutters along the street had become rivers of blood.'
Two hours later the therapist was at home and supper was on the table. It tasted excellent. But during the washing up, when he saw the hot water run in crazy patterns over a plate, he imagined rivers of blood.

A therapist can also have nightmares about the violent events which the client has described to him (McCann & Pearlman, 1990), or be unexpectedly confronted with intrusive memories of violent events which he himself has witnessed. He may also imagine that it is he himself who maltreats or rapes the client. All this is experienced as confusing, disturbing and burdensome. On the other hand, such experiences can increase the therapist's capacity to react empathically.

The result of all this is that job satisfaction declines and activities which were previously interesting or even relaxing are now experienced as burdensome because they remind the therapist of stories heard at work. For example, the therapist develops a loathing for war films, avoids watching television documentaries about starvation and other disasters or has less interest in sexual contact. Some therapists have sleep disturbances and somatic complaints (Benedek, 1984).

In the long term

Working with seriously traumatized clients can also have long-term consequences for the therapist. For example, there may be a change in the cognitive schemes, attitudes, expectations and assumptions which he has regarding himself and others (McCann & Pearlman, 1990). Put differently, being continually confronted with the blackest side of human nature, the most horrible forms of injustice and repression, all thinkable and unthinkable forms of cruelty, as well as the most fateful forms of accident, alter the therapist's view of himself, the world and human nature. Moreover, his thoughts may be structured round images which are derived from the stories of his traumatized clients.

This may lead to a change in the therapist's attitude towards his work and his professional norms. The temptation to become indolent, not write reports, become prejudiced against certain 'minorities' among the clients, keep clients with serious problems or problems which are difficult to treat at a distance through rigid procedures or an uninviting attitude, etc., is sometimes great (cf. Bustos, 1990a).

A similar phenomenon can be observed among therapists who receive refugees—whose request for political asylum is still pending—for consultation, and are overwhelmed by the helpless situation in which their clients find themselves as long as they have to live with the fear of being deported. The lowering of professional norms then becomes visible in the following manner: the therapist concludes that he is unable to help these refugees with the means at his disposal. He fails to make a detailed study of either the client's problems, capacities and problem-solving skills, or of the point of application for psychotherapeutic methods; even if there are descriptions of various psychosocial or psychotherapeutic forms of treatment in the professional literature which are suitable for asylum seekers. The therapist also does not get round to consulting a colleague who has more experience with the problems of asylum seekers.

The same thing may occur if the refugee adopts a theatrical, coercive or manipulating attitude in the eyes of the Western therapist. What the average

European or American person considers to be theatrical can, given the cultural background of the client, be an adequate expression of emotions. Coercive, manipulating behaviour is often understandable and recognizable if one has an eye for the compelling circumstances in which the asylum seeker may find himself (Van der Veer, 1987c, 1989a). A lowering of professional norms has occurred when the therapist no longer takes the trouble to discover the background to the theatrical or coercive behaviour but, without the necessary diagnostic reflection, applies a label referring to a personality disorder, brands the client as unmotivated, or concludes, without trying even a single intervention, that he is not capable of profiting from psychotherapeutic techniques.

Changes may also occur in the way in which the therapist relates to himself and to others. This can include some dysfunction, for example, in contacts with house-mates and colleagues (Bustos, 1988). These changes will eventually lead to a personality change in which one may recognize positive and less positive aspects: the therapist loses a number of illusions but in a certain sense may possibly become milder.

Recommendations

In order to keep the particular reactions during the therapeutic interview under control and to expand one's own repertoire of adequate coping behaviour, it is useful to carefully record how the interviews pass off. If the use of recording devices is not indicated then a standardized reporting procedure may be used (see p. 168). Material thus obtained can be used to keep an eye on one's own functioning, but may also be used in consultation with colleagues or in supervision.

After some interviews with a seriously traumatized refugee the therapist needs some extra time to regain his breath. His diary and caseload should be adjusted to take this into account.

It is often useful, and sometimes necessary, to discuss some of the emotions which have been evoked in the course of the job with fellow team members. These sometimes concern intimate matters which it is better to discuss with a colleague outside the team. Such collegial contacts must be anticipated beforehand and made possible by the therapist's employer.

In order to prevent the blurring of professional norms it may be useful to regularly question them explicitly, for example, by considering, together with one or more colleagues, the diagnosis and the course of the assistance provided to each individual client. This seems rather obvious, but in practice this often does not occur for various very understandable reasons, such as the therapist being overloaded with work, or a lack of interest among colleagues for the specific problems of refugees.

Working with seriously traumatized clients also has consequences for the personal functioning of the therapist, and some of these are not particularly pleasant. As a result the therapist may wonder why he has chosen to do this work. Continual reflection on the philosophy of life, but also on the unsolved inner conflicts or unassimilated traumatic experiences, that underlie this choice can help the therapist to make working with seriously traumatized clients into a enriching experience. The continuation of the last case example may illustrate this point.

The therapist remembered what else E.V., gasping for breath and stumbling over his words, had said: how his commander had given the order to kill a large number of prisoners of war, how dogs had run wild among the bodies, and how that night he had slept between the bodies of his comrades who had been killed.

The therapist was still looking at the plate. The picture changed, and he remembered E.V.'s face, the single tear which welled up in the corner of his right eye and left a trace over his cheek. E.V. looked dead-tired, but he was now breathing more calmly.

References

Abend, S. M. (1986). Counter transference, empathy and the analytic ideal: the impact of life stresses on analytic capability, *Psychoanalytic Quarterly*, **55**, 563–575.

Adleson, J. (1975). The development of ideology in adolescence, in *Adolescence and the Life Cycle* (Eds S. Dragastin & G. H. Elder), pp. 63–78. Norton, New York.

Agger, I. (1987). The female political prisoner: a victim of sexual torture, paper presented at the Eighth World-Congress for Sexology, 14–20 June, Heidelberg.

Agger, I. (1988). *Psychological Aspects of Torture with Special Emphasis on Sexual Torture: Sequels and Treatment Perspectives.* Institute of Cultural Sociology, Copenhagen.

Agger, I. (1989). Sexual torture of political prisoners: an overview, *Journal of Traumatic Stress*, **2**, 305–318.

Agger, I. & Jensen, S. B. (1990). Testimony as ritual and evidence in psychotherapy for political refugees, *Journal of Traumatic Stress*, **3**, 115–130.

Alamos, L. (1986). *Repercusiones psicológicas en niños víctimas de la represión política*, Fundacion para la protección de la infancia dañada por los estados de emergencia, Santiago.

Alexander, A. A., Klein, M. H., Workneh, F. & Miller, M. H. (1981). Psychotherapy and the foreign student, in *Counselling across Cultures*, revised and expanded edition (Eds P. B. Pederson, J. G. Draguns, W. J. Lonner & J. E. Trimble), pp. 226–243. University Press of Hawaii, Honolulu.

Allodi, F. (1980). The psychiatric effects in children and families of victims of political persecution and torture, *Danish Medical Bulletin*, **27**, 229–232.

Allodi, F. (1982). Psychiatric sequelae of torture and implications for treatment, *World Medical Journal*, **29**, 71–75.

Allodi, F. & Rojas, A. (1983a). *The Health and Adaptation of Victims of Torture from Latin America and Their Children in Metropolitan Toronto.* Canadian Centre for Investigation and Prevention of Torture, Toronto.

Allodi, F. & Rojas, A. (1983b). *Arauco: a Study of Mental Health and Social Adaptation of Latin American Refugees in Toronto.* Canadian Centre for Investigation and Prevention of Torture, Toronto.

Allodi, F. & Rojas, A. (1985). The health and adaptation of victims of political violence in Latin America (Psychiatric effects of torture and disappearance), in *Psychiatry: The State of the Art* (Ed. P. Pichot), pp. 243–248. Plenum Press, New York.

Allodi, F. & Stiasny, S. (1990). Women as torture victims, *Canadian Journal of Psychiatry*, **35**, 144–148.

Amen, D. G. (1985). Post-Vietnam stress disorder: a metaphor for current and past life events, *American Journal of Psychotherapy*, **39**, 580–586.

Amnesty International (1991). *Geschonden rechten, geschonden levens.* Amnesty International, the Netherlands, Amsterdam.

Anthony, E. J. (1998). Special section. Children's reactions to severe stress. The response to overwhelming stress: some introductory comments, *Journal of the American Academy Of Child Psychiatry*, **25**, 299–305.

APA (1987). *Diagnostic and Statistical Manual of Mental Disorders* (third edition, revised). American Psychiatric Association, Washington, DC.

Arcos, V. & Araya, P. (1982). Claustrofobia, paralización y participación. Psicoterápia de un militante político, unpublished study, Santiago.

Ashmann, B. & Ngo, T. L. (1981). Een stukje achtergrond van de Vietnamese vrouw, in *Vluchtelingenvrouwen* (Ed. M. Meijer), pp. 37–43. Vereniging Vluchtelingenwerk Nederland, Amsterdam.

Bailly, C., Jaffe, H. & Pagella, A. (1989). *Psychological Sequelae of Torture: PTSD with Psychotic Features?* Association por les victims de la repression en exil, Paris.

Baker, N. G. (1981). Social work through an interpreter, *Social Work*, **26**, 391–397.

Bandura, A. (1977). *Social Learning Theory*. Prentice Hall, New York.

Baranger, M., Baranger, W. & Mom, J. M. (1988). The infantile psychic trauma from us to Freud: pure trauma, retroactivity and reconstruction, *International Journal of Psychoanalysis*, **69**, 113–128.

Bartels, K. & Haaijer, I. (1990). Somali Female Refugees in baseline health care, paper presented at the second European Traumatic Stress Congress, 23–27 September 1990, Noordwijkerhout, the Netherlands.

Barudy, J. (1981). *Self-help and Mutual Aid in a Mental Health Programme for Political Exiles*. Colat, Leuven.

Beck, A. T., Rush, A. J., Shaw, B. F. & Emery, G. (1979). *Cognitive Therapy of Depression*. Guilford Press, New York.

Becker, D. & Weinstein, E. (1986). La familia frente al miedo: aspetos psicodinámicos y psicoterapéuticos, *Revista Chilena de Psicologia*, **8**, 57–63.

Beets, N. (1974). *Persoonsvorming in de Adolescentie*. Bijleveld, Utrecht.

Beiser, M. (1988). Influences of time, ethnicity, and attachment on depression in Southeast Asian refugees, *American Journal of Psychiatry*, **145**, 46–51.

Benedek, E. P. (1984). The silent scream: counter transference reactions to victims, *American Journal of Social Psychiatry*, **4**, 49–52.

Benson, D., McCubbin, H. I., Dahl, B. B. & Hunter, E. J. (1974). Waiting: the dilemma of the MIA wife, in *Family Separation and Reunion: Families of Prisoners of War and Servicemen Missing in Action* (Ed. H. I. McCubbin), pp. 157–169. Center for Prisoners of War Studies, Naval Health Research Center, Washington DC.

Bettelheim, B. (1960). *The Informed Heart: Autonomy in a Mass-age*. Free Press, Glencoe, Ill.

Blank, A. S. (1987). Irrational reactions to post traumatic stress disorder and Vietnam veterans, in *The Trauma of War: Stress and Recovery in Vietnam Veterans* (Ed. S. M. Sonnenberg), pp. 69–99. American Psychiatric Association Press, Washington, DC.

Bleich, A., Garb, R. & Kottler, M. (1986). Treatment of prolonged combat reaction, *British Journal of Psychiatry*, **148**, 493–496.

Blitz, R. & Greenberg, R. (1984). Nightmare of the traumatic neurosis. Implications for theory and treatment, in *Psychotherapy of the Combat Veteran* (Ed. H. J. Schwartz), pp. 103–124. MTP Press, Lancaster, England.

Blos, P. (1962). *On Adolescence. A Psychoanalytic Interpretation*. Free Press, New York.

Boehnlein, J. K. (1987). Culture and society in post-traumatic stress disorder: complications for psychotherapy, *American Journal of Psychotherapy*, **16**, 519–530.

Boekhoorn, P. (1987). *Omvang van de immateriele hulpvraag onder oorlogs en geweldsgetroffenen in Nederland*. Stichting Research voor Beleid, Leiden.

Boman, B. & Edwards, M. (1984). The Indochinese refugee: an overview, *Australian and New Zealand Journal of Psychiatry*, **18**, 40–52.

Boon, S. & Draijer, N. (1991). Diagnosing dissociative disorders in the Netherlands: a pilot study with the structured clinical interview for dissociative disorders, *American Journal of Psychiatry*, **148**, 458–462.

Boszormenyi-Nagy, I. & Spark, G. M. (1973). *Invisible Loyalties*. Harper & Row, New York.

Brainin, E., Ligeti, V. & Teicher, S. (1990). De tijd heelt geen wonden. *ICODO-Info*, **7**, 5–25.

Brassé, P. (1987). Jonge Turken en Marokkanen: Vreemdelingen of medeburgers, in *Adolescenten in Vele Gedaanten* (Eds R. A. C. Hoksbergen, R. van der Meer & G. P. Schoor), pp. 32–39. Swets & Zeitlinger, Lisse.

Brett, E. A. & Ostroff, R. (1985). Imagery and Posttraumatic Stress Disorder: An Overview, *American Journal of Psychiatry*, **142**, 417–424.

Bromley, M. A. (1987). New Beginnings for Cambodian Refugees—or further disruptions?, *Social Work*, **32**, 236–239.

Brown, L. S. (1986). From alienation to connection: feminist therapy with post-traumatic stress disorder, *Women Therapy*, **5**, 101–106.

Buers, J. J. M. (1985). *Vervreemding, geborgenheid en integratie*. Psychiatrisch Ziekenhuis Wolfheze, Wolfheze.

Burstein, A. (1984). Treatment of post-traumatic stress disorder with imipramine, *Psychosomatics*, **25**, 681–687.

Bustos, E. & Ruggiero, L. R. (1985). El proceso de emancipación en los jóvenes exilados, unpublished study, Copenhagen.

Bustos, E. (1988). Psychopathological processes in the treatment of torture victims, paper presented at the 24th International Congress of Psychology, 28 August–2 September, Sydney, Australia.

Bustos, E. (1990a). Dealing with the unbearable: Reactions of therapist and therapeutic institutions to victims of torture, in *Psychology and Torture* (Ed. P. Suedfeld), pp. 143–163. Hemisphere Publications, New York.

Bustos, E. (1990b). The need of relatedness and the impact of introjective-projective processes in transferential and countertransferential reactions, paper presented to the symposium 'Assistance to victims of organized violence', organized by the Refugee Health Care Centre (CGV) and the Social Psychiatric Centre for Refugees (SPD-V), 28 September, Utrecht, the Netherlands.

Butcher, J. N., Egli, E. A., Shiota, N. K. & Ben-Porath, Y. S. (1988). *Psychological interventions with refugees*, report published for the Refugee Assistance Program—Mental Health: Technical Assistance Center, University of Minnesota, Minnesota.

Cancelmo, J. A., Millán, F. & Vazquez, C. I. (1990). Culture and symptomatology—The role of personal meaning in diagnosis and treatment: a case study, *American Journal of Psychoanalysis*, **50**, 137–149.

Caplan, G. (1964). *Principles of Preventive Psychiatry*. Basic Book, New York.

Castillo, M. I. (1984). Adolescencia y exílio, in *Escritos sobre exílio y retorno (1978–1984)* (Ed. C. González), pp. 37–54. Fasic, Santiago.

Cathcart, L. M., Berger, P. & Knazan, B. (1979). Medical examination of torture victims applying for refugee status, *Canadian Medical Association Journal*, **121**, 179–184.

Chandler, M., Ball, L. & Boyles, M. (1988). Relativism and stations of epistemic doubt, paper presented at the second biennial meeting of the society for adolescent development, 25–28 March, Alexandria VA.

Chu, J. A. (1988). Ten traps for therapists in the treatment of trauma survivors, *Dissociation*, **1**, 24–32.

Cienfuegos, A. J. (1982). 'Borra todas las huellas', Psicoterapia de un mujer atrapada en el miedo, unpublished study, Santiago.

Cienfuegos, A. J. & Monelli, C. (1983). The testimony of political repression as a therapeutic instrument, *American Journal of Orthopsychiatry*, **53**, 41–53.

Coelho, G. V. (1982). The foreign students sojourn as a high risk situation: the 'culture-shock' phenomenon re-examined, in *Uprooting and Surviving* (Ed. R. C. Nann), pp. 101–107. D. Reidel Publishing Company, Dordrecht.

Cohn, J. (1982). *Children and Torture*. Danish Medical Group Amnesty International, Copenhagen.

Cohn, J., Holzer, K. I. M., Koch, L. & Severin, B. (1980). Children and torture. An investigation of Chilean immigrant children in Denmark, *Danish Medical Bulletin*, **27**, 238–239.

Comision de derechos humanos de El Salvador—CDHS (1986). *La tortura en El Salvador, Penal 'La Esperanza'*, Ayutuxtepeque, San Salvador.

Cowell McFarlane, A. (1987). Post-traumatic phenomena in a longitudinal study of children following a natural disaster, *Journal of the American Academy of Child and Adolescent Psychiatry*, **26**, 764–769.

Cox, A. & Rutter, N. (1985). Diagnostic appraisal and interviewing, in *Child and Adolescent Psychiatry, Modern Approaches*, (second edition) (Eds M. Rutter & L. Hersov), pp. 233–248. Blackwell, Oxford.

Curtis Alley, J. (1982). Life-threatening indicators among Indochinese refugees, *Suicide and Life-Threatening Behaviour*, **12**(1), 46–51.

Dahl, C. (1989). Some problems of cross-cultural psychotherapy with refugees seeking treatment, *The American Journal of Psychoanalysis*, **49**, 19–32.

Daly, R. J. (1985a). Victims of torture and their rehabilitation, in *Psychiatry: the State of the Art*, **8**, (Eds P. Pichot, P. Berner, R. Wolf & K. Thau), pp. 277–282. Plenum Press, New York.

Daly, R. J. (1985b). Effects of imprisonment and isolation, in *Psychiatry: The State of the Art*, **8**, (Eds P. Pichot, P. Berner, R. Wolf & K. Thau), pp. 249–254. Plenum Press, New York.

Damon, W. & Hart, D. (1982). The development of self-understanding from infancy through adolescence, *Child Development*, **53**, 841–864.

Danieli, Y. (1980). Counter transference in the treatment and study of nazi holocaust survivors and their children, *Victimology*, **5**, 355–367.

Dare, C. (1980). Gezinsgeheimen, *Maandblad Geestelijke Volksgezondheid*, **36**, 1073–1083.

Davey, G. C. L. (1989). UCS revaluation and conditioning models of acquired fears, *Behaviour Research and Therapy*, **87**, 521–528.

Davidson, J. R. T. & Foa, E. B. (1991). Diagnostic issues in post-traumatic stress disorder: considerations for the DSM-IV, *Journal of Abnormal Psychology*, **110**, 346–355.

Davidson, J., Swartz, M., Storck, M., Krishnan, R. R. & Hammet, E. (1985). A diagnostic and family study of posttraumatic stress disorder, *American Journal of Psychiatry*, **142**, 90–93.

Davidson, J., Kudler, H., Smith, R., Mahorney, S., Lippen, S., Hammet, E., Saunders, W. B. & Cavenar, J. O. (1990). Treatment of posttraumatic stress disorder with amitriptyline and placebo, *Archives of General Psychiatry*, **47**, 259–266.

De Anda, D. (1984). Bicultural socialization: factors affecting the minority experience, *Social Work*, **29**, 101–107.

Delaney, G. M. V. (1979). *Living Your Dreams*. Harper & Row, San Francisco.

Denley, J. (1987). Personal communication, cited in *Torture and Trauma*, (Eds J. Reid & T. Strong), p. 96. Cumberland College of Health Services, Sydney.

De Silva, P. (1985). Early Buddhist and modern behavioral strategies for the control of unwanted intrusive cognitions, *The Psychological Record*, **35**, 437–443.

De Wind, E. (1969). Psychotherapie van vervolgden, *Inval*, 99–107.

De Wind, E. (1970). Psychotherapie van vervolgden (2), *Inval*, 127–138.

De Wit, J. (1987). Protectieve factoren: maatschappelijk en wetenschappelijk een uitdaging, in *Protectieve factoren in de ontwikkeling van kinderen en adolescenten* (Eds H. J. Groenendaal, R. W. J. Meijer, J. W. Veerman & J. Wit), pp. 9–16. Swets & Zeitlinger, Lisse.

De Wit, J. & Tak, J. A. (1988). Theoretische achtergronden van de klinische diagnostiek, in *Psychodiagnostiek voor de hulpverlening aan kinderen* (Eds T. Kievit, J. De Wit, J. A. H. Groenendaal & J. A. Tak). Acco, Amersfoort.

De Wit, J. & Van der Veer, G. (1989). *Psychologie van de adolescentie. Ontwikkeling en hulpverlening*, (fifteenth revised edition). Intro, Nijkerk.

Diekstra, R. F. W. (1983). Suicidal behaviour among adolescents, in *Development in Adolescence* (Eds W. Everaerd, C. B. Hindley, A. Bot & J. J. van der Werff ten Bosch), pp. 206–225. Martinus Nijhoff Publishers, Boston.

Diekstra, R. (1984). *De opgroeiende dood*. Ambo, Baarn.

Domovitch, E., Berger, P. B., Wawer, M. J., Etlin, D. D. & Marshall, J. C. (1984). Human torture: description and sequelae of 104 cases, *Canadian Family Physician*, **30**, 827–830.

Draijer, P. J. (1987). De omvang van sexueel misbruik van kinderen door verwanten. Kanttekeningen bij epidemiologisch surveyonderzoek naar pijnlijke gebeurtenissen, in *Seksuologie: Incest* (Ed. P. Cohen-Kettenis), pp. 1–16. Boerhaave Commissie voor Postacademisch Onderwijs in de Geneeskunde, Rijksuniversiteit, Leiden.

Dweck, C. S. & Wortman, C. B. (1982). Learned helplessness, anxiety and achievement motivation, in *Achievement, Stress and Anxiety* (Eds H. W. Krohne & L. Laux), pp. 93–125. Hemisphere Publishing Company, Washington DC.

Eisenbruch, M. (1984). Cross-cultural aspects of bereavement. I: A conceptual framework for comparative analysis, *Culture, Medicine and Psychiatry*, **8**, 283–309.

Eisenbruch, M. (1989). *The Cultural Bereavement Interview: a New Clinical and Research Approach with Refugees*. Royal Children's Hospital, Melbourne.

Eisenbruch, M. & Handelman, L. (1989). Development of an explanatory model of illness schedule for Cambodian refugee patients, *Journal of Refugee Studies*, **2**, 243–256.

Eitinger, L. (1960). The symptomology of mental disease among refugees in Norway, *Journal of Mental Science*, **206**, 947–966.

Elkind, D. (1967). Egocentrism in Adolescence, *Child Development*, **38**, 1025–1034.

Erikson, E. H. (1968). *Identity, Youth and Crisis*. Norton, New York.

Erikson, E. H. (1982). *Childhood and Society: the Life Cycle Completed*. Norton, New York.

Eth, S. (1986). Freud and traumatic neurosis, *American Journal of Psychiatry*, **142**, 1057.

Eth, S. & Pynoos, R. S. (1984). *Post Traumatic Stress Disorder in Children*. American Psychiatric Press, Washington DC.

Ettedgui, E. & Bridges, M. (1985). Post-traumatic Stress Disorder, *Psychiatry Clinics of North America*, **8**, 89–103.

Fairbank, J. A. & Nicholson, R. A. (1987). Theoretical and empirical issues in the treatment of post-traumatic stress disorder in Vietnam veterans, *Journal of Clinical Psychology*, **43**, 44–55.

Falcon, S., Ryan, C., Chamberlain, K. & Curtis, G. (1985). Tricyclics: possible treatment for Posttraumatic Stress Disorder, *Journal of Clinical Psychiatry*, **46**, 385–389.

Figley, C. R. (1985). The family as a victim; mental health implications, in *Psychiatry: the State of the Art*, **8** (Eds P. Pichot, P. Berner, R. Wolf & K. Thau), pp. 283–291. Plenum Press, New York.

Figley, C. R. (1988). Post-traumatic family therapy, in *Post-traumatic Therapy and Victims of Violence* (Ed. F. M. Ochberg), pp. 83–109. Brunner/Mazel, New York.

Fischman, Y. & Ross, J. (1990). Group treatment of exiled survivors of torture, *American Journal of Orthopsychiatry*, **60**, 135–142.

Folkman, S. & Lazarus, R. S. (1988). The relationship between coping and emotion: implications for theory and research, *Social Science and Medicine*, **26**, 309–317.

Frank, J. B., Kosten, T. R., Giller, E. L. & Dan, E. (1988). A randomized clinical trial of phenelzine and imipramine for post traumatic stress disorder, *American Journal of Psychiatry*, **145**, 1289–1291.

Frankenthaler, L. M. (1986). Imipramine and chlordiapoxide in depressive and anxiety disorders. II. Efficacy in anxious patients, *Archives of General Psychiatry*, **43**, 79–95.

Freud, S. (1955). Beyond the pleasure principle, *Complete Works*, Vol. 18, pp. 3–64. Hogarth Press, London.

Freud, A. (1958). Adolescence, in *The Psychoanalytic Study of the Child*, vol. 13, pp. 255–278. International University Press, London.

Friedman, M. J. (1988). Towards rational pharmacotherapy for post traumatic stress disorder: an interim report, *American Journal of Psychiatry*, **145**, 281.

Furman, E. (1986). On Trauma. When is the death of a parent traumatic?, *The Psychoanalytic Study of the Child*, **41**, 191–208.

Galante, R. & Foa, D. (1986). An epidemiological study of psychic trauma and treatment effectiveness for children of a natural disaster, *Journal of the American Academy of Child Psychiatry*, **25**, 357–363.

Galli, V. A. (1984). Terror, silencio y enajación, unpublished study, Buenos Aires.

Garcia, M. O. & Rodriguez, P. F. (1987). Psychological effects of political repression in Argentina and Central America. Covert political repression: the Argentinian experience, paper presented at the Third Annual Meeting of the Society for Traumatic Studies, Baltimore.

Garmezy, N. (1985). Stress resistant children, in *Recent Research in Developmental Psychopathology* (Ed. J. E. Stevenson), pp. 213–233. Plenum Press, New York.

Garza-Guerrero, A. C. (1974). Culture shock: its morning and the vicissitudes of identity, *Journal of the American Psychoanalytic Association*, **22**, 408–429.

Genefke, I. K. (1984). *Rehabilitation of Torture Victims*. International Rehabilitation and Research Centre for Torture Victims, Copenhagen.

Giel, R. (1984). *Vreemde zielen. Een sociaalpsychiatrische verkenning in andere culturen.* Boom, Meppel.

Gielis, A. (1982). Geleerde hulpeloosheid all depressiemodel, een literatuurstudie, *Gedragstherapie*, **15**, 3–31.

Gilligan, C. (1982). *In a Different Voice.* Harvard University Press, Cambridge, Mass.

Glassman, J. G. (1988). PTSD in Refugees, *American Journal of Psychiatry*, **145**, 1486–1487.

Glover, H. (1988). Four syndromes of post-traumatic stress disorder: stressors and conflicts of the traumatized with special focus on the Vietnam combat veteran, *Journal of Traumatic Stress*, **1**, 57–78.

Goddijn, H. P. M. (1969). *De sociologie van Emile Durkheim.* Academisch Paperbacks, Amsterdam.

Goodwin, J. (1985). Credibility problems in multiple personality disorder patients and abused children, in *Childhood Antecedents of Multiple Personality* (Ed. R. P. Kluft), pp. 2–19. American Psychiatric Press, Washington.

Graafsma, T. (1987). Coping en veerkracht: enkele psychoanalytische kanttekeningen, in *Protectieve factoren in de ontwikkeling van kinderen en adolescenten* (Eds H. Groenendaal, R. Meijer, J. W. Veerman & J. de Wit), pp. 137–150. Swets & Zeitlinger, Lisse.

Greenson, R. (1967). *The Technique and Practice of Psychoanalysis.* International Universities Press, New York.

Grigsby, J. P. (1987). Single case-study. The use of imagery in the treatment of posttraumatic stress disorder, *The Journal of Nervous and Mental Disease*, **175**, 55–59.

Grimberg, L. & Grimberg, R. (1984). *Psicoanálisis de la migración y del exílio*. Alianza Editorial, Madrid.

Grinker, R. & Spiegel, J. (1945). *Men under stress*. Blakiston, Philadelphia.

Groenenberg, M. (1984). *Psicoterapia con refugiados Latinoamericanos*. Social Psychiatric Centre for Refugees, Amsterdam.

Groenenberg, M. (1991). Female refugees, paper presented at the conference on Mental Health and multicultural societies in the Europe of the nineties, 15–18 September, Rotterdam.

Grosjean, F. (1982). *Living with Two Languages*. Cambridge University Press, Cambridge.

Gross, A. M. & Levin, R. B. (1987). Learning, in *Handbook of Adolescent Psychology* (Eds V. B. Van Hasselt & M. Hersen), pp. 77–90. Pergamon Press, New York.

Gunderson, J. G. (1986). Pharmacotherapy for patients with borderline personality disorder, *Archives of General Psychiatry*, **43**, 698–700.

Guscott, R. & Grof, P. (1991). The clinical meaning of refractory depression: a review for the clinician, *American Journal of Psychiatry*, **148**, 695–704.

Haley, S. A. (1974). When the patient reports atrocities: specific treatment considerations in the Vietnam veteran, *Archives of General Psychiatry*, **30**, 191–196.

Haley, S. A. (1978). Treatment implications of post-combat stress response syndromes for mental health professionals, in *Stress Disorders among Vietnam Veterans* (Ed. C. Figley), pp. 254–268. Brunner/Mazel, New York.

Hall, R. C. W. (1981). Paradoxical reactions to benzodiazepines, *British Journal of Clinical Pharmacology*, **11**, 995–1045.

Handford, H. A., Dickerson Mayes, S., Mattison, R. E., Humphrey, F. J., Bagnato, S., Bixler, E. O. & Kales, J. D. (1986). Child and parent reaction to the Three Mile Island nuclear accident, *Journal of the American Academy of Child Psychiatry*, **25**, 346–356.

Harter, S. (1988). Developmental and dynamic changes in the nature of the self-concept: implications for child-psychotherapy, in *Cognitive Development and Child Psychotherapy* (Ed. S. R. Shirk), pp. 119–160. Plenum Press, New York.

Hartmann, E. (1984). *The Nightmare: the Psychology and Biology of Terrifying Dreams*. Basic Books, New York.

Hauff, E. (1990). Vietnamese boat refugees: casualties of war and its aftermath, paper presented at the Second European Conference on Traumatic Stress, Noordwijkerhout, the Netherlands.

Hayley, J. (1963). *Strategies of Psychotherapy*. Grune & Stratton, New York.

Hendin, H. & Pollinger Haas, A. (1991). Suicide and guilt as manifestations of PTSD in Vietnam combat veterans, *American Journal of Psychiatry*, **148**, 586–591.

Herrera Rivera, S. (1986). *El taller terapeútica. Un recurso para el rescate de la salud mental en grupos de familiares afectadas por la represión del régimen dictatorial*, Fundación para la protección de la infancia dañada por los estados de emergencia, Santiago.

Hertz, D. G. (1987). *Research on Migrants and Psychological Effects of Uprooting*. Lecture as a visiting professor at the University of Amsterdam, 29 April 1987.

Horowitz, M. J. (1976). *Stress Response Syndromes*. Aronson, New York.

Horowitz, M. J. (1986). Stress-response syndromes: a review of post-traumatic and adjustment disorders, *Hospital and Community Psychiatry*, **37**, 241–249.

Huijbregts, V. (1985). Chileense vluchtelingenvrouwen in Nederland, *Antroplogische Papers VU 2*, VU uitgeverij, Amsterdam.

Jacobson, E. (1938). *Progressive Relaxation*. University of Chicago Press, Chicago.

Janoff-Bulman, R. (1989). The benefits of illusions, the threat of disillusionment, and the limitations of inaccuracy, *Journal of Social and Clinical Psychology*, **8**, 158–175.

Janoff-Bulman, R. & Frieze, I. H. (1983). A theoretical perspective for understanding reactions to victimization, *Journal of Social Issues*, **39**, 1–17.

Jaranson, J. M. (1988). *Psychotherapeutic Medication in the Treatment of Refugees*. University of Minnesota, Department of Psychiatry, Minnesota.

Kabela, M. (n.d.). *Transculturele aspecten van depressie*. Elizabethsgasthuis, Haarlem.

Kalix, P. (1988). Khat: a plant with amphetamine effects, *Journal of Substance Abuse Treatment*, **5**, 163–169.

Kaptanoglu, C. (1991). *Iskencenin Ruhsal Etkiliri*. Eskisehir Anadolu Üniversitesi, Uzmanlik Tezi.

Kazdin, A. E. (1987). *Conduct Disorders in Childhood and Adolescence*. Beverly Hills, Sage Publications.

Keilson, H. (1979). *Sequentielle Traumatisierung bei Kindern*. Ferdinand Enke Verlag, Stuttgart.

Kerkhof, A. J. F. M., Van der Wal, J. & Hengeveld, M. W. (1988). Typology of persons who attempt suicide with predictive value for repetition, in *Current Issues of Suicidology* (Eds H. J. Möller, A. Schmidtke & R. Welz), pp. 42–60. Springer Verlag, Berlin.

Kernberg, O. (1975). *Borderline Conditions and Pathological Narcissism*. Jason Aronson, New York.

Kinzie, J. D. (1978). Lessons from cross-cultural psychotherapy, *American Journal of Psychotherapy*, **32**, 110–120.

Kinzie, J. D. (1987). Anti-depressant blood levels in South East Asians: clinical and cultural implications, *Journal of Nervous and Mental Diseases*, **175**, 480–485.

Kinzie, J. D., Frederickson, R. H., Ben, R., Fleck, J. & Karls, W. (1984). Post traumatic stress disorders among survivors of Cambodian concentration camps, *American Journal of Psychiatry*, **141**, 645–650.

Kinzie, J. D., Sack, W. H., Angel, R. H., Manson, S. & Rath, B. (1986). The psychiatric effects of massive trauma on Cambodian children: the children, *Journal of the American Academy of Child Psychiatry*, **25**, 370–376.

Kinzie, J. D. & Fleck, J. (1987). Psychotherapy with severely traumatized refugees, *American Journal of Psychotherapy*, **41**, 82–94.

Kinzie, J. D. & Boehnlein, J. J. (1989). Post-traumatic psychosis among Cambodian refugees, *Journal of Traumatic Stress*, **2**, 185–198.

Kinzie, J. D., Boehnlein, J. K., Leung, P. K., Moore, L. J., Riley, C. & Smith, D. (1990). The prevalence of Post-traumatic Stress Disorder and its clinical significance among Southeast Asian Refugees, *American Journal of Psychiatry*, **147**, 913–917.

Kitchner, I. & Greenstein, R. (1985). Low dose lithiumcarbonate in the treatment of post-traumatic stress disorder: brief communication, *Military Medicine*, **150**, 378–381.

Klein, D. F. (1987). Anxiety reconceptualized, in *Anxiety: New Research and Changing Concepts* (Eds D. F. Klein & J. G. Rabkin), pp. 1–35. Raven Press, New York.

Knudsen, J. C. (1991). Therapeutic strategies and strategies for refugee coping, *Journal of Refugee Studies*, **4**, 21–38.

Kohlberg, L. & Gilligan, C. (1972). The adolescent as a philosopher: the discovery of the self in a postconventional world, in *Twelve to Sixteen: Early Adolescence* (Eds J. Kagan & R. Coles), pp. 144–179. Norton, New York.

Kolb, L. C. (1984). The post-traumatic stress disorders of combat: a subgroup with conditioned emotional response, *Military Medicine*, **149**, 237–243.

Kolb, L. C. (1987). A neuropsychological hypothesis explaining post-traumatic stress disorders. *American Journal of Psychiatry*, **144**, 989–995.

Kolb, L. C., Burris, B. C. & Griffiths, S. (1984). Propanolol and clonidine treatment of post traumatic disorders, in *Post-traumatic Stress Disorder: Psychological and Biologi-*

cal Sequelae (Ed. B. A. Van der Kolk), pp. 97–106. American Psychiatric Press, Washington DC.

Kordon, D. R. & Edelman, L. I. (1986). Efectos psicológicos de la represión política. II, in *Efectos psicológicos de la represión política* (Eds D. R. Kordon, L. I. Edelman & Equipo de Asistencia Psicológica de Madres de Plaza de Mayo), pp. 149–178. Sudamericana Planeta, Buenos Aires.

Kordon, D. R., Edelman, L. I., Nicoletti, E., Lagos, D. M., Bozzolo, R. C. & Kandel, E. (1986). in *Efectos psicológicos de la represión política* (Eds D. R. Kordon, L. I. Edelman & Equipo de Asistencia Psicológica de Madres de Plaza de Mayo), pp. 87–100. Sudamericana Planeta, Buenos Aires.

Korrelboom, C. W., Kernkamp, J. H. B., Eelen, P., Hoogduin, C. A. L. & Duivenvorden, H. J. (1989). Panic and UCS-revaluation, presentation held at the first European Congress of Psychology, Amsterdam.

Kortmann, F. (1986). *Problemen in transculturele communicatie.* Van Gorcum, Assen.

Kosteljanetz, M. & Aalund, O. (1983). Torture: a challenge to medical science, *Interdisciplinary Science Review*, **8**, 1–9.

Kramer, M., Schoen, L. S. & Kinney, L. (1987). Nightmares in Vietnam veterans, *Journal of The American Academy of Psychoanalysis*, **15**, 67–81.

Krystal, H. (1978). Trauma and Affects, *Psychoanalytic Study of the Child*, **31**, 81–116.

Krystal, H. (1984). Psychoanalytic views on human emotional damage, in *Post-traumatic Stress Disorder: Psychological and Biological Sequelae* (Ed. B. A. Van der Kolk), pp. 2–28. American Psychiatric Press, Washington DC.

Krystal, H. (1987). Speech to the third annual meeting of the Society for Traumatic Studies, 25 October, Baltimore.

Lansen, J. (1988). A critical view of the concept: post traumatic stress disorders, paper presented at the meeting of the Advisory Group on the Health Situation of Refugees and Victims of Organized Violence, World Health Organization, Regional Office for Europe, Gothenburg.

Laufer, R. S., Brett, E. A. & Gallops, M. S. (1985). Symptom patterns associated with posttraumatic stress disorders among Vietnam veterans exposed to war trauma, *American Journal of Psychiatry*, **142**, 1304–1311.

Lavelle, J. (1987). Contribution to a panel on 'The countertransference of torture and trauma' during the third annual meeting of the Society for Traumatic Studies, 25 October, Baltimore.

Lee, E. (1988). Cultural factors in working with Southeast Asian refugee adolescents, *Journal of Adolescence*, **11**, 167–179.

Lee, E. & Lu, F. (1989). Assessment and treatment of Asian-American survivors of mass violence, *Journal of Traumatic Stress*, **2**, 93–120.

Lerer, B., Bleich, A., Kotler, M., Garb, R., Hetzberg, M. & Levin, B. (1987). Post-traumatic Stress Disorder in Israeli combat veterans, *Archives of General Psychiatry*, **44**, 976–981.

Lerner, H. (1987). Psychodynamic models, in *Handbook of Adolescent Psychology* (Eds V. B. Van Hasselt & M. Hersen), pp. 53–76. Pergamon Press, New York.

Levine, H. B. (1982). Toward a psychoanalytic understanding of children of survivors of the holocaust, *Psychoanalytic Quarterly*, **51**, 70–92.

L'Hoste, M. (1986). La desaparición: effectos psicosociales en Madres, in *Efectos psicológicos de la represión política* (Eds D. R. Kordon & L. I. Edelman), pp. 105–112. Sudamericana Planeta, Buenos Aires.

Lin, M. (1982). Experiences of Chinese immigrants in Canada: patterns of help seeking and socio-cultural determinants, in *Uprooting and Surviving* (Ed. R. C. Nann), pp. 175–184. D. Reidel Publishing Company, Dordrecht.

Lin, K. M., Masuda, M. & Tazuma, L. (1982). Problems of Vietnamese refugees in the United States, in *Uprooting and Surviving* (Ed. R. C. Nann), pp. 11–24. Reidel Publishing Company, Dordrecht.

Lindy, J. D. (1988). *Vietnam, a Casebook*. Brunner/Mazel, New York.

Lira, E. (1986). Personal communication.

Lira, E. (n.d.). *Tortura y psicoterapia: una experiencia de trabajo*. Fasic, Santiago.

Lira, E. & Weinstein, E. (1986). La tortura sexual, Ponencia para el seminario 'Consecuencias de la represión en el Cono Sur: sus efectos médicos, psicológicas y sociales', Montevideo, Uruguay.

Lukmann, B. & Mortensen, N. B. (1988). *Treatment of Children in Exiled Families Who Have Been Exposed to Torture*, The International Research and Rehabilitation Centre for Torture Victims, Copenhagen.

Luna, M. (1982). 'Brindemos!... porque los monos tendrán a quién contar sus secretos'. Psicoterapia de un niño chileno exiliado y retornado, unpublished study, Santiago.

Lunde, I. & Ortmann, J. (1990). Prevalence and sequelae of sexual torture, *The Lancet*, **336**, 289–291.

Lyons, J. A. & Keane, T. M. (1989). Implosive therapy for the treatment of combat-related PTSD, *Journal of Traumatic Stress*, **2**, 137–152.

Malan, D. H. (1979). *Individual Psychotherapy and the Science of Psychodynamics*. Butterworths, London.

Malmquist, C. R. (1986). Children who witness parental murder: posttraumatic aspects, *Journal of the American Academy of Child Psychiatry*, **25**, 320–325.

Marcos, L. R. (1979). Effects of interpreters on the evaluation of psychopathology in non-English speaking patients, *American Journal of Psychiatry*, **136**, 171–174.

Marx, E. (1990). The social world of refugees: a conceptual framework, *Journal of Refugee Studies*, **3**, 189–203.

Maslach, C. & Jackson, S. E. (1986). *Maslach Burnout Inventory: Manual*, second edition. Consulting Psychologists Press, Palo Alto, CAN.

Matthijs, K. (1987). Zelfdoding bij jongeren. Sociologische kanttekeningen, in *Suicidaal gedrag bij kinderen en adolescenten* (Eds W. H. G. Wolters, R. F. W. Diekstra, C. W. M. Kienhorst), pp. 61–71. Ambo, Baarn.

Mavissakalian, M. & Perel, J. (1985). Imipramine in the treatment of agoraphobia: dose-response relationships, *American Journal of Psychiatry*, **142**, 1032–1036.

McCann, L. & Pearlman, L. A. (1990). Vicarious traumatization: a framework for understanding the psychological effects of working with victims, *Journal of Traumatic Stress*, **3**, 131–149.

McCormick, R. A., Taber, J. I. & Kruedelbach, N. (1989). The relationship between attributional style and post traumatic stress disorder in addicted patients, *Journal of Traumatic Stress*, **2**, 477–487.

McDaniel, K. D. (1986). Clinical pharmacology of monoamine oxidase inhibitors, *Clinical Neuropharmacology*, **9**, 207–234.

McDougle, J. C., Southwick, S. M., James, R. L. & Charney, D. S. (n.d.). An open trial on fluoxetine in PTSD, unpublished study.

Meichenbaum, D. (1979). *Cognitive-Behaviour Modification—an integrative approach*. Plenum Press, New York.

Meier, A. (1985). Child psychiatric sequelae of maternal war stress, *Acta Psychiatrica Scandinavia*, **72**, 505–511.

Mellman, T. A. & Davis, G. C. (1985). Combat-related flashbacks in posttraumatic stress disorder: phenomenology and similarity to panic attacks, *Journal of Clinical Psychiatry*, **46**, 379–382.

Mernissi, F. (1985). *Achter de sluier. De islam en de strijd der sexen*. Nijgh en van Ditmar, Amsterdam.

Mikulas, W. L. (1978). For noble truth of Buddhism related to behaviour therapy, *The Psychological Record*, **28**, 59-67.

Miller, P. M., Surtees, P. G., Kreitman, J. G., Ingham, J. G. & Sashidharan, S. P. (1985). Maladaptive coping reactions to stress; a study of illness inception, *Journal of Nervous and Mental Disease*, **173**, 707-716.

Minuchin, S. & Fishman, H. C. (1981). *Family Therapy Technics*. Harvard, Cambridge.

Mollica, R. F. (1987). The trauma story: the psychiatric care of refugee survivors of torture, in *Post-traumatic Therapy and Victims of Violence* (Ed. F. M. Ochberg), pp. 295-314. Bruner Mazel, New York.

Mollica, R. F. & Son, L. (1988). Cultural dimensions in the evaluation and treatment of sexual trauma: an overview, unpublished study.

Mollica, R. F., Wyshak, G. & Lavell, I. (1987). The psychosocial impact of the war trauma in Southeast Asian refugees, *American Journal of Psychiatry*, **144**, 1567-1572.

Mollica, R. F., Wyshak, G., De Marneffe, D., Khuon, F. & Lavelle, J. (1987). Indochinese versions of the Hopkins Symptom Checklist 25: a screening instrument for the psychiatric care of refugees, *American Journal of Psychiatry*, **144**, 497-500.

Mollica, R. F., Wyshak, G., Lavelle, J., Truong, T., Tor, S. & Yang, T. (1990). Assessing symptom change in Southeast Asian refugee survivors of mass violence and torture, *American Journal of Psychiatry*, **147**, 83-88.

Monelli, C. (1982). Soledad y el vacío: un caso de psicoterapia con un familiar de ejecutado, unpublished study, Santiago.

Montessori, M. M. (1987). Problemen rond de indicatiestelling voor psychotherapie bij ernstig getraumatiseerden, *Icodo-info*, **4**, 30-39.

Mueser, K. T. & Butler, R. W. (1987). Auditory hallucinations in combat-related post traumatic stress disorder, *American Journal of Psychiatry*, **144**, 299-302.

Murdock, G. P. (1965). *Social Structure*. Macmillan, New York.

Murphy, L. B. (1960). The problem of defense and the concept of coping, *Bulletin of the Menninger Clinic*, **24**, 65-86.

Mussen, P. H. & Bouterline Young, H. (1964). Relationships between rate of physical maturing and personality of boys of Italian descent, *Vita Humana*, **7**, 106-200.

Newman, C. J. (1976). Children of disaster: clinical observations at Buffalo Creek, *American Journal of Psychiatry*, **133**, 306-312.

Ochberg, F. M. (1988). Post-traumatic therapy and victims of violence, in *Post-traumatic Therapy and Victims of Violence* (Ed. F. M. Ochberg), pp. 3-19. Bruner Mazel, New York.

Oei, T. I. (1987). Psychisch dysfunctioneren en de rol van sociale steun, *Nederlands Tijdschrift voor de Psychologie*, **42**, 55-61.

Op den Velde, W. (1989). Posttraumatische stress-stoornissen, *Nederlands Tijdschrift voor Geneeskunde*, **133**, 1586-1593.

Pallmeyer, T. P., Blanchard, E. B. & Kolb, L. C. (1986). The psychophysiology of combat-induced post-traumatic stress disorder in Vietnam veterans, *Behaviour: Research and Therapy*, **24**, 645-652.

Parry, G. & Shapiro, D. A. (1986). Social support and life events in working-class women, *Archives of General Psychiatry*, **43**, 315-323.

Parson, E. R. (1984). The reparation of the self: clinical and theoretical dimensions in the treatment of Vietnam combat veterans, *Journal of Contemporary Psychotherapy*, **14**, 4-56.

Pavlov, I. P. (1960). *Conditioned Reflexes. An Investigation of the Physiological Activity of the Cerebral Cortex*. Dover Publications, New York.

Pederson, P. B. (1981). The cultural inclusiveness of counselling, in *Counselling across Cultures*, (revised and expanded edition) (Eds P. B. Pederson, J. G. Draguns, W. J. Lonner & J. E. Trimble), pp. 22-58. University Press of Hawaii, Honolulu.

Pellegrini, D. (1985). Training in social problem-solving, in *Child and Adolescent Psychiatry: Modern Approaches*, (second edition) (Eds M. Rutter & L. Hersov), pp. 839–850. Blackwell, Oxford.

Pennebaker, J. W. & Klihr Beall, S. (1986). Confronting a traumatic event: toward an understanding of inhibition and disease, *Journal of Abnormal Psychology*, **95**, 274–281.

Pentz-Moller, V., Hermansen, A., Bentsen, E. & Knudsen, I. H. (1988). *Interpretation in the Rehabilitation of Torture Victims at the RCT*, International Research and Rehabilitation Centre for Torture Victims, Copenhagen.

Perez, J. M. (1987). Personal communication.

Perren-Klinger, G. (1991). Confrontation as a tool in the therapy of tortured clients, paper presented at the XIth World Congress for Sexology, 18–22 June, Amsterdam.

Peterson, C. & Seligman, M. E. P. (1984). Causal explanations as a risk factor for depression theory and evidence, *Psychological Review*, **91**, 347–374.

Phan, B. N. (n.d.). Vietnam en mijn Utopia, unpublished study.

Pi, E., Simpson, G. & Cooper, T. (1986). Pharmacokinetics of desipramine in Caucasian and Asian volunteers, *American Journal of Psychiatry*, **143**, 1174–1176.

Piaget, J. (1973). The affective unconscious and the cognitive unconscious, *Journal of the American Psychoanalytic Association*, **21**, 249–261.

Piaget, J. (1983). Piaget's theory, in *Handbook of Child Psychology. I: History, Theory and Methods* (Ed. P. H. Mussen), pp. 103–128. John Wiley & Sons, New York.

Pincus, L. & Dare, C. (1978). *Secrets in the Family*. Faber & Faber Ltd, London.

Pope, B. & Siegman, A. W. (1972). Relationship and verbal behaviour in the initial interview, in *Studies in Dyadic Communication* (Eds A. W. Siegman & B. Pope), pp. 69–89. Pergamon Press, New York.

Price, J. (1975). Foreign language interpreting in psychiatric practice, *Australian and New Zealand Journal of Psychiatry*, **9**, 263–267.

Protacio-Marcelino, E. (1984). *Stress and Coping among Children of Political Prisoners in the Philippines*. University of the Philippines, Department of Psychology, Manila.

Protacio-Marcelino, E. (1989). Children of political detainees in the Philippines: sources of stress and coping patterns, *International Journal of Mental Health*, **18**, 71–86.

Puget, J. (1986). Psicoanalizar en estado de amenaza, unpublished study, Buenos Aires.

Putsch, R. W. (1985). Cross-cultural communication. The special case of interpreters in health care, *JAMA*, **254**, 3344–3348.

Pynoos, R. S. & Eth, S. (1986). Witness to violence: the child interview, *Journal of the American Academy of Child Psychiatry*, **25**, 364–369.

Pynoos, R. B., Frederick, C., Nader, K., Arroyo, W., Steinberg, A., Eth, S., Nunez, F. & Fairbanks, L. (1987a). Life threat and posttraumatic stress disorder in school-age children, *Archives of General Psychiatry*, **44**, 1057–1063.

Pynoos, R. B., Nader, K., Frederick, C., Gonda, L. & Stuber, M. (1987b). Grief reactions in school age children following a sniper attack at school, *Israeli Journal of Psychiatry and Related Sciences*, **24**, 53–63.

Rachman, S. J. (1979). The concept of required helpfulness, *Behaviour Research and Therapy*, **17**, 1–16.

Reid, J. & Strong, T. (1987). *Torture and Trauma*. Cumberland College of Health Sciences, Sydney.

Reinoso, D. G. (1985). El niño bajo el terror de estado, unpublished study, Buenos Aires.

Rendon, M. (1989). Discussion of 'some problems of cross-cultural psychotherapy with refugees seeking therapy', by Carl-Ivar Dahl, *American Journal of Psychoanalysis*, **49**, 45–50.

Rigamer, E. F. (1986). Psychological management of children in a national crisis, *Journal of the American Academy of Child Psychiatry*, **25**, 364–369.

Roth, S. & Lebowitz, L. (1988). The experience of sexual trauma, *Journal of Traumatic Stress*, **1**, 79-107.

Roth, S. & Newman, E. (1990). The process of coping with sexual trauma, *Journal of Traumatic Stress*, **4**, 279-297.

Rümke, H. C. (1960). *Psychiatrie II: de psychosen*, pp. 319-321. Scheltema & Holkema, Amsterdam.

Runia, E. (1986). Ruth Cohen over tegenoverdracht, *Tijdschrift voor Psychotherapie*, **12**, 271-278.

Rutter, M. (1987). The role of cognition in child development and disorder, *British Journal of Medical Psychology*, **60**, 1-16.

Sabin, J. E. (1975). Translating despair, *American Journal of Psychiatry*, **132**, 197-199.

Sack, W. H., Angell, R. H., Kinzie, S. J. D. & Rath, B. (1986). The psychiatric effects of massive trauma on Cambodian children. II. The family, the home and the school, *Journal of the American Academy of Child Psychiatry*, **25**, 377-383.

Saigh, P. A. (1986). In vitro flooding of a 6-year-old boy's posttraumatic stress disorder, *Behaviour, Research and Therapy*, **24**, 685-688.

Santini, I. (1985a). *A propósito de la identidad en el exílio y el retorno*. Social Psychiatric Centre for Refugees, Amsterdam.

Santini, I. (1985b). *Experiencia de un grupo de jóvenes en el exilio*. Social Psychiatric Centre for Refugees, Amsterdam.

Santini, I. (1986a). *Retornar no solo es volver, sino también irse (análisis de la decisión)*. Social Psychiatric Centre for Refugees, Amsterdam.

Santini, I. (1986b). *Post Traumatic Stress Disorder, Tratamiento corto*. Social Psychiatric Centre for Refugees, Amsterdam.

Santini, I. (1986c). *De gevolgen van onderdrukking en ballingschap voor adolescenten uit Latijns Amerika*. Social Psychiatric Centre for Refugees, Amsterdam.

Santini, I. (1987). *Hasta puedo soñar lindo*. Social Psychiatric Centre for Refugees, Amsterdam.

Santini, I. (1989). *Trauma tratamiento y recuperación. Tratamiento de larga duración*. Social Psychiatric Centre for Refugees, Amsterdam.

Santini, I. (1990). *Grupo de terapia alternativa*. Social Psychiatric Service for Refugees, Amsterdam.

Santini, I. & Escardo, M. (1981). *Onderdrukking en ballingschap van kinderen en adolescenten*. Social Psychiatric Centre for Refugees, Amsterdam.

Santini, I., Groenenberg, M. & Vladár Rivero, V. (1987). *Verslag van het International Seminar te Frankfurt*. Social Psychiatric Service for Refugees, Amsterdam.

Sarrel, P. M. & Masters, W. H. (1982). Sexual molestation of man by women. *Archives of Sexual Behavior*, **11**, 117-131.

Schoepf, J. (1981). Ungewohnliche Entzugssymptome nach Benzodiazepin-langzeitbehandlungen, *Der Nervenartz*, **15**, 282-292.

Schumacher, W. (1982). Ueber coping-Verhalten bei schwerer NS-Verfolgung (Ueberleben im Vernichtungslager), in *Trauma, Konflikt, Deckerinnerung* (Eds R. Berna-Glanz & P. Dreyfuss (herausgeber)), pp. 121-144. Fromann Hoizboog Verlag, Frankfurt.

Schutz, A. (1975). in *Strukturen der Lebenswelt* (Ed. A. Luckman), pp. 33-55. Neuwied, Darmstadt.

Schwartz, L. (1982). Mi puerta vieja en la casa nueva: el caso de Fernando, unpublished study, Santiago.

Schwartz, H. J. (ed.), (1984a). *Psychotherapy of the Combat Veteran*. MTP Press, Lancaster, England.

Schwartz, H. J. (1984b). Conscious guilt and unconscious guilt in patients with traumatic neurosis, *American Journal of Psychiatry*, **141**, 1638-1639.

Schwartz, L. S. (1990). A biopsychosocial treatment approach to post-traumatic stress disorder, *Journal of Traumatic Stress*, 3, 221–238.

Seifert, K. L. & Hoffnung, R. J. (1987). *Child and Adolescent Development*. Houghton Mifflin, Boston.

Seligman, M. (1975). *Helplessness: on Depression, Development and Death*. Freeman, San Francisco.

Seligman, M. E. P., Maier, S. F. & Geer, J. (1968). The alleviation of learned helplessness in a dog, *Journal of Abnormal Psychology*, 73, 256–262.

Selman, R. L. (1980). *The Growth of Interpersonal Understanding: Developmental and Clinical Analysis*. Academic Press, New York.

Shapiro, R. B. (1984). Transference, countertransference and the Vietnam veteran, in *Psychotherapy of the Combat Veteran* (Ed. H. J. Schwartz), pp. 279–340. MTP Press, Lancaster, England.

Shen, W. W. & Park, S. (1983). The use of monoamine oxidase inhibitors in the treatment of traumatic war neurosis: case report, *Military Medicine*, 148, 449–454.

Silver, R. L. & Wortman, C. B. (1980). Coping with undesirable life events, in *Human Helplessness. Theory and Application* (Eds J. Gorber & E. P. Seligman), pp. 279–340. Academic Press, New York.

Silver, J. M., Sandberg, D. P. & Hales, R. E. (1990). New approaches in pharmacotherapy of Posttraumatic Stress Disorder, *Journal of Clinical Psychiatry*, 51, 33–38.

Simons, A. D., Murphy, G. E., Levine, J. L. & Wetzel, R. D. (1986). Cognitive therapy and pharmacotherapy for depression. Sustained improvement over a year, *Archives of General Psychiatry*, 43, 43–48.

Skinner, B. F. (1974). *About Behaviourism*. Knopf, New York.

Sluzki, C. E. (1990). Semantic and somatic effects of political repression in a family seeking therapy, *Family Process*, 29, 131–143.

Smeulers, J. (1985). Overeenkomsten en verschillen tussen de (late) gevolgen van de Tweede Wereldoorlog en die van andere vormen van geweld, in *Problematiek van oorlogsgetroffenen* (Ed. J. Dane), pp. 71–78. ICODO, Utrecht.

Solomon, Z. & Bebenishty, R. (1986). The role of proximity, immediacy and expectancy in frontline treatment of combat stress reaction among Israelis in the Lebanon war, *American Journal of Psychiatry*, 143, 623–627.

Solomon, Z., Weisenberg, M., Schwarzwald, J. & Mikulincer, M. (1987). Post-traumatic stress disorder among frontline soldiers with combat stress reaction: the 1982 Israeli combat experience, *American Journal of Psychiatry*, 144, 448–454.

Solursh, L. P. (1989). Combat addiction: overview and implications in symptom maintenance and treatment planning, *Journal of Traumatic Stress*, 2, 451–662.

Somnier, F. E. & Genefke, I. K. (1986). Psychotherapy for victims of torture, *British Journal of Psychiatry*, 141, 1628–1639.

Spiegel, D. (1981). Vietnam grief work using hypnosis, *American Journal of Clinical Hypnosis*, 24, 33–40.

Spolyar, L. (1974). The grieving process in MIA wives, in *Family Separation and Reunion: Families of Prisoners of War and Servicemen Missing in Action* (Ed. H. I. McCubbin), pp. 77–85. Center for Prisoners of War Studies, Naval Health Research Center, Washington DC.

Srinivasa, D. K. & Trivedi, S. (1982). Knowledge and attitude of mental diseases in a rural community of South India, *Social Science and Medicine*, 16, 1635–1639.

Steinberg, M., Rounsaville, B. & Cicchetti, D. V. (1990). The structured clinical interview for DSM-III-R Dissociative Disorders: preliminary report on a new diagnostic instrument, *American Journal of Psychiatry*, 147, 76–82.

Stierlin, H., Ruecker-Embden, I., Wetzel, N. & Wirsching, M. (1980). *The First Interview with the Family*. Brunner/Mazel, New York.

Strunz, F. (1987). Ätiologie und Therapie der Alptraume, *Fortschritte der Neurologie Psychiatrie*, **55**, 306–321.

Sue, D. & Sue, S. (1987). Cultural factors in the clinical assessment of Asian Americans, *Journal of Consulting and Clinical Psychology*, **55**, 479–487.

Sundberg, N. D. (1981). Research and research hypotheses about effectiveness in intercultural counselling, in *Counselling across Cultures*, revised and expanded edition (Eds P. B. Pederson, J. G. Draguns, W. J. Lonner & J. E. Trimble), pp. 304–342. University Press of Hawaii, Honolulu.

Swartz, L. (1987). Transcultural psychiatry in South Africa. Part II. Cross cultural issues in mental health practice, *Transcultural Psychiatric Research Review*, **24**, 5–30.

Tailor, S. E., Wood, J. V. & Lichtman, R. R. (1983). It could be worse: selective evaluation as a response to victimization, *Journal of Social Issues*, **39**, 19–40.

Terr, L. C. (1981). 'Forbidden games'. Post-traumatic child's play, *Journal of the American Academy of Child Psychiatry*, **20**, 741–760.

Terr, L. C. (1983). Chowchilla revisited, *American Journal of Psychiatry*, **140**, 1543–1550.

Terr, L. C. (1985). Remembered images in psychic trauma, *The Psychoanalytic Study of the Child*, **40**, 493–533.

Terr, L. C. (1989). Treating psychic trauma in children: a preliminary discussion, *Journal of Traumatic Stress*, **2**, 3–20.

Terr, L. C. (1991). Childhood traumas: an outline and overview, *American Journal of Psychiatry*, **148**, 10–20.

Teter, H., Mauldin, D., Nhol, S., Conkin, D. & Sum, S. (1987). *Treatment Through Training: a Cambodian Mental Health Workshop*. International Institute of San Francisco, San Francisco.

The Anne Frank Foundation (1987). *Vreemd gespuis*. Ambo/Novib, Amsterdam.

Thompson, J. (1989). Torture by tradition, *Nursing Times*, **85**, 16–17.

Tiedemann, J. (1987). Angst in de therapeutische relatie, *ICODO-info*, **4**(1), 27–35.

Truong, T. D. (1987). Contribution to a panel on 'The countertransference of torture and trauma', the third annual meeting of the Society for Traumatic Studies, 25 October, Baltimore.

Truong, T. D. (1989). *Vietnamese Women and Sexual Violence*, CGV-report no. 1, English version, Centrum Gezondheidszorg Vluchtelingen, Rijswijk.

Tsui, A. M. (1985). Psychotherapeutic considerations in sexual counselling for Asian immigrants, *Psychotherapy*, **22**, 357–362.

Tsui, P. & Schultz, G. L. (1985). Failure of rapport: why psychotherapeutic engagement fails in the treatment of Asian clients, *American Journal of Orthopsychiatry*, **55**, 561–569.

Tuiavii (1985). *De Papalagi*. Heureka, Weesp.

Tuk, B. (1988). Vietnamese jongeren in Nederland, *Jeugd en samenleving*, **18**, 243–254.

Turiel, E. (1983). *The Development of Social Knowledge*. Cambridge University Press, Cambridge.

Tyhurst, J. S. (1951). Individual reactions to community disaster. The natural history of psychiatric phenomena, *American Journal of Psychiatry*, **1071**, 764–769.

Ulman, R. B. (1987). A self-psychological reevaluation of post-traumatic stress disorder (PTSD) and its treatment: shattered fantasies, *Journal of The American Academy of Psychoanalysis*, **15**, 175–203.

University Teachers for Human Rights (1989). Report no 3: January–August 1989, Jaffna, Sri Lanka.

Van Blaaderen-Stok, C. L. (1986). Gezinsgesprekken ter preventie van transgenerationele traumatisering, in *Praktijk van de hulpverlening aan oorlogsgetroffenen* (Ed. J. Dane), pp. 61–80. Swets & Zeitlinger, Lisse.

Van Bork, J. J. (1986). Forum: de beinvloeding van onbewuste afweermechanismen door maprotiline en mianserine: een psychodynamische verklaring van het therapeutisch effect van antidepressive medicamenten, *Tijdschrift voor Psychiatrie*, **28**, 573–581.

Van Dantzig, A. (1990). *Psychotherapie: een vak apart*. Boom, Meppel.

Van de Lande, J. (1980). Gezinsgeheimen, *Maandblad Geestelijke Volksgezondheid*, **36**, 1071–1072.

Van der Kolk, B. (1985). Adolescent vulnerability to post-traumatic stress disorder, *Psychiatry*, **48**, 365–370.

Van der Kolk, B. (1988). The traumaspectrum: the interaction of biological and social events in the genesis of the trauma response, *Journal of Traumatic Stress*, **1**, 273–290.

Van der Kolk, B., Greenberg, M., Boyd, H. & Kristal, J. (1985a). Inescapable shock, neurotransmitters, and addiction to trauma: toward a psychobiology of post traumatic stress, *Biological Psychiatry*, **20**, 314–325.

Van der Kolk, B., Boyd, H., Krystal, J. & Greenberg, M. (1985b). Post-traumatic stress disorder as a biologically based disorder: implications of the animal model of inescapable shock, in *Post-traumatic Stress Disorder: Psychological and Biological Sequelae* (Ed. B. A. Van der Kolk), pp. 123–134. American Press, Washington DC.

Van der Kolk, B. & Van der Hart, O. (1989). Pier Janet and the breakdown of adaptation in psychological trauma, *American Journal of Psychiatry*, **146**, 1530–1540.

Van der Ploeg, H. M. & J. Vis. (redactie) (1989). *Burnout en werkstress: ieders verantwoordelijkheid*. Swets & Zeitlinger, Amsterdam.

Van der Ploeg, H. M., Van Leeuwen, J. J. & Kwee, M. G. T. (1990). Burnout among Dutch psychotherapists, *Psychological Research*, **67**, 107–112.

Van der Veer, G. (1987a). Zeven manieren om een Tamil gek te maken, *VU Magazine*, oktober 1987, 12–14.

Van der Veer, G. (1987b). Psychische problemen van jonge Iraanse vluchtelingen (Psychological problems of young Iranian refugees), *Jeugd en samenleving*, **17**, 354–365, Social Psychiatric Service for Refugees, Amsterdam.

Van der Veer, G. (1987c). *Verslag van een bezoek aan het Canadian Centre for Investigation and Prevention of Torture in Toronto*. Social Psychiatric Centre for Refugees, Amsterdam.

Van der Veer, G. (1987d). Chileense jongeren: opgroeien in een onveilige en uitzichtloze situatie. *Jeugd en samenleving*, **17**, 499–506.

Van der Veer, G. (1989a). Om gek van te worden. De psychische gevolgen van het asielbeleid, *Jeugd en samenleving*, **19**, 160–164.

Van der Veer, G. (1989b). Dilemma's bij de hulpverlening aan suicidale asielzoekers, *ICODO info*, **6**, 9–21.

Van der Veer, G. (1990a). Yesterday's patients. Psychotherapy with traumatized political refugees, paper presented at the Second European Conference on Traumatic Stress, Noordwijkerhout, September, the Netherlands.

Van Leeuwen, J. J. & Van der Ploeg, H. M. (1989). Burnout bij psychotherapeuten, in *Burnout en werkstress: ieders verantwoordelijkheid* (Eds H. M. Van der Ploeg & J. Vis. (redactie)), pp. 129–139. Swets & Zeitlinger, Amsterdam.

Van Ree, F. (1987). De blinde vlekken van de therapeut en joodse oorlogsslachtoffers, in *Kinderen van de oorlog* (Eds R. Beunderman & J. Dane), pp. 73–94. Icodo, Utrecht.

Van Willigen, L. (1988). Women in exile, in *Politische Fluchtlinge: integration und rehabilitation im exil* (Ed. J. Schopfel), pp. 78–86. Amnesty International, Hamburg.

Viñar, M. (1985). *Trauma psiquico, trauma social?* Fasic, Santiago.

Vladár Rivero, V. M. (1986). De Latijnsamerikaanse vluchtelingen, in *Agressie, door psychiaters bezien* (Ed. R. E. Offerman), pp. 123–135. Swets & Zeitlinger, Lisse.

Vladár Rivero, V. M. (1989). *Diagnostic Evaluation and Indications for Treatment with Victims of Organized Violence*. Social Psychiatric Centre for Refugees, Amsterdam.

Vladár Rivero, V. M. (1991). Sexual torture, consequences for psychological health, paper presented at the 10th World Congress on Sexology, SPD for Refugees, Amsterdam.

Vontress, C. E. (1981). Racial and ethnic barriers in counselling, in *Counselling across Cultures* (revised and expanded edition) (Eds P. B. Pederson, J. G. Draguns, W. J. Lonner & J. E. Trimble), pp. 87–107. University Press of Hawaii, Honolulu.

Walker, L. J. (1989). A longitudinal study of moral reasoning, *Child Development*, **55**, 677–691.

Watzlawick, P., Beauvin, A. B. & Jackson, D. (1967). *Pragmatics of Human Communication*. Norton, New York.

Weinstein, E. & Ortic, E. (1985). Estudio psicosocial de 25 familias retornadas, in *Escritos sobre exilio y retorno* (Ed. C. González), pp. 47–60. Fasic, Santiago.

Westermeyer, J. (1988). DSM-III Psychiatric Disorders among Hmong refugees in the United States: a point prevalence study, *American Journal of Psychiatry*, **145**, 197–202.

Westermeyer, J. (1989). Cross-cultural care for PTSD: research, training, and service needs for the future, *Journal of Traumatic Stress*, **2**, 515–536.

Williams, C. L. (1987a). *Prevention Programs for Refugee Mental Health*, (Contract No. 278-85-0024 CH). National Institute of Mental Health, Washington DC.

Williams, T. (1987b). Diagnosis and treatment of survivor guilt—the bad penny, in *Post Traumatic Stress Disorders: a Handbook for Clinicians* (Ed. T. Williams), pp. 75–92. Disabled American Veterans, Cincinnati, Ohio.

Williams, C. L. & Westermeyer, J. (eds). (1986). *Refugee Mental Health in Resettlement Countries*. Hemisphere, Washington.

Winston, A., Pinsker, H. & McCullough, L. (1986). A review of supportive psychotherapy, *Hospital and Community Psychiatry*, **37**, 1105–1113.

Winston, A., Pinsker, H. & McCullough, L. (1986). A review of supportive psychotherapy, *Hospital and Community Psychiatry*, **337**, 1105–1113.

Wortman, C. B. (1983). Coping and victimization: conclusions and implications for future research, *Journal of Social Issues*, **29**, 195–221.

Wren, C. S. (1986). Hulp aan slachtoffers van marteling. Opnieuw leren leven, *Intermediar*, **43**, 19–27.

Yamamoto, J., Fung, D., Lo, S. & Reece, S. (1979). Pharmacology for Asian Americans and Pacific Islanders, *Psychopharmacological Bulletin*, **15**, 29–31.

Yang, Y. (1985). Prophylactic efficacy of lithium and its effective plasma levels in Chinese bipolar patients, *Acta Psychiatrica Scandinavia*, **2**, 171–175.

Yost, J. F. (1987). The pharmacological management of post-traumatic stress disorder (PTSD) in Vietnam veterans and in civilian situations, in *Post-traumatic Stress Disorders: A Handbook for Clinicians* (Ed. T. Williams), pp. 93–102. Disabled American Veterans, Cincinnati, Ohio.

Yüksel, S. (1991). Therapy of sexual torture, paper presented at the XI World Sexology Congress, 18–22 June, Amsterdam.

Yule, W. & Williams, R. M. (1989). Post-traumatic stress reactions in children, *Journal of Traumatic Stress*, **3**, 279–295.

Author index

Subject index